The Immigrant Rights Movement

The Immigrant Rights Movement

The Battle over National Citizenship

Walter J. Nicholls

Stanford University Press
Stanford, California

Stanford University Press
Stanford, California

© 2019 by the Board of Trustees of the Leland Stanford Junior University.
All rights reserved.

No part of this book may be reproduced or transmitted in any form or by any
means, electronic or mechanical, including photocopying and recording, or in any
information storage or retrieval system without the prior written permission of
Stanford University Press.

Printed in the United States of America on acid-free, archival-quality paper

Library of Congress Cataloging-in-Publication Data

Names: Nicholls, Walter, author.
Title: The immigrant rights movement : the battle over national citizenship / Walter J.
    Nicholls.
Description: Stanford, California : Stanford University Press, 2019. | Includes
    bibliographical references and index.
Identifiers: LCCN 2018051367 | ISBN 9781503608887 (cloth : alk. paper) |
    ISBN 9781503609327 (pbk. : alk. paper) | ISBN 9781503609334 (epub)
Subjects: LCSH: United States—Emigration and immigration—Government policy. |
    Immigrants—Civil rights—United States. | Citizenship—United States. | Social
    movements—United States.
Classification: LCC JV6483 .N52 2019 | DDC 323.3/291209730973—dc23
LC record available at https://lccn.loc.gov/2018051367

Cover design by Kevin Barrett Kane
Cover photo by Katrina Brown

Typeset by Motto Publishing Services in 10/14 Minion Pro

To my children, Emile and Louise Nicholls

Contents

Illustrations

Tables

Acknowledgments

THIS BOOK HAS BENEFITED from the support of many different people over the years. First and foremost, I would like to thank my wonderful research assistant, Marieke de Wilde. It is fair to say that this book would not have come to fruition without her extraordinary investigative work. I am deeply appreciative of everything she has done. I would also like to thank the editorial team at Stanford University Press and Gretchen Otto for their excellent work and professionalism.

I have been fortunate to know many different people involved in immigration politics in one way or another in Los Angeles. Through informal chats over lunches, coffees, and an occasional beer, these people have provided nuanced and fascinating insights into the issue of immigration and the immigrant rights movement. Although I did not use these conversations directly in the book, they certainly drew my attention to certain issues and dynamics. There are too many people to include here. But I would like to express my special gratitude to a core group including Pablo Alvarado, Carlos Amador, Teresa Borden, Nancy Meza, Victor Narro, and Chris Newman.

There are many colleagues and students who have been helpful in commenting on various drafts of this work and talking to me about immigration politics. At the University of Amsterdam, I continue to benefit from two excellent comrades and colleagues, Justus Uitermark and Floris Vermeulen. These friends have patiently listened to my long rants on immigration politics and carefully read various papers. I would also like to thank other Amsterdam colleagues, including Christian Broer, Sebastien Chauvin, Jan Willem Duyvendak, Tara Fiorito, Davide Gnes, Sander van Haperen, and Mariska de Vries, among others. At the University of California, Irvine, I would like to thank all my colleagues for providing such a supportive environment. I would especially like to thank Virginia Parks and Rodolfo Torres for being great supports and the School of Social Ecology for funding.

Parts of the book have benefited from engagement with my broader network of colleagues. First, I would like to express my deepest gratitude to Cecilia Menjívar. She has been a friend, family member, and mentor. Her generosity has been limitless. She also allowed me to tag along on some of her fascinating new research in Kansas. This journey to middle America provided much-needed respite from this book project! I would also like to thank Chris Tilly, the former director of UCLA's Institute for Research on Labor and Employment (IRLE), for providing funding and allowing me to present one chapter at a UCLA Labor Center workshop. Finally, I would like to extend my deepest gratitude to Kim Voss and Irene Bloemraad for inviting me to participate in their workshop, "Ten Years after the 2006 Marches." I presented a part of the book at the workshop, and it benefited greatly from the feedback of Xóchitl Bada, Irene Bloemraad, Hana Brown, Caitlin Patler, and Kim Voss.

The years during which this book was written presented many challenges. My family and I moved back from our charmed lives in the Netherlands to disorderly, anonymous, and car-dependent Los Angeles. To make matters even more challenging, a xenophobic demagogue was elected to the presidency of the United States a little more than a year after our return. We spent a lot more time at demonstrations and fretting over the possibilities of fascism. In the midst of this tumult, I continued to move forward with the book. My family was generous enough to allow me the time to write and rewrite the pages of this book and patient enough to endure my interminable talk about editing. My family stuck it out in spite of the destabilizing move, endless political demonstrations, obsessions with fascism and editing, and absences for work trips. My wife and children brought joy to life in a way that seemed impossible. We walked around the city, ate a lot of different foods, traveled to interesting cities, and occasionally took a grueling hike. Without the pleasure and joy of being a part of this group, I would not have had the emotional energy to finish this book. I thank Marie, Emile, and Louise for making everything possible.

Introduction

DURING THE SUMMER OF 2016, I conducted a batch of interviews during the heady days of the presidential campaign. Several executive directors of prominent advocacy organizations expressed bewilderment. They marveled at the spectacle of Donald Trump. He was boorish and wholly unqualified. But more important, he channeled a vision of America that contrasted sharply with their own liberal views of national citizenship. For ten years, they had argued that this was a nation of immigrants and that immigrants deserved membership because they were de facto Americans. This nation's exceptionalism did not stem from closed borders, immutable cultural boundaries, and blood ties. Instead, the country was exceptional because of its capacities to absorb strangers and make them into Americans. Strong borders were necessary but so too was a large door for Americans-in-waiting. Donald Trump was not a normal political adversary. His words and vision were anathema to their vision of liberal America.

Although many advocacy organizations looked on the Trump campaign with dismay, they were confident that Hillary Clinton would defeat him. Trump would lose and take down the xenophobic wing of the Republican Party with him. Republicans would suffer a terrible defeat and would never weaponize the issue of immigration again. High Latina/o turnout and the loss of the presidency and Senate would, many believed, ensure the passage of comprehensive immigration reform within the first six months of the new Clinton administration. When listening to these predictions, there was no reason for me to doubt my informants. Liberal hegemony was ascendant in the summer of 2016.

But since the election, the country has been experiencing the consequences of its outcome. Few, if any, observers now suggest that ethnonationalism is on the ropes. The president's advisors have hailed from the extreme right, and his first attorney general was the most vociferous anti-immigrant voice in the Senate. These officials and their colleagues in Homeland Security have worked to refashion government norms and policies to align with a restrictionist worldview. The Trump administration has implemented a ban on travel from Muslim countries, justified the actions of white supremacists in Charlottesville, pardoned the infamous Joe Arpaio, rescinded Deferred Action for Childhood Arrivals (DACA) and Temporary Protected Status (TPS), and separated migrant children from their parents, among other things. These spectacles of malice have been embraced by the base of the Republican Party. Migrant children sleeping in cold warehouses have been viewed by many as an unpleasant yet necessary step to stop immigrants from infesting the nation. Ethnonationalism has become legitimate for most rank-and-file Republicans. The liberal triumphalism of summer 2016 has given way to liberal dread.

The fight over the boundaries of national citizenship did not begin in 2016. Advocates on both sides of the debate have been pushing and pulling these boundaries since the creation of national citizenship. This book analyzes the immigrant rights movement as one recent emanation of these battles. As a genealogy of a social movement, it traces the massive and well-developed social movement of the 2010s to the small struggles for the rights of immigrants in countless localities across the country. Immigrants, allies, organizations, ideas, discourses, money, emotions, and politicians assembled in different places and times, metastasizing over a twenty-year period into a multimillion-dollar, politically potent, and nationally consolidated social movement. The book traces how the movement scaled up into a national social movement, but it also suggests that the battle for immigrant rights became a struggle over the very meaning of national citizenship. The leading advocates from the mid-2000s onward embraced a liberal variant of nationalism that depicted America as welcoming and immigrants as highly deserving subjects. Rather than call for the dismantlement of borders or for postnational citizenship, the mainstream immigrant rights movement celebrated the nation and wrapped immigrants in the American flag. The movement, consequently, became a vehicle for buttressing citizenship's nationalist underpinnings while seeking to make it more inclusive for those immigrants deemed sufficiently deserving.

Localities as the Breeding Grounds of Citizenship

For the past thirty years, the United States has been in a heated battle over where to set the boundaries of citizenship. The first part of the book takes the reader back to early struggles in the 1990s. Local residents struggled with one another over the new immigrants in their towns. They argued over what constitutes a national community and who deserves a place in it. To illustrate the process, the book focuses on local conflicts over immigrant day laborers. Because these workers moved into suburban areas and searched for work on public street corners, they became an early flash point of conflict between immigrant foes and supporters.

Contracting the Boundaries of Citizenship

For two generations, the lives of citizens in the United States were relatively fixed within a nationalized cultural, political, and economic system. The federal government had achieved unparalleled power, national interests were clearly defined, and the whiteness of national identity had come into sharp relief.[1] From the 1920s to the early 1960s, immigration dropped to historical lows. There was Mexican immigration, but most immigrants were either temporary or had settled in ethnic barrios and rural towns.[2] New immigrants during the mid-twentieth century remained far from the eyes and lives of most white Americans.

At a time when national citizenship was reaching its apogee, globalization began eating into its foundations. Multilateral trade agreements, offshoring of manufacturing, and growing international migration perforated borders. The more globalizing forces ate into the nation, the more people became aware of the nation's importance for their moral, cultural, and material lives.[3] For Seyla Benhabib, globalization diminished state sovereignty, which in turn spurred efforts to fortify the nation even more. She observes that "while state sovereignty in economic, military, and technological domains has been greatly eroded, it is nonetheless vigorously asserted."[4] Globalization also heightened feelings of status deprivation among many middle- and working-class white nationals.[5] Justin Gest defines status deprivation as the difference between expectations of power and positioning in a social system and "perceptions of fulfillment."[6] The sense of deprivation among white nationals was exacerbated by the perceived advances of outsider reference groups such as immigrants and minorities. This gave rise to a feeling that good, normal Americans were being left behind by lower-status others. Whereas good white nationals paid their dues and did the right thing, foreigners cut in line and cheated to get ahead.[7] Many white nationals consequently became, according to Gest, "consumed by their loss of social and political status in social hierarchies, particularly in relation to immigrant and minority reference groups. Their politics are motivated and pervaded by a nostalgia that reveres and seeks to reinstate a bygone era."[8]

Ethnonationalism bubbled up from the four corners of America in the 1990s.[9] It did not emerge as a fully formed ideology but as utterances informed by common-sense framings of citizenship. Notions of rights and belonging latched onto one another and slowly amassed into a relatively coherent understanding of citizenship that was narrow and structured by a friend-enemy binary. Citizenship centered on common culture, habitus, and sense of belonging, and as Michèle Lamont and Nicolas Duvoux argue for the case of France, an increasingly "narrowed definition of those worthy of attention, care and recognition."[10] Aggrieved citizens targeted immigrants because they were a direct expression of globalization and denationalization.[11] Immigrants were the enemies that undercut jobs and imposed high costs on public services. They were intent on making the country Mexico and displacing—symbolically and territorially—Americans from their own country. Ethnonationalism pitted Americans against immigrants in a zero-sum conflict over the very survival of the country.

These conflicts were experienced and played out in localities. Larger gateway cities have, according to much of the literature, been more accommodating to immigrants because they have immigrant traditions, greater ethnic and racial diversity, supportive organizations, and more liberal political cultures.[12] Suburban areas, by contrast, have had a long history of racial and class exclusion.[13] The demographic, ideological, and civic conditions found in the suburbs have made them less accommodating to newcomers. Benjamin Newman[14] adds that the rapid influx of immigrants in conservative and homogenous suburban areas has increased the likelihood of xenophobic responses. New immigrant businesses, public signs in foreign languages, and day laborers gathered on street corners were viewed as undermining good, normal society. The immigrant was no longer an abstract figure looming in distant border areas or in the barrios of big cities. The immigrant was now a real person who was invading intimate lived spaces and competing with good citizens for a rightful place in their own towns. The crisis of national identity was therefore experienced locally on thousands of street corners, neighborhoods, parking lots, and main streets. These were places in which immigrants disrupted the normal codes of belonging and helped, in Mabel Berezin's terms, "transform differences from a social fact to a social exacerbation."[15]

Many established residents had long believed in the nation and also in the federal government's awesome capacities to protect it from foreign intruders. But the continued settlement of immigrants in their neighborhoods signaled the government's inability to realize its authority over borders and national citizenship. It signaled a crisis of legitimacy. The perceived vacuum of power motivated locals to devise their own restrictions. Aggrieved locals produced policies to bar undocumented immigrants from settling in their towns.[16] They passed restrictive measures such as bans on soliciting work in public, street vending, renting apartments to undocumented immigrants, and the use of foreign languages in public records. These restrictions were aimed at plugging the holes that ostensibly allowed so-called illegals to take root in communities. Creating this protective mesh required the participation of different actors (for example, police, landlords, store owners, employers, and contractors). These different actors assumed responsibility for checking the legal status of immigrants in various areas of life. They served as relays of the bordering state, providing it with the means to monitor immigrants and keep them from slipping through the cracks.[17]

Mitchell Dean and Kaspar Villadsen remind us of Foucault's argument that social-control mechanisms often grew from local communities responding to the perceived incapacities of the state.

> In effect Foucault described how localized social domains, the *Gemeinshaft*, constituted the breeding ground for pioneers in policing mechanisms "from below" that would pave the way for the subsequent state-controlled apparatuses of order, hygiene, and discipline. Foucault's general narrative . . . tells us how techniques of intervening to modify and impose norms on human living were first invented in the context of local struggles and gradually taken up in state-administered biopolitics. . . . *Society becomes a breeding ground for dispositive of legal and disciplinary power with an expansive reach* (emphasis added).[18]

Localities became the breeding ground for experimentation in thinking about, talking about, and practicing citizenship. In the face of perceived state collapse, these experiments reflected bottom-up attempts to remake citizenship by sharpening boundaries between self and other.

Expanding the Boundaries of Citizenship

Undocumented immigrants certainly had complex identities before being rendered illegal in the United States.[19] Their placement in this category, however, became an important part of their lives. It shaped their opportunities as well as their political feelings, identities, and the will to resist.[20] When a landlord, government bureaucrat, or police officer denied a person a space or life-sustaining service because of her illegality, it was not simply the denial of crucial resources that was troubling but also the rationale (stigma, inequality, and otherness) underlying the denial. The countless small acts of denial, disrespect, and discrimination—whether at a bank, a service counter, a school, a sidewalk, or a job—reinforced stigma and feelings of marginalization. Resistance was forged in response to these everyday aggressions. Working-class undocumented immigrants also had few ways to escape their marginalization. Color, class, migration status, and limited opportunities for upward mobility conspired to make straight assimilation unlikely.[21] Many undocumented immigrants were therefore trapped in their marginalized positions, which helped, in certain cases, forge a sense of group solidarity. The stronger the barriers facing a marginalized group, Alejandro Portes and Julia Sensenbrenner argue, "the stronger the sentiments of in-group solidarity among its members and the higher the appropriable social capital based on this solidarity."[22] The stigma of illegality and everyday repression made the lives of undocumented immigrants virtually impossible, but it also produced conditions for solidarity, identity, and resistance. Some established residents sought to eradicate the so-called illegals in their midst, but efforts to do so simultaneously produced a group with the will to resist in one way (passive) or another (active).[23]

Although hostile local policies were directed at a target population (undocumented immigrants), the effects of these polices were not contained to this population. Repression spilled over and triggered grievances and moral shocks among populations not directly targeted by restrictions.[24] Local repressive policies often prompted sympathetic citizens to feel solidarity with illegalized people. Amalia Pallares calls the intermeshing of populations "tangling" and defines it as "tying together the lives and futures of the documented and the undocumented by underscoring the role played by the undocumented in the lives and caretaking of residents and citizens, and the ways in which deporting the undocumented leads to a dramatic decline in the affective, economic, and social conditions of the documented."[25] Several groups of people were negatively affected by repression and displayed some penchant for resistance. Latina/o immigrants with legal status or citizenship faced a higher likelihood of stigmatization and racial profiling when repressive measures were enacted. Many of these Latinas/os couldn't distance themselves from undocumented immigrants because of their racialized traits and cultural dispositions. Ethnic markers reduced the possibility for many Latinas/os to exit the stigmatized group and identify with the dominant group.[26] This generated grievances among established Latinas/os and provided undocumented immigrants with a reservoir of solidarity. Repressive measures also affected family members (citizens and immigrants) who stood to lose greatly from restrictive measures.[27] Undocumented immigrants were also entangled in relations with many nationals, including employers, friends, and neighbors as well as those they knew through businesses, churches, and civic associations. These people came to know and depend on immigrants. They were enmeshed in personal, professional, and moral networks with repressed immigrants. These entanglements spread the costs (financial, physical, psychic, and emotional) of repression to those with ties to undocumented immigrants. Finally, some local residents held on to liberal or religious values,[28] which conflicted with the enactment of anti-immigrant measures.[29] A sense of moral outrage emerged among such residents, stemming from the belief that their country was being usurped by ethnonationalists. Thus repression created new alignments and solidarities between outraged citizens and immigrants, helping to blur rather than clearly delineate the boundaries between them.

Repression precipitated resistance from targeted immigrants and their supporters. Family, friends, and a plethora of supportive allies fought against ethnonationalist words and deeds. Some argued that immigrants had inalienable rights that could not be superseded by the discriminatory impulses of the local and federal government and that undocumented immigrants had a right to free speech, assembly, and due process. These arguments drew from a framing of citizenship as territorial personhood, whereby any person within the United States possessed constitutionally protected rights.[30] The frames used to argue for the rights of immigrants, however, were not always consistent. Many early activists also adopted a postnational frame,[31] stressing that immigrants had fundamental human rights that were protected by the state, treaties, and international institutions. Drawing on this frame, Hinda Seif argues that the struggle for immigrant rights "challenge[s] the boundaries of citizenship and insist[s] on human rights."[32] Still other activists framed their arguments through what we may call "liberal nationalism." They argued that immigrants deserved membership because of their cultural assimilation, rootedness, and contributions to the national community. Immigrants possessing these attributes were already de facto members of the nation. National belonging and affiliation,[33] according to this framing, made them eligible for membership and full rights.

Early rights claims were produced by amateur advocates and activists. They generated undisciplined statements that slipped and slid across the spectrum of citizenship. Activists drew on preexisting and not particularly well-formed ideologies and framings of citizenship. They could easily employ liberal national, postnational, and territorial personhood frames within the same breath. These "master frames"[34] provided activists and advocates a discursive repertoire to construct concrete arguments for why the rights of undocumented immigrants in their towns should be recognized and protected. The frames provided activists with the values, sentiments, and narratives to forge specific public arguments. These early activists were blind to the inconsistencies between specific master frames because the underlying morality was the same: immigrants were rightful members of their communities, for one reason or another. Such early arguments were raw in every sense of the term. They had not been rationalized by a sophisticated communication infrastructure designed to ensure message discipline.

Repression in the 1990s onward, therefore, triggered multiple forms of resistance from friends, family, neighbors, coethnics, liberals, and others. Advocacy organizations were embroiled in fights for the protection of the basic rights of immigrants in the places in which immigrants lived. They fought forcefully for the right of day laborers to sell their labor on public street corners. They engaged in hard battles for domestic workers and street vendors. Some developed close alliances with labor unions organizing low-wage workers. These local battles drew from what John McCarthy has called "micro-mobilization contexts." Such contexts consisted of "a variety of social sites within people's daily rounds where informal and less formal ties between people can serve as solidarity and communication facilitating structures when and if they choose to go into dissent together."[35] These spaces provided the unity and resources needed to mount serious campaigns, allowing localities to become breeding grounds for more inclusive understandings of citizenship.[36] Thus, restrictive anti-immigrant measures spurred countermobilizations demanding more expansive forms of citizenship. The immigrant rights movement was born from these geographically scattered battles in response to local restrictions.

There was a distinctive geography to local proimmigrant mobilizations. Suburban areas were often seedbeds of conflict and mobilization because newly settled immigrants typically generated more political disruptions in these places than in larger, more diverse cities. But although they may have been seedbeds for early battles, the relative paucity of political and discursive opportunities, high levels of racial homogeneity, and few supportive organizations made it difficult for small campaigns to grow into big, powerful mobilizations. Suburban areas may have been incubators of conflict, but they were rarely major hubs of immigrant rights struggles. Big cities played such a role. These areas were normatively more predisposed to immigrants in particular and diversity in general. They concentrated more supportive organizations and resources and were more likely to contain friendlier political elites.[37] Large metropolitan regions therefore had an uneven political geography, with new conflicts flourishing in the suburbs but mobilization infrastructure and opportunities concentrating in traditional gateway cities. Fledgling suburban struggles often depended on the support (direction, money, media support, logistical assistance, and legal assistance) of better-resourced organizations in central cities. The supportive ties helped suburban activists acquire more resources and engage in more ambitious actions. For the purposes of this book, large local organizations located in central cities are called regional organizations. The book draws attention to these organizations and shows how they played an essential role in channeling local struggles into regional and then national mobilizations.

Rather than dismantle national citizenship, globalization has amplified national angst. It has accelerated unease that the country is being taken further and further away from the promise of national greatness. The threat has been experienced most viscerally in localities in which new immigrant populations have settled and become present in public space. In the 1990s and 2000s, this unleashed a plethora of new local struggles to define the boundaries of citizenship.[38] Efforts to constrict and racialize citizenship did not unfold without resistance. "Where there is power," Michel Foucault aptly noted, "there is resistance."[39] Struggles for immigrant rights began at the specific points at which repressive powers were enacted. Immigrants and their allies pushed back and drew from different citizenship frames to express their claims, giving rise to hybrid understandings of political community. Localities therefore became the breeding ground for new forms of citizenship, with people cobbling together context-specific arguments, policies, and practices into uneven assemblages of rights and belonging.[40]

Going National

The book begins in the local trenches, but it does not stay there. The second part of the book examines how these local battles scaled up into a powerful national social movement.[41] Growing federal restrictions at the end of the 1990s led to accelerated efforts to enter the national political arena. Regional organizations mounted one-off national coalitions, shared information on best practices with one another, and provided various kinds of mutual support and solidarity. There were also a number of countrywide coalitions advocating for narrow policies such as asylum status for El Salvadoran and Guatemalan immigrants. These, however, were singular efforts made up of organizations rooted in large, immigrant-rich cities. They did not result in a robust infrastructure that aggregated advocates across the country into a sustainable and potent social movement. The costs of building and maintaining a national social-movement infrastructure were prohibitive for financially precarious organizations. Real power over immigration policy was therefore concentrated in the federal government, but organizations and their fights were stuck in localities. Immigrant rights organizations had a strong motive to nationalize their struggle, but the costs of scaling up were too high for most to do it alone.

The movement for immigrant rights began to nationalize in earnest in the mid-2000s, bursting onto the political scene in 2006 with massive multicity mobilizations.[42] A handful of national organizations headquartered in Washington, DC, began to assert leadership. They did not limit their aspirations to fixing the system through small, piecemeal reforms but instead envisioned a comprehensive law that would overhaul the entire system. They wanted, in the words of advocates, the whole enchilada. While comprehensive federal reform had been floated before, it had never been taken up as the primary goal of the movement before the mid-2000s. The new leadership not only shifted the focus to the federal political arena but also invested heavily in a national-level infrastructure to pursue the campaign for comprehensive reform. The infrastructure served as a centrally unified space that connected geographically dispersed organizations and advocates, providing them with a common way to think, talk, and feel about immigrant rights. It was professional and rich and had relations with the country's most important elected officials. Entry into the national field also required a change in the discourse used to talk about the rights of immigrants. Communication with a national audience required the use of language that connected to the morals and values of its members. Advocacy organizations carefully studied the norms of Americans and crafted what they believed would be resonant frames and talking points. America, they argued, was a nation of immigrants and undocumented immigrants who were de facto Americans. Because they belonged to the nation, undocumented immigrants deserved citizenship and the full rights that came with it. A nationwide social-movement infrastructure was used to ensure that thousands of local activists employed the centrally produced discourse in the same way. The early days of haphazard arguments were eclipsed by an enormous effort to rationalize how activists thought and talked about citizenship. The movement was therefore nationalized in terms of its target and goal (federal immigration reform), the infrastructure needed to pursue national campaigns, and the discourse used to talk about immigrants and their rights in the country.

By 2014, the immigrant rights movement had become one of the best-organized social movements in the country. Considering the immense barriers facing rights advocates, the nationalization of the movement is little short of miraculous. The entry of the social movement into the political field was made possible by a massive concentration of different resources (economic, political, and cultural capital) from leading organizations. The leadership used these resources to invest in a countrywide infrastructure, develop tight relations with federal elected officials, and produce and disseminate a coherent discourse to a national public. As the larger organizations assumed the costs and risks of going national, local and regional organizations were able buy into the national network and assume a role within it. The emerging national leadership also laid down basic rules of collective action while generating a common identity for thousands of activists and immigrants across the country. These leading organizations formed in a leviathan of the immigrant rights movement.

The book draws on a range of resources, including interviews with leading advocates and organizers, newspaper documentation on both immigration reform and day laborer conflicts, financial documents from a sample of advocacy organizations, White House visitor data for the Obama administration, and, finally, documents from campaigns and the philanthropic foundation Open Society. The first part of the book focuses on the local origins of the movements and covers the period from the late 1980s to the early 2000s. This period marks the proliferation of small battles for the rights of immigrants in communities across the country. The second part of the book addresses the time from the early 2000s to the last years of the Obama administration. This period is important because it marks the rise and consolidation of the mainstream national immigrant rights movement. If readers are interested in the methodological details, they are encouraged to read the methods section in the appendix.

From Local Struggles to a National Social Movement

Two geographical arenas, local and national, shaped the immigrant rights movement. The local terrain was a breeding ground for emerging conflicts concerning immigration and citizenship. Anti- and proimmigrant forces disputed the meaning and boundaries of citizenship. They were responding to the concrete reality of immigrants moving into towns. Proimmigrant advocates were made up of immigrants and various allies who worked together in loose coalitions to expand the boundaries of citizenship. By the early 2000s, regional organizations had formed in large cities throughout the country. They worked to connect, steer, and support numerous campaigns that were unfolding throughout these metropolitan areas. This was the golden age of local immigrant organizing, as organizers worked with unions, legal advocates, churches, and so on to defend the rights of immigrants.

The move to the national political field precipitated important changes in the structure and logic of the social movement. Entry into national politics required enormous concentrations of economic and political capital. The more that leading organizations accumulated these forms of capital, the more they came to depend on elites for key resources and the more they moved away from the precarious working-class base that had fueled the early movement. Moreover, these organizations rationalized how they talked about the rights of immigrants. Rather than mixing and matching various frames, the mature immigrant rights movement prioritized liberal national discourse over alternatives. The leadership studied through focus groups and surveys how the national audience responded to mobilization frames. They came to understand that nationalist discourses resonated strongly with general audiences but especially those in conservative places. They subsequently wrapped immigrants in the language of the virtuous nation to assert their deservingness. The discursive strategy was devised to change the hearts and minds of average Americans and, in doing so, caged the rights of immigrants within the confines of the nation.

The intent of this book is not to recommend the best strategy, discourses, or organizing model but simply to highlight the dilemmas facing advocates and activists when moving into this political field. The movement became powerful in national politics by accumulating resources and employing nationalist discourses to make rights claims. Whereas resource accumulation made organizations dependent on elite benefactors, its framing of citizenship reinforced national belonging as a condition of membership and rights. The 2010s witnessed the emergence of a very rich and powerful social movement but one that could not effectively challenge its political patrons or denounce the exclusionary underpinnings of national citizenship. The conditions that allowed the immigrant rights movement to become a political force consequently bound the movement inextricably to the system that it was seeking to change. A movement for the rights of foreigners was paradoxically transformed into another political force contributing to the reproduction of national citizenship.

Although the book focuses on the mainstream immigrant rights movement, it must be stressed that not all organizations and activists cooperated with the national leadership. Some organizations certainly cooperated and played important roles within this national movement. Others, however, were dismayed by the hierarchical nature of the movement, its nationalist mobilizing frames, and its unwillingness to criticize the Obama administration for its aggressive enforcement policies. There were certainly important advantages to centralizing and rationalizing the movement, but this process produced cleavages that spurred the formation of an influential left flank.

CHAPTER 1

The Rights of Immigrants in the Nation

A NUMBER OF SCHOLARS have suggested that globalization is weakening the underpinnings of national citizenship and increasing the salience of universal human rights. For instance, some have maintained that the growing importance of transnational political solidarities and institutions whittle away at national solidarity and give rise to postnational citizenship.[1] Other scholars have made forceful arguments that the resurgence of the bordered nation-state reflects a polity in deep crisis.[2] There may certainly appear to be more nationalism than ever, they claim, but these are the violent spasms of waning power. And still others have argued that the process of state deterritorialization has made it possible for cities to assume a much greater role in defining the terms of citizenship[3] and that the connections between cities result in translocal political communities that bypass the nation-state. These different arguments suggest that globalization and international migration have weakened state sovereignty and its capacities to exert its monopoly over citizenship. New spaces are opening up in the wake of the nation-state's decline and creating possibilities for experimentation in the form and substance of citizenship.

This book maintains that neoliberal globalization and transnational immigration have indeed disrupted national citizenship but that most of these battles have been circumscribed by the caging powers of national citizenship. Social movements are not free to imagine, frame, and push for policies of their own choosing. They are confined by political fields with specific rules of engagement. Activists increase their power to redefine boundaries of citizenship by following a recognized playbook. Many proimmigrant advocates have worked to amass resources and generate language that resonate with the values and sensibilities of the public. To maximize resonance, they must ensure that their messages are delivered to the national public with consistency and discipline.[4] The fight for the rights of immigrants was, the book maintains, confined by national citizenship. Immigrant rights advocates pushed to expand the boundaries of national citizenship but not to dismantle them. Instead, the movement became one vehicle among others propagating nationalism, albeit a liberal and multicultural version, in the United States.

This wasn't always the case. Local battles in the 1990s and 2000s sometimes displayed more radical and less polished qualities. Activists and allies fought alongside one another for the protection of immigrants living in their vicinities. They fought against restrictions that targeted people on the basis of their national origin and immigration status. They drew on various framings of citizenship, some status quo and others more radical. This cacophony of local voices and frames, however, gave way to an increasingly singular voice that stressed the centrality of the nation and the deservingness of immigrants. Within the span of ten years, one specific vision of citizenship came to dominate how many activists, advocates, and allies talked about citizenship and rights. This is not to say that one particular model is better than another but just to stress that one model of organizing and talking about citizenship became prominent as the movement entered the national political field.

To analyze the sticking power of national citizenship, this chapter draws on various theoretical traditions, including social-movement theory, political sociology, citizenship theory, and immigration studies. The book uses field analysis as a general framework to weave these theoretical strands together. The field approach taken here draws as much from Pierre Bourdieu[5] as it does from recent applications of the concept to organizational, social-movement, and race theory.[6] The political field is a space in which actors (elected officials, government agents, social-movement organizations, media, and individuals) struggle to shape public issues and policies. These actors, as Neil Fligstein and Doug McAdam suggest, "interact with knowledge of one another under a set of common understandings about the purposes of the field, the relationships in the field (including who has power and why), and the field's rules."[7] Within the field, different actors use the resources at their disposal to engage in battles "over the conservation or transformation of relations of domination."[8] Although challengers within the field aim to change these relations of domination, their legitimacy requires them to abide by established rules and norms. Abidance, however, can result in supporting a system that one was seeking to change. In the field of national citizenship, immigrant rights advocates fight to expand (symbolic as well as legal) national boundaries and make them more inclusive.[9] But they feel compelled to obey rules and norms that reify the nation and favor groups of immigrants who cohere to nationalist norms (deserving) over those who do not (undeserving). Thus, in response to the constraints of the field, the mainstream immigrant rights movement played a major role in legitimating national citizenship and contributing to its reproduction.

National Citizenship as a Political Field

This section examines the foundational norms of national citizenship. It suggests that these norms are often expressed through institutions and networks, which naturalize nationhood as a necessary condition of citizenship.

Foundational Norms: Borders, Identity, Rights, and State

There are four basic norms that hold the field of national citizenship together: the border, national identity, recognition of rights on the basis of national belonging, and state monopoly over citizenship. These norms give the field its coherency and provide actors with basic rules for pursuing their political goals.

The border is a foundational concept. State sovereignty has historically rested on a well-bordered territory made up of mutually exclusive peoples. Wendy Brown explains that "sovereignty is a peculiar border concept, not only demarking the boundaries of an entity but through this demarcation setting terms and organizing the space both inside and outside the entity."[10] Furthermore, the bordered territory lays down the foundations for a national community and identity. The border demarcates the community from what it is not.[11] The demarcation is meaningful because it is structured through a binary logic of good and bad, sacred and profane.[12] These binaries, according to Jeffrey Alexander, "reveal the skeletal structures on which social communities build the familiar stories, the rich narrative forms, that guide their everyday, taken-for-granted political life."[13] The border makes the nation-state possible while providing the boundary needed to construct a potent national identity. Consequently, national citizenship cannot exist without a border that excludes, no matter how liberal and expansive its vision of citizenship.

A common identity is another necessary condition of national citizenship. National identity provides members of the community with shared values and a common culture that make collective political action possible in a country. Damian Tambini suggests that "we are unlikely to contribute to the making of a collective good if we do not believe that we shall be among those who share in it, and that free-riders will be excluded. Some argue that this is the reason that citizenship engagement is stronger where national identity is stronger."[14] Members of the community agree to play by the rules and contribute to the national enterprise because they know they will benefit from their efforts and free riders will not. Also, national identity has an ethnic core, even when the citizenship regime is civic or liberal. Anthony Smith argues that "examination always reveals the ethnic core of civic nations, in practice, even in immigrant societies with their early pioneering and dominant (English and Spanish) culture in America, Australia, or Argentina, a culture that provided the myths and language of the would be nation."[15] Identity therefore provides citizens with common moralities and symbols and a common culture serving to demarcate insider from outsider while offering reasons for solidarity and collective action.

Rights within the nation-state are not universal, inalienable, or natural, because rights stem from national belonging.[16] A person is recognized as a full-rights-bearing human being because of her membership within the political community and not because of the simple fact that she is human. Nation-states are, therefore, institutions that are by their very logic discriminatory. The early nation-state, however, struggled to accommodate universal and national norms of rights. Norbert Elias notes that

> sovereign interdependent nation-states . . . produced a two-fold code of norms whose demands are inherently contradictory: a moral code descended from that of rising sections of the third estate, egalitarian in character, and whose highest value is "man"—the human individual as such; and a nationalist code . . . , inegalitarian in character, and whose highest value is a collectivity—the state, the country, the nation to which an individual belongs.[17]

Facing interstate rivalries and internal class conflict in the late nineteenth century, the bourgeoisie, according to Elias, deemphasized the universalism of its youth and prioritized national belonging and solidarity as a condition of rights. Such a system would be further institutionalized with the League of Nations and the enactment of the Minority Treaties.[18] Rights would be accorded equally to national citizens, while a restricted set of protections, if any at all, were granted to nonnationals.[19] For Hannah Arendt, the case of state-

less people in the years following World War I exemplifies this. Stateless people had rights in an abstract sense but the recognition and realization of those
rights depended on membership in a national state. Arendt observes that

> the conception of human rights, based upon the assumed existence of a hu-
> man being as such, broke down the very moment when those who professed
> to believe in it were for the first time confronted with people who had indeed
> lost all other qualities and specific relationships—except that they were still
> human. The world found nothing sacred in the abstract nakedness of being
> human.[20]

Universal human rights had become subsumed by an exclusionary and discriminatory nation-state. Arendt goes on to note that "the nation had con-
quered the state, national interest had priority over the law long before Hitler
could pronounce 'right is what is good for the German people.'"[21] As citizenship and rights were nationalized, eligibility for full rights became dependent
on membership in the nation-state. Although there would continue to be tensions between national and human rights,[22] states, in the last instance, developed citizenship regimes that clearly made national membership the most
important criterion for full rights.

The last condition of national citizenship is the central state's monopoly
over the legal and symbolic boundaries of citizenship.[23] The state's very legitimacy became tied to its ability to carry out its national mandate. This, according to John Torpey, prompted states to exert a monopoly over the legitimate
means of movement and to expand their capacities to identify and surveil individuals within their borders.[24] States developed legal criteria for determin-
ing national membership, methods to discern membership, and an array of
techniques to detect and expel people who did not belong. Securing borders
and the movement of people across them therefore became the primary responsibility of the state. States also exerted enormous symbolic power over
national citizenship.[25] The "statements of the state," according to Philip Corrigan and Derek Sayer, "define, in great detail, acceptable forms and images of
social activity and individual and collective identity; they regulate, in empiri-
cally specifiable ways, much—very much, by the twentieth century—of social
life."[26] The state consequently became the arbiter of national membership, legally and symbolically, and assumed responsibility for the discriminatory
distribution of rights. In the United States, the struggle to assert the federal
government's authority over these matters has been ongoing since the 1880s.[27]

When cities and states attempted to pass immigration policies, courts ruled more often than not that the federal government preempted such policies.[28] Localities may serve as the breeding ground for fights over the boundaries of citizenship, but the central state retains its monopoly over which boundaries gain legitimacy and legal standing and which ones do not. Changing the rules of citizenship, consequently, requires political engagement in the halls of national power.

National citizenship, therefore, is underpinned by several foundational norms: sacralized borders, common identity, unequal rights, and the overwhelming legal and symbolic power of the central state. These norms serve as guardrails that guide the political action of those seeking to expand, conserve, or roll back the boundaries of national citizenship.

Naturalizing the Nation

The norms just described are naturalized and serve as basic rules of collective political action. Naturalization makes it possible for people to believe in national citizenship and to fight to modify or defend it rather than abolish it. In their theorization of race, Mustafa Emirbayer and Matthew Desmond argue that belief in the illusion of race makes collusion in the racial field possible. As they put it, "An underlying consensus in the relations of this 'well founded illusion' [or *illusio*] must exist—'a *collusio* in the *illusio*, a deep-seated complicating in the collective fantasy'—for race to have salience in social experience" (emphasis in original).[29] Similarly, the naturalization of national citizenship makes it real enough to ensure mass collusion by defenders and challengers alike. When people engage in these struggles, they collude with the illusion of national citizenship and contribute to its reproduction.

The state historically played a decisive role in naturalizing national citizenship. An internally expansive and bureaucratically sophisticated state helped produce and naturalize a national political community. "From being fairly insignificant [in the late eighteenth century]," Michael Mann argues, "states suddenly loomed large in the lives of their subjects, taxing them, conscripting them, attempting to mobilize their enthusiasm for its goals. States were becoming cages, trapping subjects within their bars."[30] The infrastructural powers of the state increased dramatically in the years following World War II.[31] Whereas militarism and international institutions (for example, the United Nations and Bretton Woods) buttressed the legitimacy of the bordered territorial state, the welfare state reinforced the links between national membership, solidarity, and rights.[32] Moreover, modern state infrastructure consisted of a series of organizational networks that permitted the circulation of powerful discourses and norms across society.[33] Public officials making up these networks—from the president to schoolteachers—served as relays that circulated national language, norms, and rules of citizenship.[34] Similar discourses were diffused through these different institutional networks, embracing the people in mutually reinforcing norms, feelings, and language.[35] The profusion of these state networks saturated inhabitants with the culture of the nation and the idea that rights should depend on national membership. Mann maintains that, in this way, "intense feelings of national community attachment have been fused into a single caging institution."[36]

As the tentacles of the nation-state embraced its people, citizens developed what Norbert Elias called a "national habitus."[37] *Habitus* refers to the process of internalizing external structural categories (for example, nation, class, and gender), which in turn shapes how people perceive, feel about, and act in the world. The nation, according to Elias, helped "form an integral part of the we-images and the we-ideals of most of the individuals. . . . This, in short, is one of the many instances of correspondence between specific types of social structure and specific types of personality structure."[38] Viewed from this perspective, the nation was not something that was "out there." The nation became a part of a person's feelings, thoughts, and actions. It was embodied by individuals and expressed through dispositions such as accents, gestures, fashion styles, tastes, and the use of colloquialisms.[39] Because dispositions were reflective of national belonging, they became important markers of membership and distinction. The nation consumed its people, and the people became relays of national norms, with each person assuming specific responsibility for reproducing nationalist culture, dispositions, and ethos in everyday life.

The norms underlying national citizenship undergo a process that render them natural and sacred. The nation comes to serve as the foundational grammar for how nationals think, talk, and feel about rights and citizenship. It provides a common set of references (border, identity, rights, and state) that make discussion about rights and citizenship legible. Thinking and talking about immigrant rights beyond the nation can be incomprehensible for those held by the nation's tight embrace. Articulating rights claims beyond commonsense understandings of the nation places these claims on the margins of legitimate politics. Arendt wryly describes the advocacy organizations fighting for the protection of the "Rights of Man." These efforts were, according to her, "sponsored by marginal figures—by a few international jurists without political experience or professional philanthropists supported by the uncertain sentiments of professional idealists."[40] She goes on to portray their utter marginality in the field of national citizenship.

> The groups they formed, the declarations they issued, showed an uncanny similarity in language and composition to that of societies for the prevention of cruelty to animals. No statesman, no political figure of any importance could possibly take them seriously; and none of the liberal or radical parties in Europe thought it necessary to incorporate into their programs a new declaration of human rights.[41]

Although "professional idealists" continued to mount campaigns for human rights, their claims and language had no legitimate place within the field of national citizenship. Thus, people are free to say what they want about rights and citizenship, but utterances are more likely to be recognized as intelligible and legitimate when they stay within the parameters of the nation.

Proimmigrant forces push the boundaries of citizenship but not under conditions of their own choosing. The nation is an essential part of the habitus and "moral ontology"[42] of its citizenry, and the state continues to exercise inordinate power—symbolic, political, and legal—over its boundaries. These conditions impose constraints on how proimmigrant forces go about expanding the boundaries of national citizenship. Radicals who eschew the rules of the game may certainly disrupt the field with assertive tactics, but without sufficient support they are likely to be pushed to the margins of the political field.

Framings of National Citizenship

National citizenship is stable but not fixed.[43] For nearly thirty years, the immigrant rights movement has been struggling to expand its symbolic and legal boundaries. Most of these battles have employed different framings of citizenship. These master frames help structure how activists make concrete claims about rights and nationhood.[44] These frames are not merely symbolic weapons to win over support for a cause. Successful framings of citizenship provide policy makers with the conceptual categories to draw the legal lines of inclusion and exclusion. This section identifies four common master frames used to inform debates about citizenship. These are arranged from most to least restrictive. The master frames highlighted here are not exhaustive or mutually exclusive. They simply cover prominent ways to talk about citizenship in the United States.

At the most restrictive end of the spectrum lies ethnonational citizenship. Ethnonationalism frames citizenship as a "community of descent," with membership depending on jus sanguinis or on common cultural traits.[45] The legal, physical, and symbolic boundaries separating "national self" and "foreign other" are viewed as sacred, bright, and immutable.[46] Without a sharp and inviolable line there could be no nation. The continued presence of undocumented immigrants on national territory violates the sanctity of the border, national sovereignty, the rule of law, and national identity.[47] This makes undocumented immigrants an existential threat. The immigrant population is also conceived as a contagion, with each single undocumented immigrant attracting hundreds through chain migration. "Illegal," in this discursive context, is not a description of a person who crossed a border without government authorization. It is a label indicating that a person is beyond the pale[48] of the established legal order. They are, consequently, without rights and are legitimate targets of zero-tolerance repression. Ethnonationalists therefore view members of the national community as exceptional and sacred and undocumented immigrants as "barbarians" and an "enemy of all."[49]

Further to the left on the spectrum is liberal nationalism.[50] Liberal nationalism is more expansive than ethnonationalism but still upholds the inviolability of national identity and borders. It maintains that a well-bordered nation with a strong national identity remains a precondition of a solidary, egalitarian, and democratic political community.[51] Damian Tambini explains that "in the absence of the nation as the embodiment of the public good, and with no recognizable identity, civic culture, or project, citizenship is impossible."[52] While upholding borders and identity, liberal nationalism also posits that this is a nation of immigrants, open to some but not all immigrants. Several attributes make some immigrants deserving of full membership, including cultural assimilation, embeddedness,[53] and economic contribution. Undocumented immigrants bearing these qualities are conceived as de facto Americans who merit a pathway to becoming de jure Americans. The concept of affiliation has been used to denote the qualities that make certain immigrants deserving of recognition and membership. Hiroshi Motomura notes that

> according to affiliation-based arguments, *the ties that unlawful migrants have built within the United States deserve recognition.* These ties might be based,

for example, on migrants' lives as productive members of their communities who contribute to the economy through work, taxes, and civic participation, and whose U.S. citizen children make or will make similar contributions (emphasis added).[54]

Motomura later adds that "contributions to American society, especially if substantial, can offset prior acts even if those acts are viewed as clear violations."[55] Whereas the concept of affiliation provides a path for some undocumented immigrants, it does not provide a path for all. Not all immigrants are equally affiliated, because some are more assimilated, rooted, and contributing than others. The least affiliated immigrants in American society (for example, recent arrivals, the unassimilated, and the poor) may be considered ineligible for membership and, consequently, suitable for deportation. Distinctions based on the degree of affiliation generate a normative hierarchy of deservingness, which informs how lawmakers draw the legal lines between inclusion and exclusion. Thus, liberal nationalism expands the boundaries of national citizenship while also ranking immigrants in order from most to least deserving. For much of the past half century, this particular framing of citizenship enjoyed much bipartisan support. Only with the growing dominance of ethnonationalism in the Republican Party did liberal nationalism become the reserve of the Democratic Party.

Territorial personhood suggests that presence in the territorial United States provides undocumented immigrants with constitutionally protected rights.[56] Undocumented immigrants possess civil rights that are firmly protected by the equal protection clause of the Fourteenth Amendment, the due process clause of the Fifth Amendment, and a series of Supreme Court rulings.[57] Michael Walzer[58] maintains that recognition of rights should not stem from the degree of affiliation (that is, assimilation, rootedness, and contributions) but simply by the fact that an immigrant is a human being living within a constitutional democracy. Linda Bosniak summarizes the position.

> The territorial conception repudiates the notion of differential levels of inclusion, regarding the maintenance of partial membership statuses as illegitimate under liberal and democratic principles. It thus treats the conception of belonging as more of a binary than a continuum. It says: once someone is in the geographical territory of the state, that person must, for most purposes, be treated as fully in. The fact of a person's "hereness" itself triggers the extension of extensive rights and recognition.[59]

In spite of its inclusiveness, territorial personhood recognizes the continued significance of borders and national identity. Borders are conceived as a necessary condition for a solidary and democratic political community. Bosniak characterizes this conception as "boundedness governs at the community's edges, while inclusiveness prevails within."[60] The state, according to this framing, should ensure the equal protection of all residing within its territory while enforcing borders to keep unwanted people out. These two principles, equal rights for those within *and* the maintenance of exclusionary borders, present important and unresolvable contradictions. Thus, like liberal nationalism, territorial personhood recognizes the centrality of borders. But unlike liberal nationalism, it rejects status distinctions on the basis of affiliation and asserts the equality of all people residing within a national territory.

At the least restrictive end of the spectrum stands postnationalism. This is the only framing of citizenship that rejects the nation-state as a condition of rights and equality and as an institution with a monopoly over the governance of citizenship.[61] Yasemin Soysal argued in the 1990s that the political conditions were ripe for postnational citizenship. At a juncture of rapid globalization and transnational immigration, communities were extending beyond the boundaries of the nation-state, and governing institutions (both national and transnational) were adopting legal norms that recognized and protected the human rights of immigrants. Soysal suggested that "solidarities are shaped beyond national boundaries; and the referent is no longer exclusively the national citizen, but increasingly an abstract individual entitled to claim the collective and bring it back to the public sphere as her 'natural' right."[62] Activists, Soysal went on to argue, "connect the claims of individuals and groups to broader institutionalized agendas and globally dominant discourses, rather than simply reinvent cultural particularisms,"[63] such as national identity. Thus, like territorial personhood, postnationalism asserts that all people merit equal rights simply because they are human. Unlike territorial personhood, postnationalism disavows the centrality of borders and national identity as necessary conditions for a democratic and egalitarian citizenship regime.

Anti- and proimmigrant activists therefore draw on these framings of citizenship to make their public arguments. It goes without saying that proimmigrant activists draw from the last three. Although the frames described here are analytically distinct, scholars and activists often make use of multiple framings to construct their arguments. Early immigrant rights activists frequently used liberal, territorial, and postnational framings concurrently, without recognizing inconsistencies between them. Later in the chapter, I will argue that when battles mature and shift scale into the national political arena, field constraints (that is, the need to achieve resonance and the need to counter the frames of adversaries) can encourage activists to select one frame (liberal nationalism) over others (territorial personhood or postnationalism).

Gaining Power within the Field of National Citizenship

In the 1990s and early 2000s, immigrant rights mobilizations were literally stuck in place. While immigration policy was made by the federal government, actual campaigns continued to concentrate in scattered localities. The early movement faced a geographical mismatch between the spaces that enabled emerging mobilizations (local) and the growing concentration of central state power (federal). This changed in the mid-2000s when a robust social-movement infrastructure emerged that tied many different organizations into a cohesive network with a relatively unified identity.

A central puzzle of this book concerns the process of moving from local battles to a national social movement. Such a process is by no means straightforward. It entails building a countrywide infrastructure, creating relations and influence with federal government officials, and constructing a compelling voice that resonates with the norms and moral sensibilities of nationals. How did resource-poor, maligned, local immigrant activists scale up to one of the most robust social movements of our time? This section draws inspiration from resource mobilization theory (RMT)[64] and field analysis to respond to the question. It suggests that the movement's growing prominence in the field of national citizenship was made possible by the accumulation of economic, political, and cultural capital.

Becoming active in national politics requires money.[65] Economic capital enables organizations to grow, acquire staff with specialized and professional skills, plan for long-term goals, lobby high-ranking political officials, invest in countrywide infrastructure, and enact far-reaching mobilizations. Economic capital also allows actors to develop sophisticated organizations with vertically integrated divisions of labor, with legal, communication, lobbying, and mobilization teams working in-house. By contrast, organizations with limited economic resources have difficulty securing their own survival. Staff may have few professional skills, and there may be high turnover rates because of long hours, low pay, and organizational uncertainty. The lack of financial resources prioritizes short-term survival over long-term goals and planning. Also, poorer organizations lack the capacity to mount large, costly campaigns and to lobby federal officials. The accumulation of economic capital is therefore a necessary condition for building a national, integrated social movement. Whereas organizations in the past depended more on dues from local members, modern organizations with national aspirations attract substantial sums of money from large foundations and elite donors. This places foundations in a strategically important position in today's social-movement ecology.[66]

Political capital is defined here as relations with strategically important political officials that allow organizations to exercise influence over public policy. Access to government officials lets organizations and officials develop trusting, interdependent relations. Organizations with political capital gain insights into the inner workings of government. Such information is valuable because it provides advocates with a clear understanding of political opportunities and constraints. This allows them to better identify political targets and develop more effective methods to exert pressure. Organizations lacking political access have greater difficulty exercising influence. Influential political officials may not know, count on, or trust the outside organization, making officials less likely to respond to their demands. Additionally, the lack of access provides organizations with few if any insights into the political machine, compelling activists to make decisions on the basis of incomplete information, unconfirmed hearsay, and media stories. The absence of good information introduces great uncertainty to organizations, which makes it less likely for them to mount costly political campaigns. They are more likely to opt out of contentious politics entirely, invest in political arenas in which they have more access, or tag onto the campaigns of other organizations that have greater political access.

Cultural capital is defined as inherited cultural dispositions (for example, taste, manners of speech, and interests) used to mark one's position in the class hierarchy. Pierre Bourdieu argued that there is a direct correlation between class and culture.[67] Dispositions such as taste and consumption preferences serve as markers of class distinction and weapons in the struggle over class positioning. For political advocacy purposes, cultural capital can be redefined as the cultural attributes that allow activists to produce politically potent symbols such as discourse, clothes, flags, and performances. Although much of this cultural capital is inherited, it can also be acquired through formal education (university in particular) and sustained engagement—in the form of retreats, workshops, and the like—in professional advocacy circles. The growing importance of communication in social movements has increased demand for cultural skills. This has given rise to the growing number of middle-class people filling the ranks of national advocacy organizations. They assume greater responsibility in crafting discourses and symbols to represent an issue and the people experiencing an injustice. Established communication specialists in advocacy organizations also have durable contacts with journalists and media producers, which allows them to direct how the movement is represented in news reports.

Each form of capital identified here is important in its own right for national political campaigns. But the value of each is enhanced because it can be used to leverage other forms of capital. Pierre Bourdieu[68] calls this a process of conversion. For instance, money allows an organization to invest in middle-class staff with high levels of cultural capital. They can then use that capital to produce compelling frames and narratives about the plight of immigrants. Money is also essential for developing strong relations with political officials. Organizations can use high levels of political access to demonstrate their influence and justify funding decisions among foundations and to improve their status within the media. Cultural capital is useful not only in communicating to the general public but also in establishing good relations with funders and politicians. The habitus of culturally endowed actors provides them with the codes, norms, backgrounds, and dispositions needed to communicate and interact easily with elite funders and politicians. Cultural capital is not a necessary condition for tapping economic and political capital, but it definitely helps to lubricate elite networks. Thus, the importance of each resource is enhanced because of its potential conversion to other forms of capital. Losing one form undercuts the ability to acquire others, eating into and weakening any single organization's power within the field.

The central state's inordinate power over immigration policy draws advocacy organizations into the federal political arena. Doing so, however, is a costly affair. Enormous levels of economic capital are required to finance an organizational infrastructure, develop complex media campaigns, hire professional staff, and so on. Advocacy organizations also need political capital and access to elite federal officeholders. This allows these organizations to communicate regularly with policy makers and obtain scarce, valuable information about government, policy, and politics. Finally, they need cultural capital to cultivate and disseminate far-reaching and morally resonant discourses. Thus, elevating the voice of a marginalized group and achieving change in national politics require enormous resources. Those organizations that fail to accumulate these resources risk being cast into the margins of the national political field.

The Paradox of Power

Starting in the mid-2000s, several prominent advocacy organizations began to invest heavily in immigrant rights activism. These investments transformed what was a largely local movement in the 1990s and early 2000s into a robust national social movement in the late 2000s and early 2010s. The advocacy groups built a national infrastructure that would connect local and regional organizations to the national leadership. They possessed the money and skills to plan long-term campaigns for comprehensive immigration reform. They lobbied politicians, mounted legal battles, and ran sophisticated media campaigns. They effectively drew on American norms to craft resonant arguments about immigrants, rights, and citizenship.

Their growing power, however, came at a price. The leadership embraced nationalism and was constrained by political and financial benefactors. The concentration of resources also engendered conflicts between national leadership and grassroots activists. These, among other consequences, limited how hard the movement could push to change the system and weakened its unity and political resolve. The pathway to power within this political field ultimately constrained what the movement could do and say. The movement would, consequently, become another contribution to the reproduction of national citizenship rather than pushing for its transformation.

Nationalizing the Immigrant Voice

Resonance, according to Robert Benford and David Snow, depends on "how essential the beliefs, values, and ideas associated with movement frames are to the lives of the targets of mobilization."[69] Social-movement organizations prioritize and amplify the values that they believe will resonate the most with their target audience.[70] Given that nationalism has a stranglehold over the political imaginations of most Americans, the use of national norms and discourse makes communication about citizenship, rights, and belonging comprehensible. Nationalism shapes what the public understands to be legible and legitimate claims.[71] Marco Giugni and Florence Passy argue, for instance, that "contentious politics is enabled or constrained not only by (political) institutions, but also by the shared (cultural) understandings and collective definition of the groups involved and of the ways in which the members of those groups should be included in or excluded from the larger community—in this case, the national state."[72] The path to rights, therefore, travels through the discursive and cultural landscape of the nation. Reaching a target audience also requires a clear and consistent message. Robert Benford and David Snow note that "a frame's consistency refers to the congruency between the SMO's articulated beliefs, claims, and actions."[73] The absence of consistency results in a cacophony of utterances, which obscures the impact of a well-developed message.[74] Consequently, activists are encouraged to cultivate a resonant frame, continually refine that frame, and suppress other frames that may generate inconsistences.

Generating a resonant and consistent message in the field of national citizenship favors one framing of citizenship (liberal national) over others (territorial personhood or postnational). Liberal nationalism proposes greater inclusion while simultaneously embracing core national norms (border, identity, discriminatory rights, and authority of central state). Tropes such as "a nation of immigrants" and narratives concerning the hardworking, family-loving migrants are well entrenched in commonsense understandings of citizenship of many, but certainly not all, Americans. Although the need for resonance elevates liberal nationalism over alternatives, the need for consistency favors organizing messaging, talking points, and stories according to this master frame and silencing alternatives.

Countering the frames of anti-immigrant adversaries further locks the movement into liberal nationalism.[75] Anti-immigrant forces argued that the boundaries of the nation were sharp and the carrying capacities of the nation limited. Moreover, undocumented immigrants were polluting agents (for example, rapists, murders, cultural inferiors, and usurpers),[76] making it impossible to consider them as legitimate residents, let alone citizens.[77] Proimmigrant forces felt compelled to counter powerful frames that aimed to disqualify all undocumented immigrants from the possibility of becoming American. They argued that America's exceptionalism did not stem from its walls and chauvinistic isolationism. The country was exceptional because it was a nation of immigrants.[78] Advocates also cleansed the stigmas attributed to immigrants by inverting them. If anti-immigrant forces disqualified immigrants because of their cultural otherness and supposed freeloading, proimmigrant advocates represented as culturally assimilated, hardworking contributors,[79] ultimately producing a public image of undocumented immigrants as an upright model minority.[80] Thus, movement-countermovement dynamics further hemmed the movement within the confines of liberal nationalism.

Framing is not merely a symbolic activity. A discursive infrastructure is required to ensure that a central message is articulated and disseminated in a consistent and disciplined way. This can precipitate leaders investing in such an infrastructure to ensure message discipline.[81] Such investments are aimed at producing mobilizing frames, talking points, and narratives.[82] Communication professionals perform research on resonant language and devise their strategies accordingly.

Ensuring that a message is delivered in a consistent way by thousands of advocates and activists also requires training. Message training can unfold in various ways, ranging from informal suggestions among activists to more formal workshops. Activists learn how to construct a story that effectively conveys the message of the movement to the target audience. They learn how to express urgency and how to deliver basic talking points to media outlets. The movement's leaders therefore construct a discursive infrastructure consisting of methods to manufacture language, circulate it to the public and to movement members, and train members in the discourse's proper usage. The discursive infrastructure becomes a method to instill and naturalize nationalist discourses among the thousands of activists in the movement.[83] It serves to normalize the nation among activists and control their talk and actions.

The field of national citizenship therefore presents proimmigrant advocates several constraints on how to talk about immigrants and their rights in the public sphere. First, proimmigrant advocates need to create a message that can resonate with a broad, mainstream, and thoroughly American audience. This favors a master frame that is nationalist enough to speak to American sensibilities but also liberal enough to provide those deemed deserving a pathway to citizenship. Second, proimmigrant advocates need to counter adversaries who seek to disqualify undocumented immigrants from national membership. The constant effort to invert disqualifying stigmas can lock proimmigrant forces into the use of liberal nationalism. Finally, the need to generate a consistent message in a countrywide social movement requires an infrastructure to train grassroots activists in the use of the movement's language and ideology. Thus, the rules of the game favor the selection of liberal nationalism over other framings of citizenship and the construction of a discursive machine to ensure the disciplined delivery of the movement's message into the public sphere.

Constraining the Professional Leadership

The growth of well-resourced, professional, national advocacy organizations has been a general trend. It is by no means limited to the immigrant rights movement.[84] Scholars have shown that starting in the late 1960s and 1970s, many organizations relocated their headquarters to Washington DC, far away from the population centers of their members. These moves were precipitated by the growing regulatory and fiscal powers of the federal government.[85] Liberal advocacy organizations, in particular, began to focus on shaping federal policy. Their entry into federal politics helped to spur a process of professionalization. Organizations rationalized their operations, introduced complex divisions of labor, and hired college-trained experts. "The proliferating new organizations," Robert Putnam observes, "are professionally staffed advocacy organizations, not member centered, locally based associations. The newer groups focus on expressing policy views in the national political debate."[86] Although professionalization made organizations more effective in certain ways, it also introduced significant constraints on what could be done.

The massive influx of money from large foundations has made large advocacy organizations more accountable to affluent foundations than to the precarious communities they are supposed to represent. The growth of sizable, professionally staffed organizations increased dependency on large philanthropic foundations from the late 1960s onward. This marked an important change in how organizations acquired revenue. Prior to this time, organizations received most of their funding from membership fees. Under this model, advocacy groups seeking to expand their national prominence needed to increase the number of members in local branches across the country. The organizations would have to recruit people through personal networks, build trust with communities, and sustain local legitimacy.[87] An organization's national prominence was therefore tied to the health and growth of its grassroots base. This changed with the massive funding influx from foundations. Organizations with national aspirations no longer needed to cultivate local members to increase revenue. Instead, they needed to hire professionals with expertise in identifying grants, writing grant proposals, and cultivating strong ties to program officers in large foundations. According to Theda Skocpol, organizations now had "a greater need to pay attention to foundations and the wealthy."[88] The growing power of a handful of large funders within a field has compelled different organizations to adopt the same organizing model, resulting in what Paul DiMaggio and Walter Powell have called "institutional isomorphism." DiMaggio and Powell suggest that "the greater the extent to which an organizational field is dependent upon a single (or several similar) source of support for vital resources, the higher the level of isomorphism."[89] Thus, large professional organizations have become far more dependent on and accountable to elite foundations than to precarious communities.

More access to the federal government presented its own distinctive constraints on advocacy organizations. Access required professional skills because of the sheer complexity of federal policy and politics, which in turn spurred the further professionalization of organizations. "After all," Skocpol notes, "there were now more decision makers to contact about policy concerns, new levers to pull in Washington, DC. And it was usually a matter of professionals contacting fellow professionals, people with similar policy interests, or perhaps fellow college classmates."[90] As professionals in advocacy organizations connected to professionals in government, their intellectual and political norms overlapped, increasing the likelihood of convergent worldviews and policy preferences. Additionally, political access could be used to leverage more money from foundations, more attention from the media, and more status and power from the social movement. Skocpol remarks that "they [liberal advocacy organizations] must cultivate access to government professionals in order to be able to claim to their public audiences that they have an impact on public policy making."[91] Government officials have been quite aware of the value of access and have used the threat of denial of access as leverage to ensure organizational compliance. The mere threat of denying access to an organization could be enough to ensure compliance with government goals. Thus, growing access to the halls of federal power spurred more professionalization, created convergent worldviews among advocates and government officials, and rendered advocacy organizations reliant on their political benefactors.

Professionalization has long been associated with the suppression of radical goals. National advocacy organizations reflect trends identified by Robert Michel in Germany's trade-union movement a hundred years ago.

The complex of tasks—and the financial and technical requirements of the structure which the trade unions create as they grow out of their swaddling clothes—demand the replacement of the agitator by the schooled official with specialized knowledge. The merchant adventurer who deals in class struggle yields his place to the dry and unimaginative accountant, the glowing idealist to the lukewarm materialist, the democrat, firm at least in theory, to the conscious autocrat.[92]

The radicalism of the German labor movement fell by the wayside as it became professionalized, bureaucratized, and imbricated with the field of capitalist social relations. The contemporary immigrant rights movement has faced a similar dilemma. Growing professionalization prioritizes organizational reproduction while dependency on systemic elites binds the professional leadership to the system it had once sought to transform. Thus, becoming a prominent organization in a national political field requires professionalization and resource dependency, which ultimately constrains what organizations can do.

Generating Hierarchy and Engendering Conflict

The conditions (accumulation of resources) that make it possible for movements to enter national politics also contribute to creating significant hierarchies within the social movement. Because national organizations have strong advantages, they are more likely to assume a leadership role within the national network. Dominant organizations set the strategy, targets, goals, and discursive frames of the struggle while also extracting a greater share of profit from the collective enterprise. The leading organizations are in a stronger position to benefit further from additional foundation support, political access, and media coverage, reinforcing their dominant position in an already stratified movement.

Moreover, the resources needed to articulate a legitimate political voice are not evenly distributed.[93] Kay Lehman Schlozman, Henry Brady, and Sidney Verba demonstrate that not all groups have an equal voice because of the unequal distribution of resources. Smaller, local organizations made up of actual immigrants may not have the financial resources to sustain a sophisticated communication infrastructure. They may not have the cultural capital and national habitus needed to craft discourses that resonate with white Americans in the suburbs of Ohio or Michigan. National, professional organizations are more likely to have the financial resources, technical skills, and cultural capital to produce clear and compelling discourses. They are also in a better position to hire professionals to perform focus groups and surveys, develop a messaging strategy, and connect to allies in the media. As a consequence, national advocacy organizations often become the representational leaders of social movements. They devise the legal arguments that justify rights claims, craft representations of immigrants that resonate with the norms and moralities of Americans, and represent immigrants in the media, to funders, and in negotiations with elected political officials. This results in a stratified structure in which rich national organizations tend to play a dominant role in producing the public representations of mostly working-class, undocumented immigrants.

The "stratification of political clout and voice"[94] plants seeds of conflict over leadership; the distribution of money, political access, media exposure, and general recognition; and who should be representing whom. These different points of conflict overlap and fortify one another, forming into the basic cleavages that fracture social movements into different parts. The process of fragmentation can ultimately undermine the capacities of a social movement to exert pressure on its principal targets.

Larger, national organizations have the resources to mount big campaigns, but this has come at the cost of severing ties to local members and grassroots support.[95] This creates a dilemma. Without grassroots support, national organizations may have trouble gaining recognition as the legitimate representatives of a population when in negotiations with White House and congressional officials. They may also have difficulty presenting themselves as trustworthy and legitimate in local communities. This, in turn, reduces their capacity to call on local organizations and activists to mobilize in support of a countrywide campaign. The thin grassroots infrastructure of national organizations results in low mobilization capacities and feeble campaigns.[96] Thus, in spite of greater resources and organizational sophistication, large, professional advocacy organizations headquartered in Washington, DC, still need grassroots support to achieve legitimacy and mobilize substantial numbers in national campaigns.

To make up for deficient grassroots infrastructure, some national organizations develop partnerships with prominent local organizations to tap into their grassroots social capital. They effectively outsource mobilization capacities to local allies. In the immigrant rights movement, the most strategic local allies are large regional organizations that possess strong ties to a variety of grassroots groups throughout their metropolitan region. During the 1990s and 2000s, these regional organizations served as the engines of immigrant rights advocacy.[97] For instance, the Illinois Coalition for Immigrant and Refugee Rights (ICIRR), located in Chicago, served as a coalition of many different local advocacy organizations working on issues related to immigration throughout the Chicago metropolitan region. For national organizations without members, regional organizations serve as gateways into the grassroots. National organizations can also draw on regional organizations for source material to construct compelling and morally resonant arguments for politicians, media, and the public. Regional organizations likewise are drawn to partnerships with national organizations. Regionals are rich in social capital, but they are comparatively poor in economic, political, and cultural capital, which limits their abilities to become important political players in the national field. Partnerships with larger organizations allow them to enter national politics without assuming the heavy costs. Such partnerships also provide new funding sources, greater media exposure, and access to a wide variety of government officials. Thus, the changing nature of national advocacy organizations has precipitated new interdependencies between organizations operating at different geographical scales.

This structure places regional organizations in a contradictory position. The conditions of organizational prominence in local and national political arenas differ greatly. Local organizations need to maintain their legitimacy among grassroots activists by demonstrating their commitment to community issues. National organizations, by contrast, must invest in maintaining good relations with national economic, political, and cultural elites. Moreover, national organizations are embedded in social and cultural worlds that are removed from their base. They are ensconced in different structural, political, and cultural worlds and, consequently, face different sets of pressures. Sometimes, what is urgent for national organizations is less urgent for grassroots organizations and vice versa. This sociopolitical disjuncture is exacerbated by the deep inequalities that arise within the social movement.

When strategic differences arise between national leaders and grassroots activists, regional organizations are stuck between the need to express loyalty to the national leadership because of the benefits derived from the leadership (that is, economic capital and political access) and the need to retain their legitimacy among grassroots allies and members. Too much loyalty to the national leadership can weaken local relations, diminish grassroots legitimacy, and give rise to recriminations. Regional organizations must therefore balance between maintaining legitimacy in the local social-movement milieu and maintaining loyalty to the national leadership. They are wedged in a contradictory position, perpetually being tugged at by competing obligations in national and grassroots political arenas.

Thus, the stratification of the social movement contributes to conflicting and contradictory relations. National organizations often become the centers of power within the social movement because of their abilities to amass enormous amounts of economic, political, and cultural resources. Their leadership position allows them to prosper from additional capital flowing into the movement, and their ability to capture the inflow of resources allows them to further improve their positioning within the political field. Doing so, however, unleashes irresolvable contradictions and conflicts. The constant tug between the local and the national, between the grassroots base and the leadership, has resulted in much discord, with several defiant factions losing faith in the leadership and starting their own campaigns for immigrant rights. Between these poles stand the regional organizations that are beholden to allies in both national and grassroots arenas. They face constant pressure from both sides to adhere to their strategies, framings, and worldviews. Failure to do so can, and often does, result in disapproval, censures, and, in some cases, the cessation of relations.

Organizations moving into the field of national citizenship face a pressing dilemma. Increasing positioning in the field requires the accumulation of important resources and the use of resonant frames. But by following these rules, the movement ends up further locked into national citizenship's iron cage. It produces language that reifies national belonging as a condition of rights and equality while generating organizations that look, act, and think like the government institutions they are seeking to change. And finally, emerging oligarchies induce complex cleavages that make unity nearly impossible. The movement's rise within this field does not constrict national citizenship's iron cage, but it thoroughly fragments the movement, thereby limiting the movement's ability to generate systemic change. Not playing by the rules of the game, however, risks producing a movement of what Arendt would call "professional idealists,"[98] pure in mind, spirit, and word but ignored by all and with little to show for their efforts.

Becoming Players in the National Field

The immigrant rights movement began in the grassroots but quickly scaled the heights of national political power. The federal government's growing command over immigration required organizations to shift their political focus to national politics. National organizations in the 2000s began to increase their power by developing strong relations with funders, government officials, and, to a lesser extent, the media. Accessing these elite venues allowed these organizations to amass more power and wealth, which made it possible for them to become players in the field of national citizenship. They produced discourses, built a national social-movement infrastructure, circulated discourses through their infrastructure and national media, and lobbied federal officials. Thus, they pushed to expand the boundaries of citizenship and introduce laws to translate liberal symbolic boundaries into reality.

The paradox of the social movement is that the conditions that made its power possible also restrained the full realization of that power. Advocacy organizations became more susceptible to the demands of government officials and elite funders. Leaders chose not to forcefully criticize the Obama administration's fierce enforcement and deportation policies. They became dependent on Democratic allies. And they employed language that reinforced the nationalist underpinnings of citizenship. The mainstream immigrant rights movement therefore eventually became a prisoner of the political field it was seeking to transform.

The fate of the mainstream immigrant rights movement is symptomatic of contemporary American civic life. Skocpol explains that "early-twenty-first-century Americans live in a diminished democracy, in a much less participatory and more oligarchically managed civic world."[99] Kay Lehman Schlozman, Henry Brady, and Sidney Verba make a slightly different point, suggesting that movements are increasingly run by privileged people who draw other privileged people into the leadership ranks. Such movements "are less likely to transform than to replicate representational outcomes of a participatory system in which the privileged speak more loudly than the disadvantaged."[100] There is more advocacy than ever, but the new advocacy tends to favor elite voices over precarious ones and status quo solutions over radical and more egalitarian ones. It is an advocacy that is decidedly liberal, and even progressive, yet oligarchic and prone to gently nudging political boundaries rather than forcefully subverting them.

PART I

THE LOCAL FIGHT FOR IMMIGRANT RIGHTS

CHAPTER 2

Suburbia Must Be Defended

DURING THE 1990S, towns and cities across the United States became front-line battlegrounds in the immigration debate. Immigrants were no longer invisible in out-of-sight fields, factories, kitchens, and barrios. They were not fading silently into the shadows. They were on the streets—taking public transportation, enrolling in schools, and opening businesses in highly trafficked areas. Immigrant day laborers were the most public of immigrants. In the hope of finding work, they congregated in large groups on streets and in busy retail areas. Many longtime residents viewed these immigrant workers as problematic interlopers. Most of those who complained focused on their visibility. Viewed as frightening, uncivilized, and bellicose, they were accused of swarming passing cars, acting aggressively toward women, urinating in the open, and deviating from all forms of decent conduct. Their continued presence threatened to displace residents from their own towns. Many believed that they were losing their right to the city.

Up to this time, many Americans had never thought or talked about national citizenship. There had certainly been surges of xenophobia in the country's history, but it was generally a nonissue for much of the postwar period. For most, national citizenship was a settled and largely naturalized category that didn't elicit much thought or passion. This changed with the settlement of immigrants in towns across the country. People began to reconsider the boundaries of citizenship. They deliberated over who merited inclusion (and exclusion) and rights in their communities. Many believed that the conduct, culture, and legal status of immigrants made them ineligible for a rightful place in the community. Newly invigorated nationalists demanded that government officials (federal, state, and local) wall off barbaric immigrants from good national citizens. And although local officials could not build a wall around towns, they could introduce policies to make the lives of immigrants impossible, at least in their own towns. The day laborer was viewed as a "barbarian"[1] who needed to be banished through whatever means necessary, including zoning restrictions, enhanced antiloitering measures, and police repression.

This chapter explores the local conditions that helped foment ethnonational citizenship by examining responses to immigrant day laborers. This chapter and the next draw on a day-labor newspaper data set (see the appendix for further detail). The chapter uses material mostly from the 1990s to suggest that the open assembly of Latina/o immigrants disrupted everyday life and introduced sharp conflicts between groups. Such disruptions propelled thousands of people to step in and debate the meanings of citizenship. From this cauldron of conflicting passions emerged a particular understanding of citizenship that was ethnonationalist, exclusionary, and revanchist. The criteria for belonging became stricter as new policy instruments were devised to enforce the separation of self and the barbaric other. This was an ethnic understanding of citizenship backed by an increasingly violent and exclusionary state.

The Disruption

In the late 1980s and the 1990s, day laborers emerged as a visible population. Before this time, most unauthorized immigrants found employment in established businesses and out of public view. In 1986, Congress passed the Immigration Reform and Control Act (IRCA), which introduced sanctions for hiring unauthorized immigrants.[2] These sanctions increased the risks of hiring immigrant workers. One employer complained to a newspaper reporter about the rampant fear and confusion in his industry. The feelings were "unanimously of total and absolute fear and confusion. They [business owners] don't understand why, when they fail to dot an 'i,' cross a 't' or date a form, they should get a $1,000 fine."[3] The enforcement of sanctions at specific work sites made it more difficult for immigrants to find traditional employment in industries such as retail, light manufacturing, and office cleaning. This, in fact, was the intent of the IRCA's employer sanction. As the director of the New York district of the Immigration and Naturalization Service (INS) remarked, "We're hoping that word goes back home that there is no more 'pull' factor, that if you come up here you'll be standing on the street corner with us."[4]

The thirst for immigrant labor went unabated. The growing demand for workers in a restrictive labor market resulted in a two-prong shift in the geography of immigrant labor. First, suburban areas emerged as important poles for immigrant labor as demand for personal services and construction increased. This induced a shift from core urban hubs to outlying suburban areas that previously had little experience with immigrants. "In suburban communities and the rest of the country," Douglas Massey explained, "you can expect to see more immigration. Immigration goes where the low-wage jobs are. And as those jobs shift from the cities to suburbs, they will be there."[5] The geographic shift in the labor market resulted in more immigrants seeking opportunities in historically white suburban areas.

Second, there was a shift in the physical spaces where jobs were sought. Instead of seeking employment largely in private firms, immigrant workers increasingly began to seek it in public spaces. Streets and parking lots became sites for laborers to find temporary jobs. Immigrant workers assembled at these places waiting for employers to approach and offer employment for a day. These areas essentially functioned as spot markets where the terms and conditions were negotiated between prospective employees and employers. Many workers complained about the precarity of these spot markets. Others, however, preferred the freedom of day-labor work, because it allowed them direct connections to potential employers. Workers did not need to access employment through their typical social networks. They could bypass family, friend, and employer networks and make a go of it simply by standing on a corner.

Day laborers first emerged in large cities and were often located in marginalized areas such as industrial districts and immigrant neighborhoods. City residents were traditionally more tolerant of diversity, and day laborers found support from a variety of immigrant advocacy organizations. Considering the political culture of these environments, big-city officials were more apt to respond to day laborers by adopting pragmatic policies such as the sponsorship of regulated hiring or worker centers. Los Angeles administrators, for example, directly operated several hiring centers throughout the city in the early 1990s. The concentration of day laborers in more tolerant and supportive cities helped mitigate the politicization of the day-labor issue.

This began to change when new immigrants began moving into suburbs that had been designed—through discriminatory zoning and exclusionary ordinances—to meet the needs of white American residents. Many suburban residents experienced the influx as a major disruption of their well-established order. It was difficult for many to fathom the ethnic changes unfolding in their towns. Residents often expressed moral outrage that they were losing control of their communities. Their implicit understanding of belonging, rights, and boundaries was unhinged by a handful of immigrant workers assembled on street corners. Intensifying outrage contributed to the fast politicization of immigration and citizenship as residents demanded that their local politicians act fast on this issue.

The Barbarians among Us

Local residents began to articulate an understanding of citizenship that was ethnonationalist and revanchist. Locals highlighted qualities (discussed as follows) that made immigrants barbarian[6] and a threat to their community.

Dirty, Scary, and Bellicose

Many established residents (but certainly not all) expressed a visceral fear associated with the public assembly of immigrant bodies. The conduct of some day laborers may have resulted in annoyances, but such troubles in and of themselves did not pose an existential threat to society. It was the publicness of Latina/o immigrants that transformed small irritants into deep, profound anxieties. For example, the former mayor of Mount Kisico, New York, recognized that littering at street corners was an irritant but felt this and other problems would not have led to high levels of public outrage if the laborers had not been Latinas/os. As he put it, "If it was 50 Irish carpenters on the corner, I don't think there would be a voice raised."[7]

In addition to these workers being from a denigrated ethnic group, they were also very public. One early observer remarked that the problem was not really with the conduct of the immigrants but with their publicness. The spokesperson of a community organization in Encinitas, California, stressed, "If you just put these guys on balloons after work and they just disappeared so people would not have to see them, then the problem would go away."[8] The public assembly of immigrant workers produced feelings of fear that drove people away from highly trafficked areas of the city. "It's not because they're Hispanic," noted one resident of Silver Spring, Maryland. "It's because it's a multitude of men."[9] These and other statements suggest that the public assembly of laborers disrupted a sense of order and precipitated deep anxiety.

Coupled with the fear of publicly assembled Latinas/os, there was a per-

ception that immigrant workers were dirty and uncivilized. Residents repeatedly raised issues concerning the bodies and hygiene of immigrants.[10] A resident of Chamblee, Georgia, exclaimed that "they're just terrible filthy people.
I don't want them in Chamblee."[11] The mayor of Chamblee exclaimed, "We're
not going to have these people coming in here going to the bathroom wherever they want."[12] In Alpine, New York, the owner of a shopping center remarked, "It would help if they were more respectful of our property." He went
on to add, "It gets filthy and it looks like Tijuana."[13] The perceived lack of
cleanliness and hygiene were troublesome to the residents partly because it
signaled the profound otherness of day laborers ("looks like Tijuana").

Immigrant day laborers were also viewed as scary and bellicose. Many
residents complained that they were constantly attacking passersby. The
owner of a Dunkin' Donuts in Queens, New York, remarked, "Look at them.
Every time a van or truck pulls up, they're all over it like seagulls on crumbs.
People don't want to get out of their cars, they're so afraid, and it's costing
me money."[14] Their behavior was gendered, with many residents expressing
complaints of aggressive sexual behavior. Fears of predatory behavior kept
residents from accessing public spaces and retail outlets. Margaret Bianculli
of Long Island, New York, remarked that, "my daughter is solicited for sex
every time she is in town and goes to Kmart."[15] The alleged solicitations of
Ms. Bianculli's daughter motivated the mother to become a formidable opponent of day laborers and unauthorized immigration. She went on to create
one of the most potent local anti-immigrant organizations in the country, Sachem Quality of Life. Rumors frequently circulated in these suburbs that the
day laborers were rapists. These common allegations precipitated vigilante attacks across the country. A day laborer in the New York town of Farmingville
addressed these types of rumors by remarking, "There are bad feelings here.
There is racism. They say we look at the white women. It's not true. We just
want to work."[16]

The Right to the (White American) City

Long-established residents believed themselves to be rightful citizens. Their
roots in these towns, their white backgrounds, and their Americanness gave
them standing. The appearance of scary, dirty, and hostile immigrants in
central public spaces made many feel displaced from their own towns. "It was
another country," complained one California resident. "Hispanic immigrants
were having a *paseo*, walking on the sidewalk, eyeing each other, playing loud

music. I felt displaced and alienated. They are on the attack."[17] Whereas he expressed displacement in terms of alienation from his everyday world, Margaret Bianculli of the Sachem Quality of Life talked about displacement as a community crisis. "This is a crisis in our community," she exclaimed. "We're not able to appreciate our community. We can't walk on the streets. We can't go to Kmart."[18]

Disruption of everyday activities, such as going to Kmart, fueled feelings of loss. Menacing alien bodies reduced access to normal, everyday spaces, producing a deep feeling of displacement. They felt, as Arlie Hochschild observed in the case of Louisiana, like strangers in their own lands.[19] One *New York Times* journalist reported on the attitude of a resident in Long Island, saying, "She has no animosity toward them. She just feels uncomfortable in the streets. 'You don't live here. Our town is not what it used to be.'"[20] The statement connects feelings of displacement with nostalgia for a presumably better time. A member of the World Church, a white supremacist congregation, suggested that local displacement portends the eventual eradication of the white race from the nation itself: "It doesn't take a rocket scientist to extrapolate the final result of the demographic changes that have taken place just in the 1990s—the white race in the United States is facing extinction."[21]

Feelings of displacement were coupled with a sense of rightslessness and victimhood. American residents, not the immigrants, were being deprived of rights in their own hometowns. Longtime residents were the ones without voices, the ones silenced and pushed into the shadows. An early anti-immigrant petition circulated in Chamblee, Georgia, protested that "the city does not want to violate [the immigrants'] rights." The petition went on to ask, "Well, what about our rights? This is our city, not theirs, and the city of Chamblee has surrendered this part of town to them."[22] On Long Island, Margaret Bianculli expressed a similar grievance. "The rights of foreign nationals are taking precedence over the rights of citizens," she said. This, she argued, made the longtime (white) residents of her town outsiders and underdogs. "We came to understand that we were actually the underdogs; we were actually the victims," Bianculli claimed.[23] White Americans believed that, in the words of Justin Gest,[24] they were becoming the "new minority."

Reframing white Americans as "underdogs" reinforced the displacement narrative because residents were now stripped of their political power and rights. One anti-immigrant activist from Voices of Citizens in Arizona suggested that such processes were directed by a distant and unaccountable power elite. The activist said that "the power elite have decided we have to be folded into the world village, we have to sacrifice our sovereignty." Because elite and establishment forces are aligned against *real* Americans, he argued that "you are in the biggest fight you will have to face."[25] Day laborers were now reconceived as the Trojan horse of cosmopolitan elites. The elite would eventually force its agenda of a politically correct global village on normal, hardworking Americans by allowing these laborers to establish beachheads in these towns. They, white American citizens, had become the downtrodden outsiders, displaced by global elites and invading hordes of immigrant day laborers. These local conflicts therefore opened the door to larger ideological battles over the terms of citizenship in globalizing times.

Illegality and Impossible Citizenship

Many residents believed that because immigrants lacked authorization to be in the country, immigrants ultimately surrendered all rights and protections. This made it impossible for many residents to fathom immigrants as possible or even probationary citizens.[26] They had no grounds to speak or express grievances because of their illegality. Their status deprived them of the right to expect solidarity and support. It was impossible for many to conceive of lending support to the enemy population. In Mountain View, California, a member of Citizens for Action argued that "they violate our laws and demand we feed them, clothe them and educate them in their own language. They are taking jobs away from American citizens."[27] A resident from Mount Kisico, New York, expressed identical concerns. "People must be legal," he argued. "I am a taxpayer, and I resent educating and feeding people that have no legal right to be in this country. I resent that they get free medical care while we have to pay."[28] To these residents, the boundaries of solidarity were marked by legal status. It was inconceivable to extend fraternity to people who lacked authorization to reside in the country.

Local government officials reinforced this assumption when they argued that the federal government should assume the costs of maintaining unauthorized immigrants. The mayor of Encinitas, California, remarked, "They've said, 'O.K., we're not going to enforce the border and we are not going to take charge of immigration, but it's up to your local hospitals, your local schools, your local social service agencies to provide for the needs of these indigent people.'"[29] Knowing who was responsible for ensuring resources to this population was particularly important for local and state-level government officials, but local residents were less interested in who pays (federal or local government) and more aggrieved about the principle of extending any form of solidarity to a population that was considered illegal.

Although there were certainly problems associated with day laborers (for example, litter and crowding on corners), most of these problems were by no means catastrophic. They could have been addressed with easy, pragmatic solutions. But because the problems involved a highly stigmatized population, many residents viewed day laborers as symptomatic of a deep, underlying, existential threat. Left untreated, the places they knew and loved would become uncontrollable, alien, hostile spaces; these towns would become Tijuana.

Defending Suburbia

Immigrant day laborers had been conceived as barbaric illegals who threatened the white right to the city (or suburb for that matter). Perceived in this way, good citizens had little choice but to sharpen boundaries and oust the barbarians. "Society must be defended," Michel Foucault once noted, by banishing society's barbarians. Illegality placed immigrants beyond the pale of the rule of law.[30] Many residents believed that the normal rules of lawful society need not apply to this population, opening the way to brutish, violent behavior.[31] This negative perception shaped the ways in which some residents interacted with immigrants in daily life. Interactions were characterized by sharp, largely racialized boundaries between longtime (mostly white) residents and new immigrant populations. Immigrants reported repeated forms of harassment and discrimination. They were keenly aware that this aggressive behavior was driven by the racist dispositions of the dominant population. One resident of Gwinette County, Georgia, who worked with the immigrant community reported that "[day laborers] feel as if, sometimes, they are treated worse than hogs."[32]

"Illegal" was a label that placed immigrants outside the law and, as a consequence, stripped them of any rights or protections.[33] The widespread belief that immigrant laborers were rightsless gave many residents a sense of impunity. Many dishonest employers used the precarious legal status to cheat day laborers of their wages. This contributed to high levels of wage theft.[34] According to one of the most exhaustive studies on day-labor conditions, "Almost half of all day laborers experienced at least one instance of wage theft in the two months prior to being surveyed. In addition, 44 percent were denied food, water or breaks while on the job."[35] An organizer with the advocacy organization CASA Maryland reported that "you talk to these people and I guarantee you that three out of four will tell you they've worked and not gotten paid, or they were paid less than they contracted for, or they were injured on the job and got no benefits or compensation. This is their situation."[36] A contractor in Washington, DC, reported:

> Most of the men are skilled and eager to work. If I hire them, I feel obligated to pay them. But unfortunately, there are contractors out there who have no ethics at all. They have no intention of paying, and *they feel they can use these men because they are not versed in our legal system and have a limited command of English* (emphasis added).[37]

A legal assistant in Montgomery County, Georgia, reported the high numbers of wage-theft cases reported to her office. She noted that when confronting guilty employers, "I've had employers say to me, 'Why should I pay him? He's illegal.'"[38] Workers also lived in constant fear because of their unauthorized status and general ignorance of their legal rights. Because local law enforcement agencies targeted day laborers, immigrant workers had little trust in them as a source of protection.

Day laborers were also targets of criminals. Because of their status, most workers lacked bank accounts and carried substantial amounts of cash. High rates of homelessness among the workers made them vulnerable to attacks at night. Many criminals knew that the legal status of day laborers made them less likely to report criminal activities to local law enforcement officials. As one detective investigating a spate of crimes noted, "Many do not speak English. Others are suspicious of the law or, as illegal workers, are violating it by working without a visa and do not trust or report crimes to police."[39] One robbery in De Kalb, Illinois, resulted in the murder of a day laborer in 1999. The police officer investigating the case remarked, "They were obviously targeting these guys," going on to note that one crew of thieves specialized in immigrant day laborers. He concluded that, "It's common knowledge that Hispanic day laborers keep cash on them, and paid daily, send money home at the end of the week."[40]

Many other day laborers faced a range of aggressions during the course of their everyday lives. Racist aggressions and harassment became a part of normal life. According to Valenzuela and his colleagues,[41] "Almost one-fifth (19 percent) of all day laborers have been subjected to insults by merchants, and 15 percent have been refused services by local businesses." On Long Island, for instance, an organizer from the Workplace Project noted that one of the primary complaints of day laborers was the constant harassment inflicted on them.[42] In more egregious cases, immigrants were targets of violent hate crimes. In Glen Cove, New York, in 1998, one immigrant was severely beaten when a property owner found him sleeping in a wooded area in his backyard. High levels of stigmatization and discrimination reduced sympathy for victims of hate crimes. In one case concerning the beatings of day laborers in Alpine, New York, a resident responded by saying, "Good for them [the perpetrators of the crime], whoever it was. Maybe they'll get rid of the Mexicans down there."[43]

Feelings of displacement and rightslessness among nationals gave rise to collective action. Some residents repurposed homeowners' associations (HOAs) into vehicles for anti-immigrant campaigns. Many of these organizations had experience maintaining the privileges of white homeowners through the use of deeds, covenants, municipal ordinances, and zoning restrictions.[44] Other civic organizations were created in direct response to day laborers. Appearing in very different locales, these new associations often had names that included terms such as *citizen* and *quality of life* or both (for example, the Sachem Quality of Life Organization, Voices of Citizens, Citizens for Action, and Citizens for the Preservation of Local Life). The organizations consisted of a handful of particularly vocal residents who displayed a high capacity for cultivating and harnessing collective outrage and directing it at government officials. Engaged civic activists demanded that government officials develop policies that reflected their particular understanding of ethnonational citizenship. Sachem Quality of Life Organization, for instance, was made up of a handful of very dedicated residents. This small group tapped local ties, developed a strong messaging campaign, and mobilized locals to agitate for far-reaching restrictions on day laborers.

Although most neighborhood organizations stayed local, some linked up to national anti-immigrant networks such as Federation for American Immigration Reform (FAIR), Numbers USA, and white nationalist movements. This was more the case in the 2000s, when FAIR and the infamous Kris Kobach launched a national effort to support restrictive local and state-level laws.[45] Nationally connected local organizations were particularly severe in their determination to push for restrictive measures and were less willing to address problems (for example, litter and congregating in streets) through pragmatic policies. Their connections to national anti-immigrant organizations reinforced the belief that the small troubles posed by day laborers were symptoms of a deeper malady.

Complaints resulted in efforts to create laws, employ surveillance techniques, institute urban-planning measures, and adopt law enforcement tactics to effectively banish the immigrant population from their towns. In many communities, police increased their presence at day-labor hiring sites. Early on, local police were uncertain of the rights of the new immigrant population. Ignorant (willfully or not) local police engaged in various forms of repression. According to Valenzuela and his colleagues, "Day laborers report being insulted (16 percent), arrested (9 percent) and cited (11 percent) by police while they search for employment."[46] Reporting on day-labor disputes in another Georgia suburb, a newspaper journalist commented that "the police chief had labeled all the members of the labor pool as 'illegals' and added that he didn't know whether undocumented aliens had any rights under U.S. law."[47] The legal obtuseness of police officials was by no means a limited phenomenon. Local law enforcement officials across the country displayed ignorance about the rights of immigrants and the limits of their policing authority.[48] A common assumption was that the presumed legal status of day laborers deprived them of rights and provided police with unrestricted powers. Many police officers created inhospitable environments, hoping that their aggressive and often illegal tactics would drive day laborers out of their towns. The police chief of Chamblee, Georgia, argued that if they were ever going to resolve the day-labor issue, then "Hispanic workers" needed to "go back where they came from."[49] A day laborer in Palisades Park, New York, was conscious of his rights and the limits of police powers. He complained that "police ask about green cards. That's not their concern. They can just call immigration. They talk about how we live. What's it to them if grown men share a room? Isn't this supposed to be a private matter?"[50] This person knew what many local police didn't: local officials and police had no authority to discriminate against people on the basis of their presumed immigration status.

Aggrieved locals also pressed federal authorities to banish day laborers from their towns. After lamenting demographic changes in Santa Ana, California, a resident exclaimed, "We can stop [immigrant day laborers]. I think we can take the military and do it with the military."[51] More typically, residents organized letter-writing campaigns and petitions to pressure INS to raid day-labor hiring sites. In one California suburb, residents formed a local association (Save Mountain View California) to address the day-labor issue.

The coalition was formed to save the city "from becoming a Third World outpost for cheap labor."[52] It mounted campaigns to restrict the public solicitation of work and to demand more INS raids on day-labor hiring sites. The San Francisco chief of INS investigations commented that it "had received many calls from businesses along El Camino. Businesses complain that men loiter in front of their stores, scare away customers and urinate in the bushes."[53] In Marietta, Georgia, a local citizens' committee launched a similar campaign for INS raids of hiring sites. The INS responded by launching "several waves of intensive crackdowns on illegal immigrants." One INS official in Atlanta informed a journalist that "we're not going to sanction the illegal employment of these undocumented aliens. We intend to be back here, and we are looking at signing up a couple of officers with the Marietta Police Department to help."[54]

Whereas certain INS officers responded eagerly to local requests, others preferred *not* to raid day laborer sites. They used their discretion to prioritize immigrants with a criminal record. As one INS officer noted, "Day laborers can be annoying, but they are not criminals per se. Criminals are a bigger priority for us, they have more potential for harm than these day workers who are just looking for work."[55] Other INS officers complained that the work-site raids insisted on by local residents were dangerous because workers often ran away from agents and risked being struck by cars. For many INS officers, the deployment of state power at specific hiring sites was a poor use of scarce government resources. Most laborers got away and simply reassembled at other corners or in neighboring towns. Although such results might satisfy the not-in-my-backyard demands of merchants and residents, they did little to satisfy what the INS believed to be the larger mandate of the agency.

Local ethnonationalists also turned to their elected town officials. They hoped these officials would design physical environments that would criminalize the life-sustaining behavior of day laborers and encourage them to self-deport, or at least move on to the next town. But the federal government guarded its monopoly over immigration matters and prohibited local lawmakers from enacting discriminatory laws and measures. This compelled local officials to design policies that would restrict behavior closely associated with immigrants, a practice Douglas Massey[56] called "categorical discrimination." Some communities enacted laws to ban the public solicitation of work. Costa Mesa, California, enacted such a ban early on, and others followed its lead in the 1990s. Palisades Park, New York, passed a law in 1994 that made it "unlawful for any person, while standing in any portion of the public right-of-way, including but not limited to public streets, highways, sidewalks and driveways, to solicit or attempt to solicit employment, business or contributions of money or other property from any person traveling in a vehicle." The law also made it illegal for an "occupant of a moving vehicle" to solicit workers.[57]

Rather than pass restrictive new ordinances, many municipalities bolstered and enforced preexisting laws. Antiloitering and jaywalking laws were particularly effective weapons. "It's against the law to hang out on the streets in groups," reported a police officer in Glen Cove, New York. He went on to say, "That's from the Mayor himself. We'll have to give you an appearance ticket or jail, at worst, if we see you hanging around."[58] Many officials also sought to limit accessibility to immigrant workers by regulating traffic flows at popular hiring sites. Creating regulations to maintain traffic flows made it impossible for employers to pick up day laborers. Officials directed police officers to cite cars for causing congestion in popular hiring areas while introducing parking restrictions to limit the possibility of employers parking and picking up workers. Many cities targeted the housing of day laborers by actively enforcing regulations against overcrowding. Because workers were poor, they often shared housing with friends, family, and colleagues. This made them vulnerable to fines and evictions by enforcement agencies.

Reluctance by INS agents and federal prohibitions on local officials limited the possibility of banishing immigrants outright from their communities. Instead, officials were compelled to use whatever instruments were at their disposal to create restrictive environments that made the lives of immigrants virtually impossible. Immigrants faced an increasing barrage of laws that targeted the conduct associated with them. These restrictions, coupled with everyday forms of discrimination and violence, produced hostile landscapes that made the maintenance of basic life difficult. These environments contributed to greater psychological problems for the immigrants. As scholars have observed in the case of Arizona, "Feelings of having to hide in fear on a routine basis can have detrimental health consequences. Living with constant fear and internalizing social injustices without being able to speak up or challenge them is similar to the concept of 'racial battle fatigue.'"[59]

City officials were key players in the early day-labor debate. They played an active role in diagnosing the problems and devising solutions. In most cases, city officials were pushed by aggrieved businesses and residents to take a position. In response to these important constituents, officials adopted eth-nonational frames and proposed restrictive, exclusionary policies. As will be discussed in the next chapters, proimmigrant organizations pushed back through protests, supportive campaigns, and lawsuits. The pushback, how-ever, resulted in intensifying the grievances of residents and business own-ers. These persistent problems reinforced a sense of being displaced from their own communities. Feeling ignored and rightsless, residents' hostility to-ward immigrants increased, especially when these sentiments were coupled with economic insecurities. All these emotions formed into intense clusters of anti-immigrant sentiments that were channeled into restrictive political campaigns.

Under Siege in the Suburbs

The 1990s generated hostile discourses and feelings in suburban communi-ties throughout the country. Many people believed that they were under siege by threatening barbarians and that they were losing control. They had to save their towns. But locals were unable to build a big wall to protect rightful citi-zens against marauding immigrants. In lieu of this, community officials, po-lice, civic organizations, and individual residents constructed an environ-ment designed to make physical life impossible for immigrants. "Illegals" were marked as people who resided outside of the lawful order, "where civili-zations ends" and "where the brutishness of the civilized is therefore permit-ted."[60] Nationals leveraged the illegality of day laborers to discriminate, re-press, exploit, and victimize them. These practices, which were themselves illegal, were meant to produce such an inhospitable terrain that it would be impossible for workers to settle. Established residents therefore struggled to reassert control over the meaning and practice of lived citizenship. The cu-mulative outcome of many battles was the slow assembly of a racialized vi-sion of citizenship, with sharp symbolic and physical boundaries between na-tionals and foreigners. Facing these conditions, immigrants were expected to leave town, going to either a neighboring town or their home country. Most immigrants stayed, however. Moving across these towns, from home to job sites to shopping centers, presented terrifying risks. Fear of theft, violence, racist harassment, and deportation was constant.

CHAPTER 3

Resisting Ethnonationalism, One Town at a Time

IMMIGRANTS FACED growing antagonism from individuals and government officials. Simply by standing on a corner or shopping at a local market, immigrants risked repression by local police and harassment by residents. Employers treated them poorly, pedestrians insulted them, and thieves stole their money and goods. Immigrant laborers could speak out about the dreadful conditions facing them, but their status made it difficult to gain legitimacy from established residents. They were, in the words of Wendy Brown, "beyond the line,"[1] which made it impossible for many residents to recognize them as rights-bearing subjects with justifiable grievances.

In spite of the challenges facing immigrants, they did not passively accept repression. From New York to Georgia, from Illinois to California, immigrants and their allies fought back. Ethnonational discourses and policies gave rise to resistance by day laborers, Latina/o residents, local organizations and churches, sympathetic residents, and legal-advocacy organizations. With the mobilization of these groups, the public arena became subject to political disagreements over boundaries, belonging, and the right to have rights in the United States. Many supporters were motivated by basic humanistic concerns for immigrants, an aversion to xenophobic discourse, and an interest in finding a pragmatic solution to a particular local problem. Competing understandings of citizenship churned through contentious debates in town halls, local media, and community centers around the country. Towns became breeding grounds for new American understandings of citizenship.

As local mobilizations gathered steam, they drew in additional support from regional and national organizations. These networks were crucial be-

cause they provided essential resources to local campaigns. In certain instances, these larger organizations provided communication expertise, legal
services, and financial support to shoestring campaigns. Such resources allowed local groups to extend their efforts and to launch campaigns that would
have regional and national implications. Furthermore, local immigrants and
their allies talked to other organizers and discovered that the struggles of immigrants were much broader than their particular towns. They learned that
immigrants across their regions were facing political hostility. The geographic
growth of support networks allowed these small organizations to scale up into
regional coalitions.

The chapter examines how support for the rights and dignity of immigrants bubbled up from small towns around the country. It does so by describing the early resistances of day laborers and their diverse range of supporters
and then describing how some local mobilizations snowballed into sizeable
struggles mostly anchored by regional immigrant rights organizations.

The Right to Live: The Emergent Voice of Day Laborers

Many immigrant laborers were confused and outraged by the negative reac-
tions of established residents, but surprisingly few expressed a sense of powerlessness. Only one person in the day-labor database expressed powerlessness,
saying with regard to restrictive measures, "It doesn't matter what I think. We
have no power in this land."[2]

Most workers responded to the public's indignation by explaining the
physical need to ensure their physical survival as well as that of their families. "I have no choice but to stay here. I would like to go back to Mexico, but
I like to eat, too," one immigrant said.[3] He and other workers were not apolo-
getic. Given the choice between life and death, they chose life, as anyone else
in their situation would have. Another worker explained how the need to survive accounted for the desperate tactics of the day laborers. "A burning desire
to work is what drives people to rush to the vans, to the contractors," he said.
"We all have families to feed."[4] The need to work and survive was something
that cut across borders and national cultures; it was a universal trait common
to all human beings. One worker suggested, "If a policeman could see how
poor we are at home, he would feel sorry for us and say, 'Let them work here.'"
He went on to say that "the police think we're trying to take their country
away from them, but we're not."[5] Some used the language of universal need to
elicit sympathy. Others used it as a way to assert their rights claims. "I don't

think it's right for them to run us off because we're looking for work," argued a day laborer in New York. "We're not causing any problems. We're not harassing or stealing. It's rough. I think everyone deserves a chance to work."[6] The denial of recognition of basic rights, according to this and other day laborers, was fundamentally wrong.

Many immigrant workers stressed that the denial of basic rights was wrong anywhere but especially in the United States. There was a mismatch between the *promise* of equality and the *reality* of rights denied. This, to many immigrant laborers, was outrageous. Many assumed the United States to be a constitutional republic bound by the values of equality and freedom. In response to restrictive measures in Mount Kisco, New York, a reporter wrote, "Workers say they cannot believe this is happening to them here. Many say they came not only to find work but to escape Guatemala, where they watched the military overrun villages and torture dissenters." One of the reporter's sources went on to say, "This was supposed to be a free country."[7] The disbelief stemmed from the disconnection between the great promises of the United States (of freedom, equality, and justice) and the everyday realities of terrifying and humiliating exclusion. One laborer said, "It is America, yes? It is a right to stand where you want."[8] Responding to the proposed restrictive policies in his town, another laborer noted, "The whole idea makes me feel that we're not in the United States. [...] Something like this makes me feel I'm in the old Soviet Union."[9] Whereas ill treatment and injustices would have been expected in dictatorial countries, they were not what was expected in the "land of the free." The workers did not argue that their rights should be recognized because they were de facto Americans. Instead, the transcendent principles of equality and freedom guaranteed the rights of all people regardless of their affiliation to the nation. Their rights to work and live should be recognized everywhere but especially in the United States.

Immigrant day laborers were not ones to hide in the shadows and avoid rights talk. They expressed their grievances and outrage in clear, unfiltered terms. Some also had a wealth of political-organizing experience. As the director of CASA Maryland remarked in an interview, "It was a very extraordinary experience because what happened is that many of these day laborers, they have a lot of experience fighting for justice. . . . When they arrived here, they brought all of that experience, so fighting for justice, mobilizing rallies, civil disobedience, all of that kind of experience."[10]

In spite of the political experience of some day laborers, most faced barriers that blocked their abilities to create a powerful and legitimate public voice. There were many national, regional, and class divides that weakened feelings of camaraderie. Constant competition for jobs further weakened solidarity among them.[11] While diversity and job-market forces weakened collective solidarity, the laborers also lacked the resources needed to run effective campaigns. They needed safe places to meet and coordinate campaigns; they needed cultural knowledge and symbolic legitimacy to translate grievances into compelling and resonant mobilizing frames; and they needed people who could broker relations with well-placed allies (for example, political officials and journalists). Facing extreme political and discursive hostility, weak group solidarity, and the lack of essential resources, these precarious migrants faced barriers to producing a potent political voice on their own.

The Spilling Over of Grievances

Had day laborers remained an isolated group, most would not have been able to mobilize against restrictionists. Fortunately for them, assorted people and organizations came out to provide support. The lives of immigrants were, as Amalia Pallares argues, "tangled"[12] with many others (for example, family, churches, employers, and neighbors) in their communities. Hostility and restrictions targeted a single population (immigrant day laborers), but the effects of these measures spilled over and touched other segments of the population. This negative spillover caused grievances to multiply and became the basis of political solidarities between day laborers and diverse community members. Many people came out and gave different levels of support to the day laborers. Some even reached out to the laborers and worked with them to form their own distinctive political groups. Others pressured politicians to soften restrictive measures or reject them altogether. In different regional contexts, the enactment of restrictive measures triggered the formation of webs of solidarity and support for the maligned population. They were fighting against ethnonationalism and, through these fights, constructing their own understandings of citizenship.

Latina/o Residents and Immigrant Organizations

Due to racial profiling, legal permanent residents and US citizens of Latin American origin were among the first to feel the negative spillover of restrictive policies. As local lawmakers devised more comprehensive and aggressive measures (for example, targeting overcrowded housing and the hiring of workers), they depended increasingly on local enforcers such as police, land-lords, employers, and administrators to enact them. In some towns, landlords were called on to check the legal status of tenants. Contractors were threat-ened with fines if they did not verify the status of immigrants. Local police were authorized to shut down day-labor hiring sites and fine day laborers for violating a number of laws. These local enforcers used ethnic cues to fulfill their mandate. All Latinas/os, irrespective of their immigration status, be-came suspect. The expanding restrictionist net therefore drew more enforc-ers into the fold and led to more circumstances (sitting on a corner, renting an apartment, getting a job, driving a car, and so on) in which Latina/o ethnicity became cause for suspicion.

A Latina/o resident of Long Island complained that "we are not all ille-gal. I'm not illegal. My daughters are not illegal. You can't say that about all of us!"[13] This frustrated resident went on to note that restrictive policies neg-atively affected broader sectors of the population. "By attacking illegal immi-grants, they're attacking everybody because if you see me on the street, you won't be able to differentiate." On the other side of the country, a legal perma-nent resident of Mexican origin complained that restrictions resulted in in-creased stops when he went outside. "I'm a gardener. I'm not well dressed. I've been here in California 15 years. I never felt it necessary to carry documenta-tion until now. We don't have any freedom to walk along El Camino because we're afraid of being chased by immigration agents."[14] Racial profiling made it difficult for him to go out and have a normal public life, "We're not able to go to the stores anymore because we feel we'll be asked for documents." Another Latina/o resident of Mountain View, California, felt compelled to move to an-other city because of unwarranted suspicion and police repression. A jour-nalist reported, "One child [of the resident] asked, 'Why do we have to move? We like Mountain View.' 'I'm sorry,' the father answered. 'We have to move. Probably when you're older, you'll understand.'"[15] Latina/o permanent resi-dents and citizens were drawn into the restrictionist dragnet because of racial profiling. As their lives were negatively affected, many became more support-ive of recent immigrants who lacked authorization. These grievances did not automatically draw established Latina/o residents into day-labor campaigns, but they did create reservoirs of solidarity that could be activated in actual campaigns.

Larger cities such as Los Angeles and Chicago enjoyed more supportive or-ganizations for immigrants, but there were nevertheless some organizations in smaller cities and suburban towns. These ranged from moderate organizations like the Latin American Association of Chamblee, Georgia, to more combative organizations such as Latinos Unidos in Mountain View, California, and La Fuerza Unida in Long Island, New York. Some of these organizations criticized restrictions because they were too broad and risked entrapping all Latinas/os in their ever-expanding nets. California-based La Raza Centro Legal, for instance, suggested that restrictive local measures "will impact people for looking the wrong way or standing the wrong way." After asserting that restrictive laws risked ensnaring many different people (including legal Latina/o residents), La Raza Centro Legal went on to argue that day laborers had a basic right to look for work. "They live in this community—they have a right to look for honest jobs."[16] The director of Organización Hispana in Mount Kisco justified her support for day laborers on the basis of humanitarianism.[17] She described the desperate conditions facing day laborers, saying, "These people are very abused and they have to take it because they don't have a choice. They come to this country because they need to support their families and feed their children." She went on to argue that the dire conditions of workers and their lack of choices compelled Americans to be more empathetic. "Many Americans feel very frustrated and very threatened, but they need to open their eyes with more compassion."[18]

These organizations had existed before the day-labor issue but were drawn into that struggle because their constituents (Latina/o residents and new immigrants) were directly affected. Their investment in that particular issue changed the way they operated, however. The director of CASA Maryland, an early immigrant rights organization, stressed the importance of investing in this issue.

> That [day laborer fights] was a social phenomenon that our board of directors made a decision to engage in. It changed our organization forever because day laborers politicized us. Day laborers educated us about the struggle, about why they were day laborers, about the discrimination issues, about the challenges they faced, about the political reality they faced related with lack of documentation and lack of payment and abuses from many unscrupulous employers.[19]

This and similar organizations were brought into day-labor struggles and thus became deeply embedded in the lives of the most precarious immigrants in the country.

Welfare Organizations and Unions

The negative effects of anti-immigrant restrictions spilled over to other groups as well. Local welfare organizations and charities served large pools of poor immigrant workers. Although they had never considered themselves to be immigrant advocacy organizations, the fact that their clients were increasingly precarious immigrants compelled them to address the problems confronting this population. "Ten years ago we would see about 100 [immigrant] families a month; now we see about 600," reported the director of North Fulton Community Charities of Roswell, Georgia.[20] These organizations provided basic support and services to day laborers and other immigrants. The director of one welfare organization in Montgomery County, Georgia, noted, "These are truly some of the neediest people in our community. Whether they are legal or illegal is not the question. They still have the right to work."[21] The director of the organization, which had no connection to immigrant rights advocates, reiterated a common theme: the physical need to work and survive was a universal human right irrespective of legal status.

Several high-profile proimmigrant advocates in the 2000s and 2010s began their careers by working in welfare advocacy organizations. These include Deepak Bhargava (Center for Community Change), Rich Stolz (Reform Immigration for America), Ali Noorani (National Immigration Forum), and Lupe Lopez (Alliance for Citizenship, Center for Community Change). Through this work, they and many others encountered difficult conditions facing immigrants and the negative effects of restrictions on people's ability to sustain basic life. The anti-immigrant provisions in the 1996 welfare reform law, Personal Responsibility and Work Opportunity Reconciliation Act (PRWORA), reinforced and politicized the tie between welfare organizations and local immigrant populations. As the welfare state withdrew its support for recent immigrants, these organizations struggled to meet the needs of local immigrants. Many expanded and tailored service provisions to this community. They began to advocate for the rights of immigrants (authorized and unauthorized) to local, state, and national government agencies. These organizations were not immigrant rights organizations, but demographic shifts and hostile policies encouraged some to fight for immigrant rights as part of their general antipoverty mandate.

Union locals had a more ambivalent relationship with immigrants. The position of most unions in the 1980s and early 1990s ranged from vehement opposition to uncertainty concerning the possibility of organizing immigrants. On the one hand, opposition to immigration has a deep and long-standing history, even among progressive unions such as the United Farm Workers.[22] In the case of Pasadena, California, the International Brotherhood of Electrical Workers (IBEW) was the most vociferous opponent of day laborers. The unauthorized status of workers and the informal nature of the work was seen as anathema to their mission.[23] In their view, they had no choice but to fight day laborers. On the other hand, many unions doubted whether undocumented immigrants could be organized and unionized.[24] They believed that informal labor markets, high turnover rates, and the lack of legal status, made it difficult to organize immigrant workers. Day laborers, in particular, were challenging to organize because workers frequently changed hiring sites and employment. A representative of the International Ladies Garment Workers Union in New York was "unsure whether it was viable to organize labor that was constantly changing employers and job sites."[25]

In spite of opposition and uncertainty, unions in some communities believed that the they were obligated to lend their support to the exploited workers . Latina/o union members and organizers often pushed this more sympathetic position. "My essential reason to become active as a Latino is to help open the door to other Latinos," said a member of the Communication Workers of America in California.[26] He went on to argue that "a lot of social problems [confronting day laborers] are prevented with good-paying jobs." Other unions entered the fray because the growing exploitation and repression of immigrant workers was morally shocking and required a union response. This expression of solidarity reflected the union value: an injury to one, is an injury to all. The head of a Long Island union expressed his disdain for the poor treatment of day laborers by saying, "The bullies of industry who exploit people like Daniel E. [a day laborer] are going to have to deal with a new, bigger kid on the block—organized labor."[27] Supportive unions began to experiment with ways to back the day laborers. These ranged from providing political support to actually organizing immigrants on street corners. As early as 1999, the Laborers International began to organize corners in Brooklyn, Queens, and the Bronx. They reframed these immigrant workers as natural allies of the union movement. The support of these unions set an important precedent and made it more palatable for other unions to support day laborers.

Many newly established worker centers in the 1990s provided support to the incipient struggles of immigrant workers.[28] These centers were hybrids of unions and nonprofit organizations. They targeted low-income and precarious workers, advocated for their rights in courts and legislatures, mounted campaigns to support various causes, and organized some workers into nascent unions. They were eclectic in their use of tactics, drawing from the traditions of community organizing, social justice, and labor. Like the welfare advocates mentioned earlier, recent immigrants with precarious legal status began to make up the members of many worker centers. Although these organizations continued to see their role as representing all workers, they could not effectively address the problems of immigrant workers without addressing the specific legal and discriminatory challenges facing them.[29] As a consequence, many became engaged in the fight for immigrant rights. Mary Ochs, a prominent organizer who worked with worker centers at the time, remembered that "the immigration issue just kept coming up. It was just bubbling up on the ground." She went on to note, "I pulled in a lot of worker centers, and we had some groups that were involved in welfare reform that were also starting to organize immigrants."[30]

One such center was the Workplace Project in Long Island. It was created in 1992 for the purpose of advocating for low-income workers. It began its work with day laborers because they constituted the most insecure workers in the area. In addition to providing legal and social support to Long Island day laborers, the organization also worked with them to organize street corners and assist in wage-theft claims. "Workplace Project," recalls lead organizer Nadia Marin-Molina, "tried to figure out ways to organize on the street corners in Nassau County. It was focused on the day laborer corner in Franklin Square, and also supporting another organization which was working in Glen Cove."[31] As part of this, organizers launched an effort to create a regulated hiring site for the workers (a worker center or job center) where day laborers could find jobs and develop skills in a more stable and supportive environment. When municipalities on Long Island began to adopt restrictive measures, the Workplace Project invested more resources in organizing workers and fighting restrictive ordinances. In 1997, they had heard about anti–day laborer restrictions proposed by the Sachem Quality of Life in Farmingville. "We had to find out what was going on," recounted Ms. Marin-Molina. "We said we had to participate in fighting this."[32] Workplace Project opened an office in Farmingville dedicated to the issue of day-labor organizing. They worked with day laborers and other allies to organize a forceful response to the growing dominance of anti-immigrant advocates. Ms. Marin-Molina described one campaign as follows:

> The first [campaign] was against a legislator who wanted to prohibit day laborers standing on the street corner. We fought back against that and it was defeated. Then there was another resolution to sue the government for not enforcing immigration laws. There was another campaign by the town of Brookhaven to evict workers from their homes. They couldn't do it around the worker end, so they decided to do it around the housing end. We also fought against that.[33]

After a series of these campaigns, the Workplace Project became one of the premier immigrant advocacy organizations in the New York region. Like welfare organizations, the Workplace Project assumed a frontline role in local immigration battles because it had become tangled with the immigrant workers in their communities.

Religious Organizations

Religious organizations of various denominations became an important source of frontline support for immigrant workers.[34] Many immigrants joined Catholic and Protestant congregations, and as these congregants came under increased pressure by restrictionists, some pastors and priests felt compelled to come out in support of their new members.[35] Other religious organizations lent their support for humanitarian reasons[36] or because restrictions conflicted with their ethics and values. One Catholic parishioner in Farmingdale, New York, argued that, "This is our responsibility. I believe as responsible people, charitable people, we have to take care of [day laborers]."[37]

In general, religious organizations were important because there were few service and advocacy organizations in suburban communities. In Farmingville, New York, Nadia Marin-Molina remembered that there wasn't much support for their efforts in the broader community, but the local church played a supportive role. "There was a church there, which provided services to the workers, and they had a Spanish language mass. In some cases, for example, the parish social ministry person was involved and supportive of our efforts to support the workers, and so they were a good base. . . . That church and a couple of others were supportive, as far as they could be."[38]

Many religious organizations entered the fray with trepidation. They were embedded in communities in which many local residents rejected day laborers and viewed them as an enemy population. When churches provided too much support to immigrants, local parishioners would sometimes push back. Ms. Marin-Molina recounted one such experience: "The Church of the Resurrection, which is the one in Farmingville, was threatened by its parishioners, which would say, 'We're your parishioners. We give money to the church, and we're going to boycott the church if you all keep supporting these immigrants.'"[39] Churches attempted to strike a balance between the established community and the highly stigmatized newcomers. Clergy tried to validate the general concerns of established residents while stressing that the laborers in their own neighborhoods were good people deserving of support. The spokesperson for St. John Vianney Roman Catholic Church noted, for instance, that "some of [the day laborers] on Northern [Street] cause problems. There's sometimes a little drinking. But not these guys [indicating the men in her parish]. They just want to work."[40] The affiliation of day laborers to her parish consequently made them deserving of support. Politically ambivalent churches were less likely to engage in high-profile political fights, but they provided material support (such as space for meetings and administrative assistance) and public arguments for why immigrants, at least those affiliated with their neighborhood, merited recognition and respect.

Other churches went on to become vociferous supporters of day laborers. In Brookville, New York, the pastor of the Brookville Reformed Church made the struggle against restrictive measures into a major cause. Under his guidance, the Reformed Church took a leading role in organizing day laborers and mobilizing against a proposed antisolicitation law. The pastor argued that "this bill would basically prevent these new immigrants from getting work. They are already the poorest of the poor. It should not be against the law to work."[41] He, like many others, argued that the basic need to survive made finding work an inviolable right. Following a victory in the Brookville city council, the pastor stressed that the victory was important because it reinforced the rights of day laborers and enabled them to exert a voice in the political arena for the first time. "It was a solid victory for us and a wonderful way for the workers to discover how democracy works," he said. "Imagine how amazing all this is to these newcomers to America. This is something they and their children will never forget."[42]

The advocacy arms of religious organizations also played important roles in some local battles. These advocacy arms included but were not limited to Catholic Charities and the Quaker organization American Friends Service Committee (AFSC). These organizations fought for the rights of immigrants to work freely in their communities without fear of repression. For instance, AFSC branches played pivotal roles in several local battles across the country. In Pasadena, California, it provided early support to the local effort of creating a job center and fighting restrictions. The AFSC branch gave local organizers office space and administrative support, hired a part-time organizer, brokered relations with key political players in the town, and spoke forcefully on behalf of local day laborers when most other organizations ignored or scorned them.

Lawyers

Lawyers and legal advocacy organizations in a number of towns raised concerns over the poor treatment of day laborers. The East San Jose Community Law Center in California became actively involved in pursuing claims against dishonest employers. As one lawyer there said, "The workers will work all day and at the end of the day ask for wages. The boss will say, 'I'll pick you up tomorrow for more work and will pay you then.' But the employer doesn't show up the next day, of course. We hear this over and over."[43] Having taken an active role in these cases, the law center went on to play a role in fighting restrictive ordinances and INS raids in the region. In Mount Kisco, New York, a local lawyer came out to represent the cases of twenty-six men who were arrested for violating a restrictive ordinance.[44] Another law firm in the same community came out one year later against the city's discriminatory housing regulations. "The midnight housing raids were quite offensive and clearly directed at Latinos," one of the attorneys said. "So the ending of that is a major relief to our clients."[45] Many local lawyers and legal advocates worked pro bono cases for day laborers, and some initiated lawsuits against restrictive ordinances. Most local law offices lacked the resources to cover costly legal battles and typically referred litigation to more resourced and experienced legal advocates, such as Legal Aid, the American Civil Liberties Union, and the Mexican American Legal Defense and Educational Fund, headquartered in large cities like New York, San Francisco, Los Angeles, Chicago, and Atlanta. Nevertheless, local lawyers and legal organizations lent their expertise to protect immigrants against duplicitous employers and discriminatory laws.

Residents and Employers

Established residents were not homogenous in their values and views. Some with progressive or humanitarian beliefs saw day laborers sympathetically.

They talked about them as people simply trying to survive under difficult conditions. As restrictive laws and hostile discourses mounted, some residents became uncomfortable with the morally dubious motives fueling them. Commenting on a proposed restriction, a coach at Mountain View High School declared, "That law is racist, pure and simple. Whatever happened to America, the land of the free and all that."[46] A resident of Silver Springs, Maryland, suggested that day laborers were scapegoats for deeper problems facing the town. "It seemed to me those [immigrants] are an easy scapegoat," he said. "It's offensive to me to paint a whole group of people as undesirable."[47] These residents knew that hostility and proposed restrictions were motivated by a growing sense of xenophobia and racism. They were privy to discussions with their neighbors and friends and understood that deep-seated prejudices against the laborers were motivated by racism. These sentiments conflicted with their own values to respect the rights of men hoping they get work that day. According to the Workplace Project's Nadia Marin-Molina, a spate of violence directed at day laborers and the growing harshness of public debate encouraged some residents to lend their moral and political support to new immigrant residents. Thus, sharpening hostility toward the immigrants produced a growing sense of ambivalence and a search for more accommodating solutions.

Sympathetic locals attempted to soften the sharp boundaries between established residents and the newcomers by emphasizing their common humanity. For example, the board member of a homeowners' association in San Mateo, California, stressed the conflicting values of residents in her town: "The neighbors have conflicting values and rather than having compassion and understanding about it, they get hostile. They make people out like they're littering bums or unsavory characters that are some kind of threat to our well-being. But I never see this. What I see is a bunch of guys praying they get work that day."[48] The statement reflects the diversity of local values in this suburban town while also revealing contrasting discursive tactics to humanize and dehumanize this population. Anti-immigrant advocates tended to view day laborers in abstract terms. Immigrants were viewed as distant and abstract figures ("unsavory characters") rather than flesh-and-blood human beings. The tactic of discursive distancing enabled locals to draw a sharp boundary between us and them and to assert that the immigrant population posed "some kind of threat" to their well-being. By contrast, discursive tactics to humanize the population employed proximate, concrete, and normalizing terms. Rather than being "characters," they were simply "a bunch of guys" engaged in real activities that concern us all ("praying they get work that day"). In supporting day laborers, these resistant residents rejected ethnonationalist citizenship and began to imagine alternatives that were more plural and inclusive.

Many employers who came into contact with day laborers also expressed sympathy for the population. By working with day laborers, employers understood that *need* drove them to the United States, and they understood the struggles laborers faced to ensure their physical survival. An employer from Glen Cove remarked, "I feel bad. I wish I could take them all."[49] In Roswell, Georgia, another frequent employer started by hiring day laborers out of sympathy. She went on to find that they were excellent workers and recommended them to her friends. She said, "It turns out they're excellent gardeners. . . . My next-door neighbor hired them after seeing the job they were doing here." Over time, she developed relationships with certain workers, and she assisted them in various ways. "I help them fill out papers. I'll read an English letter to them or help them get lighting, gas and phone service."[50]

Some store owners were suspicious of day laborers, but others expressed sympathy with the population because they benefited from it. "I moved my business here from Mount Pleasant [New York] five years ago, and I have nothing bad to say," said one business owner. "I do not understand when people say this street is not good for business. Look out there on the street. Look at all the people. This is very good for business."[51] Rather than seeing the immigrants as a threat, this small-business owner saw them as a windfall for her and other small entrepreneurs. Other merchants expressed humanitarian reasoning. The manager of an automotive business in Chamblee, Georgia, explained, "Do I see it as a nuisance? I think the potential for that is there. But I also see it as some people trying to earn x amount of dollars for their family."[52] An Irish-born landlord in Mount Kisco expressed her opposition to restrictions because of the racist motives underlying them, "How many Italians have you arrested or called in for this? Not one. Not one Italian. Not one Jew. Not one Irish person. And we're all immigrants. Just the Spanish. Well, this has got to stop."[53] In these various instances, business owners, contractors, and landlords expressed disagreement with growing hostility. Laborers were beneficial to local economic development, and the restrictions were morally problematic. Supportive local businesspeople helped offset the influence of other businesspeople who were vehemently opposed to day laborers.

Compared to large progressive cities, suburbs and smaller cities in the 1990s had fewer organizational resources, smaller populations of immigrants, and more conservative traditions and norms.[54] Because of the growing presence of immigrant workers in public spaces, these places became flashpoints for heated debates on immigration, rights, and citizenship. Those with the loudest voices were often ethnonationalists. The proliferation of hostile discourses and practices had specific effects on different segments of the population. Day laborers felt the violent sting of xenophobic words and policies. Established Latinas/os were snared in anti-immigrant dragnets. Welfare advocacy organizations, unions, and churches had a growing number of immigrant constituents facing repressive measures and attitudes. Even some established Americans felt that the growing hostility conflicted with their values and moral worldviews. The negative spillover of restrictive policies and attitudes created a reservoir of solidarity for immigrant day laborers.

Framing Citizenship from Below

Most advocates engaged in local campaigns were not radical. They were not imagining utopias in which borders didn't exist. Most accepted the nation as a fundamental building block of citizenship, but they rejected the bright boundaries and blatant racism of ethnonationalism. Their America was made strong through the incorporation of immigrants into the national body. The welcoming ethos of America made it possible for immigrants to settle in the country and make great contributions. As one resident noted, "This is a country that has always welcomed immigrants. This [restrictive] bill would basically prevent these new immigrants from getting work. They are already the poorest of the poor. It should not be against the law to work."[55] The right to work, in this instance, was certainly a universal right held by all people, but such a right was more salient because of national values. This revisionist approach to national citizenship stretched the boundaries of citizenship, but it didn't necessarily erase them.

Hard work became an important justification for why undocumented immigrants deserved basic rights. Immigrants were not in local communities to take jobs and take advantage of welfare provisions. They were in America because of their desire to work and contribute to the sustainability of their communities. "The stereotype is that Latinos do not have a right to be here, or they're just here to take jobs," suggested a representative of the Latin American Association in Georgia. "The reality is that most Latinos who come here are looking for a better way of life, and they're willing to work."[56] Their work ethic and contributions to local life made them *deserving* of inclusion. A Latino pastor of a local church in Georgia noted, "We want to make the community aware of where we're located and of what is happening in the Hispanic community." He went on to say, "It was to communicate to the community that we are a peaceful people. We are a good people. In our congregation we have accountants, teachers and professionals and construction workers."[57] By stressing the respectable professions, the pastor asserts the deservingness of his immigrant congregants.

Many early activists also drew on territorial personhood to frame their arguments. They stressed that immigrants had a fundamental right to work. Day laborers had inalienable rights, and such rights were protected by the Constitution. A city official from San Jose noted, for example, that his city was developing a "humane approach to the problem, protecting neighborhoods and shopping centers while not depriving day laborers—often, but not always, illegal immigrants—of the right to find work."[58] While this official acknowledged the unauthorized status of many day laborers, he also recognized their fundamental right to find work in the city. The immigration status of laborers, in this and other instances, did not make them ineligible for basic rights in the city.

These different framings of citizenship came into relief through local struggles. On the one hand, many advocates and some city officials began to envision a plural community bound by liberal national values. America was not a country with sharp confines, closed off to the world. It was a country that was open and that valued its immigrant past and future. Cultural pluralism strengthened rather than threatened the community of citizens. These advocates also talked about how immigrants *deserved* inclusion in this plural country because of their affiliation. The problem was not with immigrants per se but with the barriers that blocked their integration. On the other hand, advocates also drew from territorial personhood and sometimes postnationalism to frame their arguments. They argued that the rights of all people needed to be defended first and foremost. The Constitution required local officials to recognize and protect the fundamental rights of all people in the country, irrespective of national origin, status, creed, gender, and so on. People had a fundamental right to find work not because their affiliation made them de facto Americans (as holds the theory of liberal nationalism) but because they were human beings. Citizenship was not an end state consisting of a community of equals bound by common national values; it was instead a political body that guaranteed the equality of all, with the state serving as the instrument to protect rights equally.

These locals were engaged in politics informally. Most did not have communication training and had weak and messy ideological associations. Many drew from commonsense politics to express their moral support for repressed immigrants. In this context, these various framings of citizenship served as a loose, discursive repertoire used to make concrete arguments about the place of immigrants in their communities. In different situations, advocates used their political intuitions, moral compasses, and cultural dispositions to assemble arguments for why immigrants were entitled to have rights in their towns. People criticized xenophobic words and policies, produced different understandings of rights and belonging, and began to articulate policy responses that corresponded with their own visions of good citizenship. Citizenship was therefore situational, emergent, and plural. It was a political bricolage of norms, moralities, ideologies, and pragmatic needs. These small battles were openings that allowed people to come out and engage in long, emotional, and often disorderly conversations over the meanings of citizenship.

Snowballing Local Struggles into Regional Mobilizations

Some small resistances grew into larger regional mobilizations and coalitions. These mobilizations were characterized by networks of allies and activist organizations across a metropolitan area that were anchored by prominent regional organizations. These regional organizations served as connections between smaller campaigns, organizations, activists, and allies.

Regional Immigrant Rights Organizations

In regions anchored by large central cities, such as San Francisco, New York, Los Angeles, Atlanta, and Chicago, certain activists served as brokers who helped connect local mobilizations in suburban towns to rich, well-capacitated organizations in central cities.

Many local actors in smaller suburban towns connected to larger immigrant rights organizations in central cities. These regional organizations included, among others, the Center for Humane Immigrant Rights of Los Angeles (CHIRLA), the Illinois Coalition for Immigrant and Refugee Rights (ICIRR) from Chicago, and the New York Immigrant Coalition (NYIC) from

New York City. In the early 1990s, most of these organizations were young; most emerged in response to the Immigration Reform and Control Act (IRCA) of 1986. Their original purpose was to assist immigrants undergoing the legalization and naturalization process. Some of these organizations became involved in fighting for the legalizations of many El Salvadorans and Guatemalans who had been excluded from IRCA's legalization program. The organizations also initiated campaigns to protect the workplace rights of those (documented and undocumented) who stayed in the country. For example, CHIRLA was founded in 1986 as a coalition of smaller organizations working to support the rights of Central American refugees. The coalition quickly became an independent nonprofit organization and shifted its focus to defending the rights of immigrant workers. This reflected the growing realization that many refugees (whether legally recognized or not) were staying in the United States, and they needed support in asserting their workplace rights in a context of increased employer exploitation and workplace raids. As early as 1988, CHIRLA began to prioritize the fight for day laborers' and domestic workers' rights, as these two groups of immigrant workers were the most vulnerable to exploitation and repression. Organizations such as the ICIRR and CASA Maryland shared similar histories.

These regional organizations became aware of suburban battles through personal relations, brokers, and local media. When organizers from regional organizations interceded in suburban battles, they assumed a prominent role. An organizer with CASA Maryland, for instance, became heavily involved in a campaign to block local restrictions and open up a day laborer workers' center in the suburban city of Silver Springs, Maryland. She had already been involved in a similar struggle in nearby Mount Pleasant and highlighted similarities between the cases, pointing out that "the conditions that affected the community in Mount Pleasant also exist out here . . . , the sense of oppression, the overall lack of resources and a real fear of being victimized by the police."[59] The problems facing immigrants in a particular locality were by no means unique, according to the CASA Maryland organizer. They reflected broader structural forces involving economic exploitation and state repression.

Larger regional organizations also provided financial and technical support to suburban efforts. As day-labor corners sprouted across large metropolitan regions, these organizations invested resources to support a range of different endeavors. In certain instances, they provided organizers assistance in local fights against restrictions and for opening worker centers. In other cases, they assumed a leading role in the effort to organize workers and their own hiring centers. CHIRLA, for example, provided technical and legal support to suburban struggles in Costa Mesa, Agoura Hills, San Bernardino, Harbor City, and Redondo Beach. It also assumed leadership in organizing local efforts to resist anti–day laborer measures and provided support in the Pasadena effort to create a new job center. Similarly, after CASA Maryland's initial entry into the Silver Springs struggle in 1991, the organization invested more resources in convincing locals to understand the needs of day laborers and the importance of providing a space where they could find jobs without the fear of exploitation and theft.[60] The deployment of resources to different local battles in metropolitan regions provided essential support for the small clusters of activists flowering across these metropolitan regions.

The larger regional organizations also assumed a central role in connecting activists to others in their broader network. These organizations had ties to regional news reporters and producers. This enabled them to call on journalists to expand media coverage of local conflicts and influence the frames used for these news stories. Many organizations also placed local activists into frequent contact with one another through workshops, social events, and coalition meetings, all of which permitted the circulation of mobilizing frames, resources, and best practices. Organizations such as CASA Maryland and CHIRLA organized such events for the specific purpose of creating ties between day-labor activists and their supporters. For example, day-labor leaders from different corners of Los Angeles were invited to the CHIRLA office, where the organization sponsored workshops and role-playing activities to encourage the leaders to talk about the problems, struggles, and campaigns in their particular localities (see chapter 5 for more on this). Participants stopped seeing their specific battles as isolated events. They shared stories and discussed ways to frame their struggles. They drew on these discussions to construct common narratives for understanding and expressing their fight for equal rights. They increasingly viewed the restrictions in their communities as local instances of broader inequalities and racism. Their struggles were consequently understood as individual battles in the wider war for equality and justice in the Los Angeles region. Just as important, these conversations permitted locally rooted activists to convey information on best practices and tactics to others engaged in similar conflicts.

Regional organizations located in the larger, more hospitable central cities therefore assumed important roles in elevating suburban struggles, geographically and politically. They framed local struggles in ways that helped increase attention and broaden support. They contributed tangible and intangible resources while deploying reinforcements to battles in hostile, resource-scarce suburbs. And they connected suburban advocates across metropolitan regions to one another. Rights advocates and activists quickly understood that their struggles were by no means particular or isolated. They learned about the existence of similar people engaged in equivalent struggles on the other side of their metropolises. They learned techniques from their distant comrades and came to understand that the fight was about more than the protection of a handful of immigrants down the street. They learned that they were engaged in a common struggle for the rights of immigrants in their specific regions of the United States. The hostility they faced was systemic, which required immigrant workers across a region to work with one another to achieve more just, equal communities. Thus, some small, local efforts scaled up into regional mobilizations through a process of building stronger relations with like-minded people and organizations.[61] Regional organizations stood at the center of these networks, helping to provide structure, direction, and vision.

Allied Support

Organizations with regional and national reach also contributed to regional and local campaigns. Intellectuals, the media, legal organizations, and religious institutions played particularly important roles in expanding specific, localized battles. These organizations were typically based in the central city and provided services to clients, members, and allies across metropolitan regions. Many supportive organizations were well respected. By lending their good political reputations to local struggles, they helped reinforce the legitimacy and amplify the reach of the smaller groups. The entry of these organizations into local suburban battles often tipped the outcome in favor of pro-immigrant advocates.

Working alone or in association with larger immigrant organizations, legal advocacy organizations such as the American Civil Liberties Union (ACLU), Legal Aid, the National Immigration Law Center (NILC), and the Mexican American Legal and Education Defense Fund (MALDEF) provided major support to day laborer struggles. Legal advocacy organizations often drew from territorial personhood to assert their claims. They argued that all people residing within the country possessed inalienable, constitutionally protected rights, irrespective of nationality and immigration status. The government wasn't obligated to protect the rights because immigrants were model minorities and de facto Americans but because these inalienable rights were protected by the Constitution. They argued that it was the restrictive laws, not the immigrants, that were legally deviant. Because restrictive laws violated the guaranteed rights of immigrants, these laws needed to be fought and rescinded. The local governments that continued to pass restrictions were therefore the ones viewed as lawless, rogue, and illegal, not the immigrants.

Legal organizations often worked closely with immigrant organizations. Legal advocates had overlapping connections to both kinds of organizations and collaborated on various campaigns. Marielena Hincapié, the executive director of the NILC, described her early legal advocacy work in San Francisco before she joined the organization.

> It was very grassroots. I was at a community meeting in San Francisco and heard other grassroots organizers and advocates talking about this woman who had not gotten paid and they were helping her with a wage claim. . . . We had to do something about that and I started working with that organization and some community organizers. . . . We then worked with a lot of worker centers. That was around 1996 to 2000. It was the beginning of a lot of the worker centers. They were just starting to develop and a lot of local unions, coalitions, immigrant labor coalitions that were starting to form. It was mostly immigrants; very grassroot immigrant rights.[62]

Legal organizations worked with immigrant organizers on various campaigns and activities. Whereas the immigrant organizations would mobilize activists and the press, the legal organizations would focus on lawsuits.

When facing restrictive measures, legal organizations often threatened localities with litigation. For instance, in response to restrictions placed on day laborers in Mount Kisco, New York, the ACLU denounced the constraints as unconstitutional and threatened the city with a lawsuit, arguing that "the statute you have written is unlawful, unconstitutional and likely to be an enormous nuisance to you while bringing you no benefits. Should you pass this law, and should anyone see fit to challenge it, I assure you that he would not lack support from the Civil Liberties Union."[63] Limitations on resources made it impossible for legal organizations to take action against every restrictive ordinance.[64] But high-profile threats reminded city officials of the limits on their authority and the possible consequences that could transpire if they chose to pursue restrictions. The threat of a lawsuit was often enough to deter uncertain local officials, especially when the threat was made by a powerful legal organization. All threats were not idle. Organizations prioritized cases that would produce maximum legal and political effects. The aim was not simply to fight a single ordinance but to produce broad legal precedents that would deter other municipalities from passing restrictive measures. Legal organizations launched hundreds of lawsuits throughout the country, arguing that the laws were discriminatory and violated the inalienable and constitutionally protected rights of immigrants. After warning the officials of Mount Kisco not to pass a restrictive ordinance in 1995, the ACLU of New York participated in federal class-action suit against the city. The lawsuit alleged that the town's antisolicitation ordinance restricted the First Amendment rights of workers and harassed immigrants for congregating on sidewalks and in the town's park.[65] Through this and other lawsuits, advocates imposed hard limits on ethnonationalists and reinforced the idea that the basic rights of immigrants were inviolable.

Local fights also scaled up to regional media. As local conflicts gained traction, television and print media broadened their coverage. Newspapers such as the *San Jose Mercury, New York Times, Atlanta Journal-Constitution*, and *Orange County Register* brought local conflicts to the attention of the regional public. Many residents used unfiltered language to express their negative views on immigrant day laborers. Some media reports helped paint suburban towns as xenophobic and racist. These representations broadened sympathy for day laborers while attracting more media coverage to an area. For instance, intense media coverage of local struggles on Long Island in the late 1990s attracted significant attention from the *New York Times* and eventually documentary filmmakers. The filmmakers ultimately made *Farmingville*, a feature-length film on the local fight. The film provided an unflattering account of anti-immigrant sentiment and restrictions in this New York suburb. The documentary aired on the PBS series *POV*. Other unflattering reports on Chamblee, Georgia, led one local official to exclaim, "I'm angry. In fact, I'm livid." The official went on to explain that "we have been painted as a whipping boy of the press, . . . a city of racist bigots. The problem is that [day laborers] are performing illegal acts on private property."[66] Similarly, the city manager of Mountain View, California, noted that "we're concerned about the perception issue that we have here" regarding anti–day labor restrictions.[67] Negative media coverage therefore broadened public sympathy for laborers in these localities, irritated publicity-conscious elected officials, and attracted other outsiders (from media to organizations) to contribute to unfolding struggles.

Spanish-language media was another important participant in the battle for immigrant rights. Favorable coverage made a region's Latina/o population, most of whom were not day laborers, more sympathetic to the plight of this disadvantaged group. The editor of the Atlanta-based Spanish newspaper *El Mundo Hispánico* stressed the connections between the restrictive measures in Marietta, Georgia, and the broader Latina/o community, saying, "They say this is not against Hispanics, but the effect is taking a toll on the Hispanic community." Although the intention of the ordinance was to target day laborers, the editor pointed out that its effects were community-wide. He went on to argue that "these are not criminals. They are very poor people who are trying to earn a living and support their families."[68] The editor of *El Volante*, the other regional Spanish newspaper in Georgia, remarked that "many immigrants work to send money to their native countries; others dream of returning home someday to build a house, to settle down."[69] The Latina/o regional press represented day laborers as sympathetic figures and stressed the connections between anti-day-labor laws and the broader Latina/o community. This coverage transformed the day laborer issue into a Latina/o issue, building a reservoir of ethnic solidarity for day laborer campaigns.

Region-wide religious institutions such as the Catholic archdiocese also played roles in the support of day laborers. The archdiocese often used its formidable prestige and reputation to make public statements on behalf of immigrants and against restrictive policy measures. For example, the pastoral assistant of the Archdiocese Catholic Center in Atlanta forcefully argued against a proposed measure in Chamblee, Georgia. "Just like the Hispanic community, in the Anglo community you can find people who are getting drunk and being destructive," she said. "But you don't discriminate against the whole community. You don't pinpoint the whole community just because some of them are destructive."[70] Catholic archdioceses across the country also began to invest more in their Latina/o immigrant congregants and their political struggles. Even in new-destination states such as Georgia, the archdiocese created the Hispanic Apostolate as an organization to reach out to newcomer populations throughout the Atlanta region. Others lent their support to create worker centers in receiving communities. Many viewed this as a way to address the problems associated with public day-labor work without requiring burdensome and punitive restrictions. The New York archdiocese proposed in 2000 to create a partnership with the New York Central Labor Council to sponsor community outreach centers. These were essentially worker centers that helped match day laborers with prospective employers. Other archdioceses drafted and circulated statements to parishioners to support and fight for the rights of immigrants in these communities.

Local clusters of resistance grew beyond their towns and connected to larger organizations in city centers. These links were made possible through the personal relations and networks that existed across metropolitan regions. Actors in different urban areas connected to one another in increasingly frequent campaigns concerning day laborers and other immigrant issues (for example, welfare cuts for immigrants and street vendors). These associations allowed immigrants in specific localities to scale up and recognize the broader scope of injustices and the common struggles against them. The regionalization of immigrant rights efforts helped create powerful countervailing forces against local expressions of ethnonational citizenship. At the center of these regional blocks stood organizations such as CHIRLA, CASA Maryland, NYIC, and ICIRR. These larger organizations in turn brokered relations between locals and regional support organizations like the media, legal-advocacy organizations, and religious institutions. In sum, the regional organizations served as relational hubs within large metropolitan areas. They were places in which activists and advocates across regions converged, connected, and engaged in different campaigns. By acting as hubs, the regional organizations became adept at negotiating complex relationships and harnessing diverse resources to lead concrete campaigns.

Pushing Back on Restrictions

For local officials, these mobilizations presented formidable challenges. Media-friendly protests and lawsuits limited what restrictionist officials could do. Contentious political battles increased the costs of restrictions and limited the capacities of officials to implement them. These mobilizations encouraged some officials to favor more pragmatic methods to address the day-labor issue.

Rallies and public demonstrations disrupted local life and often drew negative attention to suburban towns. Furthermore, well-organized protests could have more disruptive effects in suburban towns with little protest experience than in big cities with a long protest history. In 1997, for instance, the Brookville Reformed Church in Glen Cove, New York, organized a protest with its allies and day laborers who lived in the community. They protested the death of two laborers by carrying coffins in a cortege around town. The organizers of the event were able to reach out to regional media outlets, and they gained favorable coverage from the *New York Times* and the *New York Post*. The protesters demanded a worker center for immigrant day laborers, better shelter for the homeless, and an end to restrictive policies. The pastor of the church forcefully argued, "It is our sincere hope that the city administration will be as actively engaged in this endeavor as it has been in promoting and supporting an animal shelter."[71] An elected official criticized the hostile tone of the protesters and noted that he was "painfully aware" of the issues. Protest events also created unanticipated costs for smaller towns with shoestring budgets. In San Mateo, California, for instance, one protest resulted in the city paying thousands of dollars for additional police enforcement. Whereas large cities could absorb the costs of public protests, smaller suburban municipalities had trouble doing so. Thus, the small size and low budgets of suburbs as well as political and cultural complacency magnified the disruptive effects of protest.

When mobilizations included litigation, costs for suburban towns increased. For instance, a coalition of day laborers, immigrant organizations (CHIRLA), and legal-advocacy organizations (ACLU, MALDEF, and Legal Aid) launched a lawsuit against the suburb of Agoura Hills in California.[72] The small city invested more than one hundred thousand dollars to defend its law. An appellate court eventually upheld the restrictive ordinance but required that the local sheriff not violate the constitutionally protected rights of immigrants.

The growing number of countermobilizations and lawsuits revealed to ignorant local officials the rights of immigrants and the constitutional limits on their authority. In Mount Kisco, the former city attorney counseled against a restrictive law because of constitutional limits. He noted, "The problem is you can't embrace the . . . recommendations [of the local committee on immigration] without violating the Constitution of the United States." The village attorney went on to argue that "you can't regulate what people talk about. If I want to talk to a Guatemalan and I want to park my car, you can't stop me."[73] Because Mount Kisco's proposed law appeared to violate the First Amendment rights of immigrants, the town would be on the hook for costly litigation. Many officials enacted restrictions because they were ignorant of the rights of immigrant day laborers. Lawsuits helped bring these rights into relief for oblivious local officials.

In 2002, MALDEF, in an alliance with various immigrant rights organizations, mounted a federal lawsuit against the antisolicitation ordinances of Mountain View and Los Altos, California. When the cities banned day laborers from the streets, MALDEF argued that they provided no alternative sites where workers could search for jobs, which was a violation of their First Amendment rights. Faced with the lawsuit, both cities suspended enforcement of the ordinances. Mountain View then made a concerted effort to find a regulated hiring site and rescind its restrictive ordinance. It was able to do so in cooperation with a local church. In response to these accommodations, MALDEF dropped its case against the city. Los Altos defended its antisolicitation ordinance while altering it to make it less discriminatory. MALDEF continued its lawsuit against Los Altos, and its local allies protested the city's ordinance. Then, a federal judge blocked the Los Altos ordinance. Alongside this lawsuit, MALDEF filed lawsuits against Upland and Rancho Cucamonga, California, arguing that ordinances in those suburban towns discriminated against day laborers and violated their First Amendment rights. Facing pressure from MALDEF and its supporters, Rancho Cucamonga revised its anti–day laborer ordinance but faced an immediate backlash by local anti-immigrant activists. Positioned between these conflicting forces, city officials eventually offered a compromise by prohibiting solicitation from the streets but permitting it on sidewalks.

Lawsuits were not always successful, but they still imposed limits on what elected officials and the police could do. Commenting on his department's capacities to enforce restrictions in Agoura Hills, a lieutenant in the Los Angeles County Sheriff's Department stressed the complications with enforcement: "We say we observed [solicitation] activity, but the D.A. says, 'How do you know he wasn't asking the guy to play golf?' The only way we could really prove it is to go undercover, and our department is not going to do that. We don't need that kind of press, that our officers are going undercover to arrest people looking for work."[74] Even though an appellate court upheld Agoura Hills's ordinance, local law enforcement was restricted in how they could implement the ordinance. In Marietta, Georgia, police officers were required to take extensive training courses prior to enforcing its restrictive laws.[75] Local police officials complained that specialized trainings resulted in costs that were difficult to sustain with their small budgets. Without these trainings, however, police would inevitably violate the rights of immigrant workers, which would result in costly lawsuits.

Local officials and law enforcement agents became conscious of the legal limits on their authority. In Roswell, Georgia, the police chief said that his "officers were wrong to hand out citations [to day laborers]." He went on to add that "crackdowns can backfire and engender ill will, particularly among minority groups traditionally wary of police." The chief publicly reprimanded one of his lieutenants for giving the order to arrest and cite workers for violating the town's antisolicitation ordinance. He stressed the importance of working with the Latina/o immigrant community rather than confronting them through harsh police interventions. He said, "You have to build a relationship" with the Latina/o immigrant community.[76] A resident of San Mateo, California, raised the problems of enforcing restrictive local laws. "It's just a waste of paper. The law has been in effect now 30 days, and there's been no change. The most it's been able to do is polarize our community. It's done nothing to improve the lives of the residents or the workers."[77] A San Mateo councilperson largely agreed, noting that it was "a lot of trouble for very little result. It seemed somewhat drastic. And I'm not sure they're getting the results they expected to get."[78] The limited benefits of the ordinances came at the cost of polarizing communities and creating "a lot of trouble" for elected and law enforcement officials. Expensive lawsuits, emotional disputes, and damaged reputations for towns were viewed as heavy prices to pay for stopping immigrants from seeking work on a street corner.

INS officials also experienced limits on the scope of their actions. When they initiated raids on hiring sites, they needed the participation of local police. Officially, the role of the local police was restricted to traffic control. They did not have the authority to stop or arrest people because of their suspected immigration status. The reality, however, was different. Local police often played a role in arresting fleeing immigrant workers and handing them over to federal agents. Cooperation in apprehending immigrants was condemned by legal and community advocates because it violated the separation of authority between federal and local law enforcement agencies. These unlawful partnerships triggered protests by community members and threats of lawsuits. In a press release in 1994, the INS issued the following press release: "About 20 INS special agents and U.S. Border Patrol officers took part in the 9:30 a.m. raid. The Mountain View and Los Altos [California] police departments also helped during the raid by controlling traffic at the corner of El Camino Real and San Antonio Road."[79] Witnesses observed the participation of local police officers in detaining immigrants, and, when questioned, the police chief admitted that he had ordered as much. This resulted in heated meetings between rights advocates and representatives of the American Civil Liberties Union on one side and the police and elected city officials on the other. A representative of the ACLU informed police that they could only provide traffic control and were prohibited from detaining day laborers, even if they were fleeing the scene. The police chief responded by saying, "We got more involved than we wanted to. We won't get involved to that degree again."[80] A representative of a local immigrant organization, Latinos Unidos, expressed the local Latina/o community's fear by saying, "How do we know that won't happen again?"[81] Another representative added, "They are angry. They feel betrayed."[82] The police chief responded by stressing that his agency now understood the problem and would limit cooperation to providing traffic support and ensuring public safety. The newspaper reported that "[the police chief] has said the department should not assist the INS with its duties but is required to provide traffic control to lessen the chance of injury if someone runs into traffic during an immigration sweep."[83] Many but certainly not all INS officials viewed blowback of this kind as a costly distraction and expressed reluctance to raid day-labor sites. The INS reminded local officials in Farmingville, New York, about the limits on their authority and about problems of racial profiling, "Loitering is not a violation of immigration law. We understand the community's concern and we know the situation, but just because a person is standing on the street corner doesn't mean he's illegal. We can't tell a person's status by looking at him or by the clothes he's wearing."[84]

In response to the blowback, many elected officials began to embrace city-sponsored worker centers for day laborers. They viewed the centers as a way to get immigrants off the streets, contain them within a designated space, and provide basic resources and services that could assist integration into communities. Worker centers for day laborers were increasingly viewed as a viable alternative to the strategy of banishment. The policy options proposed by immigrant advocates became increasingly viewed as "reasonable," while those of ethnonationalists were considered to be "impossible." In Long Island, one official argued that "the town has stated that it will support a consensus of reasonable people. It looks like the *Sachem Quality of Life Organization wants to do the impossible*" (emphasis added).[85] Channels of communication also opened up between town officials and the immigrant community. A councilperson from Roswell, Georgia, claimed that "the backlash over the arrests may have helped open communication with the Hispanic community." The councilperson continued, saying, "Relationships were formed with city officials and leaders in the Hispanic community that should help policing."[86] Through various interactions between rights advocates and town officials, these politicians began to realize not only that rights advocates were a force to be reckoned with but also that they had reasonable and cost-effective solutions to address the day-labor issue.

Disruptive protests, bad publicity, and well-resourced legal advocates compelled some local officials to recognize the claims of challengers as legitimate and reasonable. Immigrants could no longer be easily dismissed as illegals, out-of-town rabble-rousers, or no-border radicals. Local rights activists and advocates demonstrated sophistication in combining legal and protest tactics. Officials listened to rights advocates and immigrant activists at council meetings, community forums, and private meetings. These struggles generated efforts to design new policies to accommodate the newcomers rather than banish them.

Local Battles over National Citizenship

Repressive practices triggered resistance in localities across the country. Efforts to construct communities with high walls and harsh interdictions were rejected by some immigrants and their local allies. In many communities, the effects of restrictions impacted broad swaths of the local population. Families, Latinas/os, employers, local organizations, churches, and others became entangled with these policies. This cross section protested restrictive ordinances, lobbied politicians for favorable policies, and created spaces of sanctuary. All these actions expanded the boundaries of belonging in their communities. Preexisting values (for example, people deserve the right to work) served as a repertoire to construct arguments for why poor and undocumented human beings should be recognized as equals. Supporters' arguments combined notions of liberal nationalism and territorial personhood, producing a mélange of words, ideas, and feelings on the rights of others. Restrictionist policies therefore generated important negative externalities that galvanized broad swaths of the population and pushed thousands into a battle over national citizenship.

Aggrieved people did not simply pour into the streets in support of repressed immigrants. Relationships developed between different actors. These relations helped to recruit, retain, and continuously extend the battle for immigrant rights far beyond the original point of conflict. Advocates in suburbs such as Pasadena and Mount Kisco connected to the media, religious institutions, regional immigrant rights organizations, and legal-advocacy organizations. These connections were essential because they bolstered the firing power of local advocates. They provided local amateur activists with professional campaign support, legal capacities, and renown. Moreover, locals encountered others like themselves, exchanged stories, and shared best practices. Day laborers participating in these struggles benefited the most because they discovered that they were a part of a larger group and began to forge a collective identity. They constructed common mobilizing frames and cobbled together ways of talking about rights and belonging in communities that had rejected them. Through repeated discussions among organizations, lawyers, immigrant workers, sympathetic journalists and editors, and various supporters, regionally based insurgencies emerged across the country. These clashes, especially the larger ones, took their toll on targeted municipalities. Heated conflicts between residents, unflattering press coverage, and the constant threat of lawsuits dissuaded some local officials from pursuing repressive measures. The success of local campaigns helped place limits on what local officials could do. Many local elected officials responded by seeking to develop more liberal methods to govern their populations. Within these limits, pragmatic officials hoped to use worker centers to discipline and integrate immigrants into their communities. These officials argued that immigrants should be integrated into the social order rather than banished. Local communities therefore served not only as seedbeds of immigrant rights activism but also as breeding grounds of new policies to govern citizenship.

CHAPTER 4

Regionalizing the Fight for Immigrant Rights in Los Angeles

IN A SHORT PERIOD OF TIME, networks formed between different advocacy organizations within metropolitan areas such as Chicago, New York, and Baltimore–Washington. Such networks helped create a common space for talking about and fighting for the rights of immigrants. People engaged in campaigns to support immigrants seeking day-labor work as well as their right to vend on streets, rent apartments without having to reveal their immigration status, and work without the fear of wage theft. Regional organizations stood at the center of these networks. They grew in power as they assumed the growing responsibility for steering specific campaigns across their areas. The regionalization of the movement helped raise the stature of the organizations leading them.

Los Angeles was one of the most important areas to emerge during this period. Battles over immigrant rights unfolded across its vast urban region. Suburban towns such as Costa Mesa, Redondo Beach, Agoura Hills, Pasadena, and North Hollywood became embroiled in these disputes. As we saw in other regions, the presence of immigrant day laborers in prominent public places spurred locals to push for restrictive measures, which then triggered resistance from day laborers and their allies. The original seeds of conflicts grew into local mobilizations. The Center for Humane Immigrant Rights of Los Angeles (CHIRLA) assumed a prominent role in connecting these different mobilizations to one another and building a regional movement in defense of the rights of immigrant workers. CHIRLA's regional successes helped boost its national profile in the 2000s, and it came to the attention of national organizations such as the Center for Community Change. CHIRLA also became an important part of national coalitions to pass comprehensive immigration reform from the late 2000s to the mid-2010s. The cases of Los Angeles in general and CHIRLA in particular provide a window into how organizations became regional and then national powerhouses in the fight for immigrant rights.

The chapter begins with the tale of a very local conflict over day laborers in the Los Angeles suburb of Pasadena and then proceeds to a discussion of the regionalization of the struggle. CHIRLA played a pivotal role in connecting and coordinating battles unfolding across the metropolitan area. The chapter draws from key stakeholder interviews and historical archives of the Pasadena Day Labor Association, La Escuela de la Comunidad, and CHIRLA. The archives are based on grant applications and reports submitted to the Liberty Hill Foundation from 1990 to 2002. The Liberty Hills Archives are available at the Southern California Library in Los Angeles.

Activating Day Laborers in the Los Angeles Suburbs

During the 1990s, day laborers were gathering on corners in suburbs such as Redondo Beach, Costa Mesa, Agoura Hills, and San Bernardino as well as at many other sites within the city of Los Angeles. Pasadena was one such place. Before the mid-1990s, most day laborers didn't consider themselves to be a distinct political group. They didn't have elaborate networks, a group identity, or common mobilizing frames. There were few, if any, mobilizations demanding recognition for these people as equal human beings. Immigrants selling their labor on street corners were individuals from different regions, social classes, occupations, races, religions, and sexualities. Before moving to the United States, most had never sold their labor on street corners and did not see themselves as belonging to a group called day laborers (*jornaleros* in Spanish).[1] Nevertheless, their experiences of trying to find work on street corners, facing unscrupulous employers and repressive police, contending with hostile citizens and public officials, and living with their illegality provided these different people with common difficulties and grievances.

The difficult conditions facing day laborers meant that organizers (mostly volunteers) were needed to reach out and support this population. Pasadena had several organizations that provided support for its rapidly growing population of new Latina/o immigrants. La Escuela de la Comunidad was a small,[2] community organization run by volunteers during the late 1980s and 1990s. It was a project of a Los Angeles–based grassroots organization, the Institute of

Popular Education of Southern California (IDEPSCA). Veteran Chicano activist Raul Añorve created IDEPSCA to use popular education as a method to organize and politically empower working-class immigrant communities. La Escuela provided Spanish literacy and English as a Second Language (ESL) classes to immigrants at the Villa Park Community Center, which was adjacent to the most-frequented day-labor sites in the city.

The educators of La Escuela used Paolo Freire's popular-education methodology in their literacy and ESL classes. The method drew on the common experiences of oppressed people to stimulate political consciousness. According to one of their documents, popular education "incorporates the experiences and the world view of participants involved in the programs. Such a methodology assists participants in recognizing and analyzing the socioeconomic conditions which prevent them from solving their own issues."[3] During Spanish literacy classes, for example, educators developed curriculum and discussions around words like *trabajo* ("work"). Students discussed the problems that they faced in their workplaces, such as wage theft, deportation raids, and discrimination. While students were learning literacy, they were also exploring common experiences as immigrant workers. Through these discussions and the assistance of voluntary educators, they came to identify the social and institutional forces that made immigrants like themselves vulnerable to repression and exploitation. Villa Park and La Escuela provided institutional spaces in which newly arrived immigrants could feel safe to come out of the shadows and share about common experiences in a hostile and stigmatizing context.

Through literacy classes, the organizers of La Escuela encountered the large population of day laborers in Pasadena. They believed that addressing the day-labor situation would provide the organization with a strategic issue around which to mobilize the broader immigrant community in Pasadena. The leaders were well aware of the grievances of Pasadena residents and the efforts to pass a restrictive ordinance. In 1994, La Escuela helped form the Pasadena Day Labor Association. The short-term goal of the association was "to establish an official, safe, clean, and healthy designated site so that the day workers of Pasadena can congregate to wait for jobs while learning and receiving English/Spanish literacy and other services."[4] Although this was the immediate goal, the longer-term goal was to politicize and empower the community. "This purpose enables us, day workers, to achieve self-determination and self-sufficiency which are our long term goals."[5] The association began to recruit day laborers from La Escuela's ESL and literacy classes. An early recruit remembered, "So I went to Villa Park because English classes were being offered there. It was through those classes that I started to learn about the work of the Association."[6] Organizers also made weekly visits to street corners and offered coffee to interested workers.

The unique characteristics of the day-labor population presented a challenge to organizers. Although day laborers occupied a similar position in the labor market, they had different backgrounds, not to mention that the constant competition for jobs and rapid turnover of workers on the corners weakened solidarity. One day laborer and an early recruit recounted that

> the corners were divided by regions. So on one corner, the workers were from Sonora and other northern regions of Mexico. On another corner were the workers from Zacatecas. And another corner over there were workers from El Salvador, Honduras, and so on. There were conflicts over where people were from. Now within each of these corners, there were around 100 people and they competed very hard for jobs. It was difficult.[7]

The Pasadena Day Labor Association addressed the challenge of diversity and labor-market competition in workshops and training sessions. One common workshop involved a puzzle-making activity between competing teams. Organizers wanted to illustrate how competition between workers undermined their abilities to solve collective problems. They also used the exercise to identify workers with leadership skills for further training. The association sponsored community events, formed a band that wrote songs about the trials and tribulations of immigrant workers, and created a day-labor soccer team. These efforts aimed to stimulate group bonds and identity based on common class and legal positions.

La Escuela worked closely with the Pasadena Day Labor Association to help mobilize broader immigrant support for the campaign to create the Pasadena Community Job Center. La Escuela's volunteers and students became involved in outreach for the campaign. The school organized a wide variety of events for volunteers, students, and immigrant residents of Pasadena. In one funding report, La Escuela's director reported, "We are attending retreats on Population Education Methodology every three months. We will be participating in the celebration of 'Youth Month' with other organizations in the month of August. We will also celebrate our 10th anniversary on August 6 with a fiesta from 12 noon to 5 p.m. and a dance from 7 p.m. to 12 midnight.

We are also planning to organize to attend the immigrant rights march on October 16."[8] La Escuela also organized neighborhood cleanups to encourage immigrants to get involved in their neighborhoods. It created a monthly newsletter (*Todos Unidos*) that provided general information about events and news in the community as well as information about the day-labor campaign. The newsletter also contained stories and images geared to create solidarity, pride, and political motivation.

Volunteers also organized annual Christmas posadas. Volunteer actors retold the Christian nativity story by suggesting that Mary, Jesus, and Joseph were humble immigrants in search of safe lodging. The actors walked through the neighborhood and visited houses asking for a place of refuge. More volunteer actors in these houses used stigmatizing language and closed the door on the migrant family. Residents followed the cortege until everyone reached the final place of sanctuary in the Villa Park auditorium. There, hundreds of neighborhood residents gathered for a play depicting the difficulties facing immigrants. The story stressed how racist employers, authorities, residents, and police officials repressed immigrants (like the family of Jesus), but in spite of these everyday humiliations, immigrants created a dignified and sacred life.

The events organized by the Pasadena Day Labor Association, La Escuela de la Comunidad, and Villa Park Community Center overlapped and reinforced one another. They provided volunteers, organizers, students, families, and day laborers with institutional spaces where they could develop friendships and trust, construct common stories and narratives, and create powerful feelings of solidarity. The safety and emotional support provided by these spaces enabled individuals to come out of the shadows and talk about the common troubles facing them. For many new immigrants, these organizations replaced the community structure that had been lost with their move to the United States. Attending ESL and literacy classes, participating in workshops, and volunteering for different events required almost a full-time commitment outside working hours. It created powerful bonds between the participants and reinforced their commitment to the cause. The organizers worked to construct a common identity that stressed the injustice of their exclusion. They used music, popular theater, events, workshops, newsletters, and the educational curriculum of La Escuela to tell moral stories concerning the plight of immigrants and day laborers. Although the medium for telling stories varied, the narrative was consistent: immigrants were engaged in a struggle to forge dignified lives in the face of daily injustices. The intent was to transform immigration status from a source of shame into a source of pride.

This process of forming a group gave undocumented immigrants the confidence to mobilize in visible spaces, including city council meetings, public forums, and the streets. They were coming out of the shadows with one another in group meetings, and they were coming out of the shadows in the broader political world. Their increased visibility as a new group in the city of Pasadena allowed them to influence local policies concerning day-labor work. Pablo Alvarado, the lead organizer at the time, reported that "because of our greater visibility to defend human and worker's rights, no one in the City [of Pasadena] has proposed to restrict day laborers from soliciting work on the streets or to pass city ordinances similar to those passed at the L.A. County level and at other cities."[9] Increasing public visibility was a crucial step in producing a political group with the capacity to claim equal rights in the city irrespective of legal status.

These highly stigmatized individuals were able to assume a visible, public role because of the availability of organizations and local leaders. La Escuela and the Pasadena Day Labor Association provided spaces with well-trained popular-education leaders. These spaces and leaders allowed immigrants to assemble and start building a collective identity on the basis of commonalities. Such processes (meeting in supportive spaces, talking to one another, cobbling together collective identities, participating in consciousness-raising events, and so on) were essential in overcoming the debilitating effects of stigma. Without them, it would have been much more difficult for these individuals to get past the barriers and come out into the public as a rights-claiming group.

Organizers at the Pasadena Day Labor Association and La Escuela de la Comunidad also worked at the Villa Park Community Center, a major center of activity for the Latina/o community. This was a significant connecting point because it placed immigrant organizers into contact with supportive political officials and nonprofit organizations in the Pasadena area. The councilperson for the district came into contact with the association and La Escuela because they were housed in at Villa Park, a prominent recreational center in his district. The lead organizer of the association reached out to the councilperson and invited him to an early organizing meeting. These interactions between the councilperson, the lead organizer, and the day laborers proved to be important in getting the councilperson to support the cause.

Pablo had a couple training sessions at the Villa Park Community Center. Pablo invited me to come. I got to know some of the guys and some of the ladies who became stalwarts in the organization of day laborers in Pasadena. *Once you know people, you hear their stories and you know what they are about. They are no longer a symbolic "they." They are people you know, that you see around. You have to figure out a way to make it work* (emphasis added).[10]

Face-to-face interactions transformed an abstract category into actual human beings with fundamental rights. The councilperson responded by thinking about pragmatic ways to address the day-labor issue in the city. He went on to become a prominent political advocate for a job center in the city.

Working at Villa Park also helped to connect day-labor organizers to the American Friends Service Committee (AFSC). The AFSC was a well-respected Quaker organization in the city. It provided the Pasadena Day Labor Association with important infrastructure support to mount a campaign, including office space, supplies, a place for community meetings, and other miscellaneous needs. Just as importantly, AFSC was a respected part of the northwest Pasadena community and connected day laborer organizers to various people and organizations in the area. It also attempted to mediate relationships with different adversaries (the unions and the African American community) in the hope of assuaging tensions. The AFSC hired the lead day-labor organizer (Pablo Alvarado) as a part-time organizer in late 1994. This released him from his day job and allowed him to commit more time and energy to the campaign.

When the day laborers started to emerge, the supportive councilperson and the AFSC brokered relations with others in the local political field. Entry into the field unleashed a fast networking process, with many new contacts serving as brokers in their own right. One early day-labor activist remembered, "In Pasadena politics, once a project starts, they [politicians and civic organizations] all start to talk to each other. I noticed that everywhere we would go, people would say, 'Oh, you need to talk to so and so. You need to talk to the Northwest Commission.' So all the players emerged out of the blue as we made our public appearance."[11] Gaining entry into the political arena required having strong relations with reputable, influential insiders (the councilperson and the AFSC) who served as gatekeepers. This permitted day-labor activists to enter the opaque world of local politics and tap information flows concerning players and rules of the game as well as the opportunities and constraints they faced.

Local Exclusions

Despite these successes, there was only so much a small local group could accomplish once it encountered entrenched opposition. The growing visibility of the Pasadena mobilization and their demands—for rights, a voice, and the job center—resulted in confrontations with several established community groups. Adversaries viewed the day laborers as a threat. They were reluctant to recognize the legitimacy of the day laborers' claims, partly because of their illegal status, and argued for their exclusion from the areas of the city in which the adversaries lived. These long, serious engagements with local adversarial groups produced a moral shock, which helped sharpen group boundaries and identities.

The first effort to create a job center, in 1994, resulted in an open discussion among day laborers; organizers from the association, La Escuela, and IDEPSCA; and a handful of sympathetic political officials. They identified several sites in the area and explored different possibilities for the center. Their first challenge stemmed from the Fair Oaks Avenue Redevelopment Project Area Committee (Fair Oaks PAC). The Fair Oaks PAC was made up of private citizens with commercial and residential interests in the Fair Oaks area of Pasadena. Many of the members of the Fair Oaks PAC were African American, reflecting the historical demographics of the area. The PAC's role was to advise the planning agency for the district.

The Fair Oaks PAC did not oppose a job center in Pasadena. It did, however, question whether this specific area was the most suitable place for it. Members argued that this part of Pasadena already had a disproportionate number of social-service providers. They accused the whiter, richer districts in the southern part of the city of "dumping" social services in the poorer northwest. An early day-labor activist remembered these misgivings and commented, "I realized that there were bigger politics behind this, not just day laborers wanting a center. We walked into historical frictions between whites and African Americans, and the city."[12] The Fair Oaks PAC endorsed the job center as long as it was not in its district. "They said, 'We will fully support you if you look for a place south of the freeway, which historically marked the division between the northwest [African American area] and the richer, whiter area of Pasadena.'"[13]

The reticence of the Fair Oaks PAC also reflected distributional politics in the area, with older African American leaders feeling increasingly sidelined by the growing population of immigrants. According to one city employee involved in these early deliberations, "There was from the Fair Oaks PAC some pushback on dollars going to support undocumented people. Their beef was that, 'Those dollars shouldn't be going to them [for the job center]; they should be going to us.'"[14] Conflicts over the distribution of public money and political influence fueled apprehension between new and older minority communities.

Day-labor activists responded by reaching out to reputable organizations they believed could broker relations with the African American community. The AFSC played an important role in mediating relations between the two communities. "You had important parts of the African American community who believed that it can't be a black versus brown thing; that you needed ways to come together. Mr. Moon from the AFSC, for example, he saw the need for the two communities to work together."[15] Day-labor activists also tried to humanize immigrants by telling their stories. They hoped to overcome resistance by demonstrating the shared values and histories of immigrant and African American communities. This effort backfired as certain members of the Fair Oaks PAC pushed back on the legitimacy of their claims.

> We tried an approach that didn't work. We tried to use this, humanizing sharing of stories. . . . Day laborers spoke about their oppression, and why they are here, and what they want for their families, and why the job center is a good idea. But the representative from the Fair Oaks PAC was politically experienced, so he didn't buy it. He responded by telling his own story. . . . It was like, "I don't care that you are oppressed. I don't care that you crossed the border and have families. We have families too. My ancestors were slaves so your oppression is not bigger than mine." So it entered all of this kind of identity politics thing. He basically said, "You tell me your story but you are still illegal. My family was forced to come here and my family suffered too."[16]

The effort by day laborers to reveal commonalities prompted a sharp response. The illegality of the immigrants was used to devalue their political legitimacy, and day-labor activists were unable to overcome the reluctance of the Fair Oaks PAC. Consequently, the planning commission of northwest Pasadena went on to deny the association's request for a job center in its jurisdiction. According to one news report, "Saundra Knox, a member of the Commission, said the day workers' plight is a citywide problem. 'I don't think solutions are always in the Northwest borders.'"[17]

The Pasadena Day Labor Association continued its search for a location. It expressed optimism about the prospects of acquiring another site outside its district. In a letter to its principal funder, Los Angeles–based Liberty Hill, the lead organizer reported, "The Association is still negotiating a leasing contract with the owner of the property. . . . We expect to open our hiring site in May 1995."[18] Shortly after that, the association encountered another obstacle. The International Brotherhood of Electrical Workers (IBEW) Local 11 had its main administrative office in a site adjacent to the proposed job center. The IBEW took a "principled" stance against the job center because they viewed it as a step back for organized labor. The union expressed this position in a stinging letter to the AFSC, the main ally supporting the Pasadena Day Labor Association.

> At present, law-abiding contractors and honest construction workers often find themselves cheated out of a living by fly-by-night operators and their unskilled, temporary workers, who are generally solicited from curbside operations such as the one proposed for the Corson Street site. . . . Our experience has been that day laborers form a willing pool of labor for employers who intend to hire them for the lowest wage possible, often below the legal minimum. . . . In addition, the workers are almost never employed under circumstances which provide for the payment of legally required taxes or social security deductions, and are not covered by workers compensation insurance. In short, the situation created is one in which unfair and illegal treatment of workers is the norm rather than the exception.[19]

According to the statement, undocumented immigrants willingly broke labor and immigration laws. This placed them in a state of illegality and made them undeserving of basic rights. Having framed the problem in this way, the author of the letter went on to state, "As an organization whose contractual agreements *require at least the minimum protection of the law* for its members, we would consider the existence of such an operation, in the very shadow of our headquarters, *intolerable* to say the least. . . . We question the wisdom of the City of Pasadena in considering such an arrangement, *which creates a sort of Third-World hiring bazaar*" (emphasis added).[20] The law was used to draw an impermeable line between groups that had a right to the city of Pasadena (law abiders) and those that didn't (illegals). The cultural attributes of the immigrants were then used to accentuate their lack of legitimacy and deservingness in the city. These factors "made the existence of such an operation [and

the people using them] . . . intolerable to say the least." For the IBEW, the legal
and cultural status of day laborers made it impossible to consider them eligible for a rightful place in the city.

The IBEW threatened legal action to stop the project, and in the event that
that failed, the union pledged to fight the day-labor activists through coercive
means. I quote the letter at length to illustrate the fierce opposition facing immigrant workers in Pasadena.

1. We will maintain a regular presence at the site, interviewing workers
    to ensure that they have been paid minimum wages and overtime.
2. We will ensure compliance with applicable federal and state tax laws.
3. We will ensure that workers who offer themselves for construction or
    similar maintenance work are licensed as contractors with the State of
    California, and will report violators to the Contractors State License
    Board.
4. We will inform prospective employers of their obligations under the law:
    a. To hire only workers legally permitted to work in the United States;
    b. To pay appropriate taxes, and to provide workers compensation
        insurance;
    c. To pay legal wages and overtime, and to provide a legal statement of
        deductions as required by law;
    d. To possess an appropriate contractor's and/or business license for
        the work in question.[21]

The letter concluded with an ominous threat: "We envision, and invite you
to imagine a scenario in which prospective employers, many of them local homeowners and small business owners, could expect to be investigated
through their license plate numbers and perhaps turned over to a government
agency for violating the law."[22] The IBEW cc'd copies of the letter to the Immigration and Naturalization Service, Department of Labor, state labor com-
missioner, Contractors State License Board, employment tax fraud unit, and
Internal Revenue Service.

The Pasadena Day Labor Association and their allies met with IBEW officials twice to find a compromise. The proponents of the job center stressed
that day laborers would not compete with IBEW members and that the union
should express solidarity with fellow workers rather than fight them. An internal document from the association noted that it "tried to shame the union
in dropping their threats through newspaper publicity, a demonstration, and

finally, a hunger strike if necessary."[23] Day-labor activists also sought support from the director of the Los Angeles County Federation of Labor, Miguel Contreras. Pablo Alvarado, the lead organizer of the association, and a delegation of three workers visited Contreras at his Los Angeles office. Contreras expressed concern during the meeting but never contacted the association about the matter again. His nonresponse to the Pasadena conflict was puzzling because it departed from Mr. Contreras's highly touted efforts to organize precarious immigrants and give them a louder voice in Los Angeles unions. We can only infer that the power of the IBEW in Southern California made him reluctant to intervene in what many believed to be a local dispute.

The union's hostile response and the unwillingness of the Los Angeles County Federation of Labor to intervene produced a "moral shock"[24] among the members of the Pasadena Day Labor Association. One member wrote in a memo, "This threat has thrown the Association into an unexpected level of struggle, mainly because it seems a contradiction for a union to be in *opposition* to our struggle" (emphasis added).[25] The association expected the union to respond with an expression of solidarity. Instead the IBEW stressed qualities—cultural deficiencies ("Third-World hiring bazaar") and their double illegality (that is, their violation of labor and immigration laws)—that made recognizing their equality as workers impossible. The treatment by the IBEW and the lack of support by the Los Angeles County Federation of Labor left the leaders of the association frustrated with organized labor. "That was my first impression of unions in the U.S.," remembered activist José Esquival. "They were no different from Mexican unions. They were bullies."[26]

Day laborers in Pasadena formed a relatively cohesive group through the work of dedicated and politicized leaders, but their entry into the local political arena led them into conflicts with more established groups. The immigrants discovered that in spite of their efforts to build bridges and find compromises (through meetings, shaming, and storytelling), adversaries used their immigration status to block their inclusion. The immigrants and day laborers were feeling empowered to come out of the shadows and assert their voices in the public sphere, but their adversaries were using their illegality to push them back into obscurity. One day laborer remembered, "It is clear that there were problems but we were also thinking about the future of Pasadena. We wanted a clean city. But others didn't want Latinos. They said that they didn't want us, that we were trash. They rejected us, there were many people who didn't want us."[27] The emotionally intense process, though, highlighted group boundaries, reinforced solidarity, and injected a sense of moral urgency into their struggle. Undocumented immigrant workers knew that they were not "trash" and would continue their struggle to exert their voices, power, and equality in Pasadena. Their political identity and will to resist was forged in the trenches of local political life. In spite of the important advances of immigrant workers, adversaries continued to block their goal of creating a safe, regulated job center for day laborers in the city. The Pasadena activists needed stronger allies and even more political power. This would be achieved through their incorporation into regional networks and CHIRLA's day-labor project.

Regionalizing the Struggle:
The Coalition for Humane Immigrant Rights of Los Angeles

The struggle for the Pasadena job center precipitated a cascade of new networks. Increased prominence of the Pasadena campaign drew the attention of larger organizations from the city of Los Angeles, which facilitated the flow of resources to the campaign. The creation of regional networks enabled the circulation of resources, discourses, stories, tactics, and strategies across metropolitan Los Angeles. Activists in specific localities could tap these networks for various resources and enhance their particular struggles. These regional networks also tied laborers in Pasadena to others in Ladera Heights, Harbor City, Agoura Hills, and Redondo Beach. Workers on street corners across this urban region began to realize that there were others out there like them and that there was a vehicle to which they could harness their voices in local and national political arenas.

Regional Organization

Advocacy groups in large cities such as Los Angeles, Chicago, Boston, Baltimore, and New York began to organize immigrant workers in the late 1980s and early 1990s.[28] Among these cities, Los Angeles provided a comparatively supportive context for immigrant rights advocacy. The city stood apart from more conservative suburbs in the metropolitan region. Progressive council members such as Michael Woo and Michael Hernandez had long reached out to immigrant organizations. In 1996, Miguel Contreras—a representative of the most progressive and immigrant-friendly faction of organized labor—was elected to the presidency of the powerful Los Angeles County Federation of Labor.[29] In assuming leadership, Contreras embraced the effort by several union locals to organize undocumented immigrant workers in the service industry. His team also worked to make his organization into a political machine to elect labor- and immigrant-friendly politicians in Los Angeles and the rest of the state.[30] Contreras was not supportive of Pasadena activists because of conflicts with a powerful member (the IBEW) of the Los Angeles County Federation of Labor. Nevertheless, he was committed to creating a supportive political environment for immigrants and low-wage workers in the city and state.

Los Angeles also had a comparatively strong activist network. As a major gateway city for Mexican and Central American immigrants, Los Angeles possessed a fast-developing social-movement infrastructure consisting of militant immigrant rights organizations, a diverse range of supportive allies, innovative and proimmigrant unions, and resource-rich university faculty and students.[31] Immigrant rights organizations had focused on addressing the needs of refugees in the 1980s. In the 1990s they turned their attention to the needs of the settled, undocumented immigrant community.[32] Several organizations[33] mounted a series of campaigns to enhance the rights of immigrant workers.[34] A local philanthropic foundation also played a strategic role in providing financial and technical support to those burgeoning organizations. The Liberty Hill Foundation—formed in 1977—provided support to most of the early immigrant rights organizations. Whereas mainstream foundations provided support for liberal, progressive organizations, Liberty Hill had a history of funding organizations that were controversial and radical. Many organizations in Los Angeles would not have received funding from traditional foundations. Organizations such as CHIRLA, CARECEN, IDEPSCA, the Pasadena Day Labor Association, and many others received initial starting grants from Liberty Hill. Thus, organizational resources in Los Angeles during the 1980s were conducive to immigrant rights activism.

In 1986, CHIRLA was founded in an environment with political opportunities and organizational resources. It became an independent nonprofit in 1993.[35] Like early immigrant rights organizations across the country, CHIRLA began as a coalition in response to the Immigration Reform and Control Act (IRCA). This law provided a pathway to legalization for immigrants who had arrived before 1982 but excluded those who had arrived afterward. The law also introduced powerful employers' sanctions on hiring undocumented workers. This made immigrant employees much more vulnerable to exploitation. CHIRLA provided assistance to immigrants seeking to legalize their status under the new law. It continued to perform these services but also turned its attention to the growing abuses stemming from the restrictive components of IRCA. Recent arrivals, many of whom were Central Americans, were not allowed to legalize their status. Central Americans were also not recognized as refugees, even those from war-torn El Salvador.[36] El Salvador was a close ally of the United States, and the Reagan administration elevated the country as a beacon of free-market democracy. Recognizing El Salvadoran migrants as refugees would be to admit the human rights atrocities perpetrated by a key US ally. CHIRLA expanded its work to provide support and services for the many immigrants who failed to qualify for IRCA's legalization program, and it responded to increased problems associated with the violation of workplace rights due to IRCA's employment verification measure.

CHIRLA framed its arguments in terms of territorial personhood and sometimes postnationalism. In an early grant application to the Liberty Hill Foundation, it stated, "Regardless of one's legal status in this country, one is still entitled to the protections of the Constitution."[37] The rights of people transcended national background and even immigration status. CHIRLA initiated a know-your-rights campaign as early as 1989. It developed and distributed pamphlets, cards, and novellas on the rights of day laborers. One of its pamphlets stated, "Did you know that you have rights in your work? Your children can register for nutritional assistance, that you have the right to free medical help in case of emergency. *You have rights regardless of your age, race, ability to speak English, or your papers*" (emphasis added).[38] Several years later, the organization continued to embrace a strong universalist position on the rights of immigrants. In a 1995 newsletter, it proclaimed that "social justice and human decency should never be undermined by unconstitutional measures mired in discrimination, fear and selfishness."[39]

CHIRLA started working with day laborers almost from its start in the late 1980s. The work grew out of its focus on immigrant workers' rights.[40] In 1988, the Los Angeles City Council was considering adopting an antisolicitation ordinance, but CHIRLA fought against the ordinance and demanded the city open a series of worker centers. As Antonio Bernabe, one of the first day-labor organizers in Los Angeles, recounted,

> The city was going to make an ordinance to prohibit day laborers from seeking work in the city of Los Angeles. Then CHIRLA and other organizations threatened to file a lawsuit against the city. The city decided to sponsor five centers all over the city, with $5 million designated for five years. But they only opened two centers. The first in Harbor City in 1989 and then North Hollywood in 1990.[41]

As was typically the case, the city of Los Angeles designed the centers to address its security and policing concerns. Los Angeles officials expected the worker centers to be places of disciplined integration. They were supposed to take workers out of public view and provide them a disciplined and well-surveilled space to find work. Bernabe, the first employee of a city-run worker center and an early CHIRLA organizer, remembered, "When I was interviewed for this position [at the city-run worker center], they were interviewing for somebody like a bouncer in a bar." The officials wanted somebody who could enforce discipline at the hiring center. Mr. Bernabe went on to say that "they only talked about when you needed to call the police. I told them that you didn't need to call the police; these are fine people looking for work. We don't need the police getting involved."[42]

By the mid-1990s, city officials grew tired of managing the centers directly. They called on local organizations to sponsor them. CHIRLA was the only organization to make a bid and obtained a contract to manage the two centers in 1996. It used the new funding from the city to expand its team of immigrant rights organizers. Mayron Payes, one of the early organizers at CHIRLA and a future organizer at the Center for Community Change (see part 2 of the book), remembered these early organizing days with great enthusiasm.

> At that time, we were good! We were very eager to work with the day laborers. That was our task. I didn't know Pablo [Alvarado, from Pasadena]. We met at CHIRLA. He was also from El Salvador. Mario Lopez was also from El Salvador. Marlom Portillo was a popular educator from Honduras. We knew what the fuck to do! We knew about organizing and we were just in the right place at the right moment. We were young and energetic. We have our differences now, but at that time we were united.[43]

Whereas city officials viewed the centers as a tool to police immigrant workers, CHIRLA's organizers believed that they could be used to reach out to workers and raise political consciousness through popular education. Their goal was to politically empower workers and encourage them to express their own voices in city politics.

Connecting Suburban Struggles to CHIRLA

CHIRLA worked closely with IDEPSCA, the organization that had started La Escuela de la Comunidad in Pasadena. When it was clear that La Escuela and the Pasadena Day Labor Association needed help with their campaign for a worker center, IDEPSCA brokered a connection between the Pasadena activists and CHIRLA. This helped to link the Pasadena activists with an organization that was centrally involved with the struggle for immigrant rights throughout the entire Los Angeles region.

In late 1995, Pasadena's lead day-labor organizer, Pablo Alvarado, moved to CHIRLA to work on their Worker's Rights Project. The move helped integrate the Pasadena campaign into CHIRLA and connect Pasadena activists to day-labor campaigns throughout the Los Angeles area. One day-labor activist from Pasadena noted, "At CHIRLA we met with other workers from other cities to talk about our common problems and to create a union. I didn't know anybody there except for Marlom [from IDEPSCA] and Pablo [from the Pasadena Day Labor Association]."[44] Pasadena activists became involved in the effort to create a countywide day-labor association made up of workers from different corners and hiring centers. CHIRLA worked with IDEPSCA to establish the Association of Day Laborers in 1997.[45] The structure of the emerging association was made up of day laborers representing different hiring sites across the Los Angeles region. IDEPSCA took up the tasks of leadership development and popular education among the workers, and day laborers went on to fill the leadership positions of the new association. One organizer recalled, "We selected officers. I was named the Treasurer. At that time, we had meetings every eight days at CHIRLA and I represented Pasadena."[46]

The new Association of Day Laborers employed territorial personhood and postnational framings of citizenship. In a 1997 newsletter, the association maintained that "all men, as human beings, have a right to look to an honest living. Work is a gift that God has given us. A person in search of a living with their work has no reason to be blocked in any part of the world, because that is the law of God."[47] Like immigrant day laborers across the country, the Los Angeles association asserted that the right to work was universal, inalienable, and sacred. Even borders couldn't take this God-given right away from workers. They drew on constitutional reasoning to legitimate rights claims.

> Free speech is a right, we speak with our voices but also with our hands and the many gestures we use to communicate, when you are on the sidewalk you are expressing yourself or communicating an idea, basically practicing free speech. No law can prohibit someone from standing on a public sidewalk, talking about religion for example. So how can one prohibit someone from talking about work?[48]

The rights of immigrants to work and live were given by God and protected by the Constitution. People's rights did not, according to this reasoning, derive from membership in the nation-state but from simply being human.

CHIRLA organizers drew from the Pasadena experience of uniting the disparate day laborers and stressed the importance of community building to overcome group fragmentation. In addition to organizing regular meetings for the leadership team, they organized conferences among the workers of different hiring sites (*Inter-Esquinales*). Meetings were complemented by social and cultural activities such as political theater, a musical group, collective meals, and parties. CHIRLA organizers also introduced a soccer league and a Day Laborer World Cup. These activities were designed to break down the geographic, social, and cultural barriers dividing day laborers by building feelings of solidarity and a postnational identity. One report by the association explained, "Through soccer, the nationalistic and cultural barriers amongst day laborers have been broken down and the idea that Latinos are a 'people without borders' has become a legitimate and inevitable truth."[49] Soccer proved to be an important vehicle for bringing day laborers together and building solidarity among them. The report went on to note that

> the corners that have formed soccer teams are those which have achieved a relatively mature level or organization. All the corners have the potential to achieve this maturity, which has meant self-sufficiency and self-determination for those that have. The organizational level developed at these corners is based not on the need for soccer clubs but on the necessity for day laborers to control the destiny of those corners from which they depend on to make a living.[50]

These efforts were also intended to improve relations with established residents. "The soccer games," the report concluded, "serve towards projecting a positive image of the day laborers to the community and show the world that day laborers are not just about work, but are capable of all types of human interaction and culture."[51] It was one of many ways to humanize the workers.

The leadership team made the popular-education methodology a central part of organizing. The methodology was applied to a wide range of CHIRLA's activities, including workshops, leadership training, and organizing campaigns. They also instituted democratic methods of self-organization at the hiring sites, which contrasted with the hierarchical methods found in professionalized nonprofit service organizations.[52] More-active workers formed executive committees in which they would propose common rules (for behavior at hiring sites and for minimum wages), set priorities, and develop strategies for the collective. Recommendations by the executive committee would then be discussed and voted on by all workers in frequent assembly meetings. These methods were crucial to the political socialization of the day laborers because they were encouraged to view work as a collective rather than an individual affair. Workers now had a space in which they could come out of their shells and discuss their common problems with others like themselves. In discussing a hiring site, Mr. Alvarado remarked to a journalist that "there is an executive committee that deals with the issues here. The guys have organized a soccer team and a musical band. And the guys write their own *corridos* [folk songs]."[53] Social and cultural activities, democratic governance, and popular education encouraged solidarity and the construction of a critical identity and consciousness at the metropolitan scale. Not every day laborer in the metropolitan area participated in these activities, but enough did that these group-making methods helped dispersed laborers to discover commonalities, strike up friendships, and start constructing identities around their shared experiences.

CHIRLA's organizers not only created the infrastructure to build bonds and identity among day laborers in the region but also helped to build bridges between the laborers and various Los Angeles organizations. CHIRLA assumed a central role in day-labor advocacy in the city of Los Angeles, but it did not act alone. Allied legal organizations such as the Mexican American Legal and Educational Defense Fund (MALDEF), the ACLU, and Legal Aid played early, decisive roles in defending day laborers and fighting local antisolicitation laws across the metropolitan region. CHIRLA's staff also had strong relationships with other Los Angeles–based organizations such as IDEPSCA, CARECEN, and El Rescate. These organizations also began to work with day laborers and went on to form a partnership with CHIRLA to manage worker centers and organize new hiring sites. As CHIRLA became a regional powerhouse for immigration advocacy, it used its prominence to connect day laborers to a wide variety of immigrant and nonimmigrant organizations. According to Pablo Alvarado, "The Day Laborer Organizing Project has developed multi-ethnic alliances [. . .] CHIRLA organized an emergency coalition of day laborers and such community allies as the American Civil Liberties Union, the Southern Christian Leadership Conference and the Multi-Cultural Collaborative."[54]

CHIRLA supported specific day laborer campaigns in different corners of the metropolitan region, and it helped fortify organizing capacities in these localities while building coalitions with different nonimmigrant actors and organizations. This helped consolidate local coalitions against restrictions and build bridges to a broader swath of the local population. CHIRLA organizers, for instance, helped form a coalition to push back on the restrictionist efforts of some residents in Ladera Heights. One CHIRLA report recounted, "Residents, Sheriff's representatives and a multi-ethnic coalition of organizations have joined together in an innovative partnership to protect the civil rights of day laborers in Ladera Heights area."[55] Two years later, CHIRLA organizers helped push a neighborhood improvement project in the same area to build bridges with residents of the community. A 1997 CHIRLA grant application read, "The Day Laborer Organizing Project at CHIRLA continues to bring Latino day laborers together with African-American residents in Ladera Heights on a joint neighborhood improvement project. The Day Laborer Association now has African American Day Laborers working jointly with Latinos as they expand into a countywide association."[56]

In a similar campaign in the suburb of Woodland Hills, local activists affiliated with CHIRLA pursued a similar strategy. The Association of Day Laborers newsletter stated that the organization was "working towards a peaceful co-existence at Woodland Hills. . . . We have had an agreement with the police, merchants, and residents of the area. . . . Since then we have worked for its expansion and implementation. We also participate in other activities related to the corner, where we look for work, and with the neighborhood."[57] Strengthening a base in localities and building local support networks helped change the balance of power in localities across the metropolitan region. When this strategy failed to push back on restrictive immigration policies, activists pursued lawsuits.

As one of the leading organizations in the fight for immigrant workers' rights (and for day laborers and domestic workers in particular), CHIRLA assumed leadership in creating a grassroots immigrant rights coalition. The organization recounted, "The Immigrant Campaign for Civil Rights will develop grassroots leadership in the Latino immigrant community . . . and, through CHIRLA's coalition, join with other people from other communities to fight racist and divisive public policy with a strong united front. The grassroots activities will be complimented by a media strategy to publicize and therefore amplify the message of each action."[58] As part of this coalition, CHIRLA created local committees throughout the Los Angeles region and connected them through regular meetings at CHIRLA. "CHIRLA will connect these fledging [Immigrant Campaign local] committees with existing organizations in their geographical areas wherever possible, for example CHIRLA member organizations Libreria del Pueblo in San Bernardino."[59] The culmination of its role as a regional player was in the creation of the Multi-Ethnic Immigrant Worker Organizing Network (MIWON) in 2000. MIWON was a coalition of five prominent Los Angeles organizations including CHIRLA, Koreatown Immigrant Workers Alliance (KIWA), the Institute of Popular Education of Southern California (IDEPSCA), the Pilipino Workers Center (PWC), and the Garment Workers Center. While these organizations played important roles in making up this coalition, CHIRLA played a founding and leading role. It was established with the twofold aim of strengthening immigrant-worker organizing and engaging in broader immigrant rights advocacy at the local, state, and national levels.

Going National

Throughout the 1990s, CHIRLA continued to amass power. Although it remained a largely regional organization, it began to fight against federal anti-immigrant policies. The Personal Responsibility and Work Opportunity Reconciliation Act (PRWORA) of 1996 restricted welfare on the basis of immigration status. In response to these restrictions, CHIRLA developed alliances with a broader coalition of organizations (for example, the March 9th Coalition) battling welfare reform. Other coalitions such as the California Immigrant Welfare Collaborative were designed to lobby state and federal politicians about the problems of new restrictions. They organized a variety of actions to pressure elected officials. One action planned in 1998 was Immigration Day, which involved a large mobilization of working-class immigrants in California's capital. A California Immigrant Welfare Collaborative grant application stated that "Immigrant Day seeks to increase civic participation in the immigrant community and to involve and organize community members and organizations from Los Angeles. We would like to enable a large delegation of low-income Los Angeles area residents to be in Sacramento for a rally and to visit their State assembly members and senators."[60] CHIRLA also began to mobilize against the Illegal Immigration Reform and Immigrant Responsibility Act (IIRIRA) of 1996. The organization criticized this harsh immigration law with the following statement: "Immigration Reform Law attacks the Constitutional and human rights of all immigrants."[61] By the late 1990s, CHIRLA had forcefully addressed restrictive national policies through regional, state, and increasingly national coalitions. Although CHIRLA continued to be firmly embedded in metropolitan Los Angeles, it was difficult for the organization to ignore federal policy because its members were being severely affected by it.

CHIRLA entered a coalition that was central to nationalizing the immigrant rights movement. CHIRLA and other regional organizations were invited to participate in the Center for Community Change's National Campaign for Jobs and Income Support (NCJIS) in late 1997. In one press release from that same year, CHIRLA reported that "this press conference kicks off a nationwide effort . . . by local and national organizations calling for the restoration of benefits to some of society's most vulnerable members."[62] Organizations such as CHIRLA joined a welfare coalition but worked with other regional immigrant rights organizations specifically on issues pertaining to immigration. This would go on to serve as the springboard for a centralized, highly professionalized, national social-movement infrastructure. This will be the subject of the next chapters of the book.

CHIRLA also sponsored a national network of organizations working with immigrant day laborers. Advocacy organizations working on day laborer issues connected to one another through various networks. As a result of these dialogues, organizers passed on information concerning challenges, tactics, and various opportunities. The flow of information and ideas allowed organizations to better map out the realm of possibilities in their local political environments. Realizing that there was a need to better coordinate efforts, worker centers and various advocacy organizations created a national organization in 2001, the National Day Laborer Organizing Network (NDLON).[63] Pablo Alvarado, leader of the Pasadena Day Labor Association and the director of CHIRLA's day-labor program, worked with other organizations to create this national organization. Gustavo Torres from CASA Maryland remembers, "I was the first president of the board of directors of the National Day Laborer Network with Pablo Alvarado and the other organizations. All of that energy was creating a great momentum right here locally but also at the national level with day laborers."[64] While CHIRLA served as NDLON's fiscal sponsor and parent organization, NDLON quickly established itself as an independent 501(c)(3) nonprofit organization in 2005 and grew from twelve founding organizations in 2001 to forty in 2015. NDLON invested heavily in fighting against restrictive ordinances and for worker centers and would go on to become one of the most important organizations in the fight against federal enforcement and deportation policies. NDLON became the left flank of the immigrant rights movement, moving further and further away from its parent organization (see part 2).

Although this regional organization effectively defended the rights of immigrant workers in greater Los Angeles area, it was drawn into the national political field. It sought to exercise greater influence in the federal political arena while also creating an organization (NDLON) to connect local efforts to organize immigrant workers across the country. Both strategies emerged from CHIRLA but they were not, as the following chapters will show, always consistent with one another.

PART II

NATIONALIZING THE FIGHT FOR IMMIGRANT RIGHTS

CHAPTER 5

The Resurgent Nation-State

SCATTERED LOCAL AND REGIONAL STRUGGLES defined much of immigrant rights activism in the 1990s, whereas centralization and nationalization characterized the mainstream movement in the late 2000s and 2010s. There were many factors that precipitated this change. The growing concentration of the federal government's power in the area of immigration was an important contributing factor. The federal government asserted its power over immigration in the late 1990s and continued to do so into the 2000s. It created a legal apparatus to reinforce its southern border, deny many rights to documented and undocumented immigrants, criminalize large sections of the population, and expedite deportations.[1] These moves were intended to reassert the power of the federal government over immigration and citizenship. State and local governments were given new responsibilities through police cooperation programs such as 287(g) and Secure Communities, but they were intended to be subordinate partners in the enactment of federal policy. The federal government's accumulation of power and resources compelled advocates to target it in their fight for immigrant rights.

The centralization of government powers was also reflected in increased activity of federal officials in public debates on immigration. Democrats and Republicans diagnosed the problem differently. When immigrant rights organizations and other advocates entered the federal playing field, certain branches were also far more open than others. In the mid-2000s government officials began to conceive and push for broad, comprehensive reform. This captured the political imagination of many advocates. They believed that making immigrants into legal permanent residents and citizens would ensure the rights of millions. The recognition of basic rights would now have to wait until membership in the national community had been obtained. Only after gaining membership would immigrants actually be recognized as rights-deserving human beings.

The federal government therefore became the preeminent force in the field of national citizenship. Its symbolic and legal power were overwhelming, helping to not only shape the parameters of national citizenship but also frame how all stakeholders were engaged in the battle to change it. This chapter draws on secondary literature to describe the centralization of government powers. It uses the immigration-reform newspaper database to assess political dynamics, policy positions, and opportunities (see the appendix for further detail). The immigration-reform newspaper database was compiled for the 2000 to 2014 period using a method developed by Ruud Koopmans and Paul Statham.[2] The database includes 1,254 newspaper articles, from which 5,422 claims were extracted. This information provides insights into the prominence of the issue, the influence of government claims makers, and their positions on immigration reform and rights.

Nationalizing Repressive Power

The local battles in the 1990s emboldened some activists and some subnational elected officials to usurp federal authority over immigration matters. The most decisive power grab was led by the Save Our State (SOS) coalition in California in the 1990s. The anti-immigrant coalition sponsored the infamous Proposition 187, a measure designed to end most public services to undocumented immigrants. The Clinton administration recognized this action in California and other states as a threat to the federal government's monopoly over immigration and citizenship. If the federal government did not want a patchwork of immigration policies, it needed to take decisive action and reassert its monopoly.

In 1996, the Clinton administration supported three decisive laws that would change immigration politics for years to come.[3] The Illegal Immigration Reform and Immigrant Responsibility Act (IIRIRA) allocated more resources to enforcement, expedited deportation procedures, restricted judicial discretion during removal proceedings, and reduced possibilities for appeals, among other changes.[4] The measure also expanded what were considered deportable criminal offenses. The law, according to Nicholas de Genova, was "the most punitive legislation to date concerning undocumented migration."

He goes on to note that the law introduced "provisions for criminalizing, apprehending, detaining, fining, deporting, and also imprisoning a wide array of 'infractions' that significantly broadened and elaborated the qualitative scope of the law's production of 'illegality' for undocumented migrants and others associated with them."[5] In a follow-up executive order, President Clinton expanded the geographic area for expedited removals (that is, the immigrants had no right to contest deportation in court) to within one hundred miles of the border. During the same year, Congress passed and President Clinton signed into law the Antiterrorism and Effective Death Penalty Act (AEDP). IIRIRA and AEDP expanded the offenses that could be considered "aggravated offense" for immigrants even when they weren't necessarily felonies.[6] The two laws enhanced the country's ability to detect and remove immigrants while restricting judicial review.

The Clinton administration and the Republican Congress also supported measures to restrict social benefits to immigrants. IIRIRA, for example, imposed new restrictions on federal financial aid and social security benefits for undocumented immigrants. In addition to this, the Personal Responsibility and Work Opportunity Reconciliation Act (PRWORA) established new restrictions on the receipt of welfare benefits. Although PRWORA was not an immigration law, it contained stipulations that strongly shaped the lives of immigrant residents, authorized and unauthorized. Immigrants were deemed ineligible for many welfare programs. The law also placed new restrictions on Supplemental Security Income (SSI), food stamps, Temporary Assistance for Needy Families (TANF), and nonemergency Medicaid. It made undocumented immigrants ineligible for state and local services unless a state passed a law "positively affirming its commitment to provide public services to this population."[7] The three laws therefore contributed to an expansion of powers of the federal government over immigration and citizenship. "Their expansive provisions (concerned primarily with enforcement and penalties for undocumented presence) were truly unprecedented," according to De Genova, "in the severity with which they broadened and intensified the ramifications of the legal production of migrant 'illegality.'"[8]

These restrictive laws were viewed by Clinton administration officials as ways to reassert the authority of the federal government over the issue of immigration. But they were also understood as good politics. The Clinton White House embraced aggressive zero-tolerance policies in order to compete with Republicans for law-and-order voters. A 1996 memorandum from then–senior advisor Rahm Emanuel to President Clinton stated, "Since Nixon's Law and Order campaign, crime has been a staple in the GOP platform. Over the past four years, your policies have redefined the issue and allowed Democrats to achieve parity."[9] IIRIRA was seen as a natural continuation of this strategy. The memorandum went on to say that "after the Crime Bill passed in 1994, we built a stronger record on crime. The illegal immigration legislation provides that same opportunity; now that the legislation is passed, we can build up a strong administration record on immigration."[10] The memo outlined several immigration policies, in addition to those already included in IRRIRA, AEDP, and PRWORA, to bolster the administration's tough posture on the issue. These included increasing immigration hearings in six states in order to "claim and achieve record deportations of criminal aliens," expanding the government's employer-verification program for the purposes of claiming "a number of industries free of illegal immigrants," instituting a one-month moratorium on naturalization, and dramatically increasing National Guard forces on the southern border. The section on immigration concluded that "if we want continued public support for trade and friendly relations with Mexico, we must be vigilant in our effort to curb illegal trade (e.g. narcotic and immigrants)."[11] The memo contained a number of handwritten annotations by President Clinton himself, including, "*This is great*" (emphasis in the original).

The election of Republican George W. Bush in 2001 presented a brief opportunity for immigrant rights advocates to beat back the policies of the previous administration. The first several months of the Bush administration occasioned a round of high-level talks between administration officials, Congress, and the president of Mexico. In a highly publicized speech to Congress, Mexico's president Vicente Fox argued that "regularization [of immigration status] does not mean rewarding those who break the law. Regularization means that we give legal rights to people who are already contributing to this great nation."[12] Presidents Fox and Bush upheld sacred national principles such as the rule of law, while stressing that legal rights should be conferred to immigrants making a contribution to "this great nation." This was an important departure from the get-tough language that had pervaded in the late 1990s.

Five days after President Fox's historic speech, the terrorist attacks of September 11 occurred. The Bush administration suddenly shifted its attention away from immigration reform to the war on terror. Immigration was now viewed as an issue of national security.[13] President Bush announced that he was "[giving] new authority to the Justice Department to arrest immigrants suspected of terrorism, accelerate the process of deporting them and curtail court appeals."[14] The tight link between immigration, national security, and border enforcement was echoed in public statements by prominent elected officials during the first half of the decade. This discourse fueled restrictive new measures and laws throughout the 2000s. Congress passed five restrictive laws during the decade, and the Department of Homeland Security introduced twelve different measures to strengthen borders and facilitate the deportation of undocumented immigrants.[15]

These initiatives added to the 1996 laws and accelerated the growth of the state's enforcement machine. According to a report from the Migration Policy Institute,[16] spending for immigration enforcement grew by fifteen times from 1986 to 2012.[17] In 2012, funding to the main immigrant enforcement agencies was nearly $18 billion. This was $2 billion more than the combined budgets of the Drug Enforcement Agency, FBI, Secret Service, US Marshals Service, and Bureau of Alcohol, Tobacco, Firearms, and Explosives. As a matter of comparison, in 1986, funding to these other federal agencies surpassed immigration enforcement by four times. By 2012, immigration had become the single most important area of federal law enforcement.

The increase in the government's enforcement capacities resulted in a surge of detentions and deportations. Department of Homeland Security spending on immigration detention grew from $900 million in 2005 to $1.8 billion in 2010.[18] Between 1995 and 2011, annual detentions grew from 85,730 to 429,247, with detainees spending on average 37.6 days incarcerated.[19] By the end of the 2000s, there were approximately 330 adult detention centers.[20] In addition to skyrocketing detentions, deportations also increased substantially. In 1990 there were 30,039 deportations from the country. This number grew to 188,467 in 2000 and 391,943 in 2011. The 1996 laws played a central role in expanding a complex deportation and detention apparatus. According to Doris Meissner and her Migration Policy Institute colleagues,

> The 1996 laws made retroactive and substantially broadened the list of crimes—including adding some relatively minor crimes—for which noncitizens are subject to removal from the country. . . . As a result, unprecedented numbers of individuals—including long-time lawful permanent residents . . . became subject to mandatory detention and removal. Armed with tough laws and generous funding, programs to "control the border" and combat illegal immigration by enforcing immigration requirements have become far-reaching.[21]

Over a relatively short period of time, the federal government intensified its immigration enforcement efforts. It passed laws that expanded its authority to detect, detain, and deport unwanted and unauthorized immigrants in the country. By doing this, it asserted its monopoly on discrimination and repression of immigrants in the country. Rather than have a patchwork of policies, the federal government was seeking to create a single, all-encompassing repressive net.

The centralization of federal government power was, interestingly enough, coupled with the devolution of immigration functions to city and county law enforcement agencies. In 1996 IIRIRA introduced a program (287 [g]) to create agreements between federal and local law enforcement agencies. The program introduced a memorandum of understanding between the federal Department of Justice and local law enforcement agencies. Local police participating in the program were given special training in immigration matters and granted authority (that is, deputized) to assume the responsibilities of immigration enforcement. But 287(g) was superseded by the Secure Communities program, which was introduced in 2008. This program required local police agencies to report on the status of immigrants in detention and to place holds on those people lacking legal status. These procedures allowed local police to serve as a force multiplier for federal immigration enforcement agencies, enhancing their capacities to detect, detain, and deport immigrants.

Nationalizing Immigration Politics

Government officials were busy not only enacting more restrictive policies but also incessantly talking about immigration, citizenship, and nationhood. This section uses the immigration-reform newspaper database to assess such talk.

Between 2000 and 2014, all government officials (elected, unelected, national, state, and local) accounted for 40 percent of the total number of statements made on the subject in the immigration-reform newspaper database. They outperformed organizations (from businesses to nonprofit advocates), which accounted for 33 percent of all claims. The remaining claims (27 percent) were made by individuals unaffiliated with an organization or government agency. The government has been, and remains, a formidable voice in the political field. Although more people and organizations entered the fray, the federal government retained a particularly prominent position in debates. Federal officials accounted for a greater share of all government claims, but state and local officials did not completely cede the field to federal officials (see

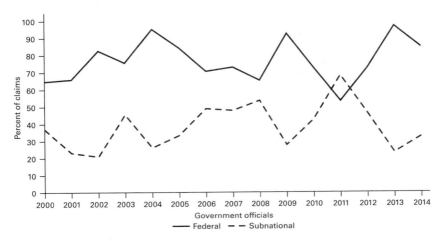

FIGURE 5.1. Percent of claims by federal and subnational government officials. Source: Newspaper database, LexisNexis.

figure 5.1). Subnational officials accounted for 25 percent of all government claimants in 2000 and climbed to almost 56 percent in 2011. This coincided with battles over Arizona's restrictive SB 1070 law and the passage of similar laws in several other states. The move into a presidential election year in 2012 and the push for a national immigration reform bill in 2013 and 2014 contributed to a surge of claims by federal officials. The federal government dominated, but its discursive power did not go unchallenged.

The federal government is not a monolithic institution. It is, as James Jasper would say, an "arena of arenas."[22] It contains various institutional arenas, with different levels of authority and party dynamics, in which political issues are debated and fought out. Political opportunities available to rights advocates varied by arena. Attitude scores have been calculated to assess the political opportunities in different arenas of the federal government. The scores are based on the degree of support for immigrant rights and reforms, with 1 being positive, 0 neutral, and −1 negative. The overall attitude score for all government claims (federal, state, and local) was −.01. This score compares poorly with the attitudes of businesses (.27), unions (.67), religious organizations (.79), and nonprofit organizations (.23). Officials in the federal government (−.04) staked out a middle ground between municipal (.22), county (−.4), and state (−.12) officials.

The attitudes of officials in different branches of the federal government varied sharply. Congress was split between a somewhat supportive and vocal Senate (.02, 388 claims) and an antagonistic and less vocal House of Representatives (−.31, 307 claims). Congress was divided not only by chamber but also by political party. Senate Republicans generally held a negative view of immigration (−.21), but they were more supportive than House Republicans (−.51). Important Republican senators such as John McCain (.04) and Lindsey Graham (.06) were influential moderate voices who helped counterbalance their more strident anti-immigrant colleagues like Jeff Sessions (−.83), Charles Grassley (−1), and Jon Kyl (−.6). The divided Republican caucus in the Senate contrasted with the unified House. Among the most moderate House Republicans was John Boehner, with an attitude score of −.32. This position can be considered moderate when compared to hard-liners such as Steve King (−.91), Tom Tancredo (−.81), Lamar Smith (−.8), and Michele Bachman (−1). For years, the Republican House presented major challenges to immigrant rights advocates. It contained some of the most vociferous anti-immigrant voices in the country. Anti-immigrant House Republicans exerted enormous influence by using immigration as a litmus test for ideological purity. Impassioned hard-liners were a minority, but their great influence among House Republicans silenced moderate voices. The Hastert Rule also forbade the Republican Speaker to send a bill for a full vote without a majority of Republican support. This rule reinforced the power of the hard-line minority faction. By contrast, the Republican Senate, while by no means friendly grounds for immigrant rights advocates, was more divided between hard-liners and moderates. The presence of some Republican reformers in the upper chamber opened up opportunities for bipartisan reform efforts.

The Democratic Congress presented immigrant rights advocates more opportunities. Democrats were consistently supportive in both the House (.31) and Senate (.32). Among Senate Democrats, Charles Schumer stood out as the leading reform advocate, but his attitude was mixed (.09) when compared to colleagues such as Edward Kennedy (.3), Harry Reid (.22), Hillary Clinton (.79), Richard Durbin (.62), and then-senator Barack Obama (.89). Senator Schumer long believed in the importance of winning bipartisan support by adopting some of the more restrictive preferences of Republicans. Commenting on the prospects of comprehensive immigration reform during President Obama's first year in office, Senator Schumer argued, "*Unless we can convince Americans we're going to be really tough, then this is not going to work*" (emphasis added).[23] An Open Society document reporting on politi-

cal opportunities noted that "Chuck Schumer stepped up his efforts for immigration reform this week by unveiling several 'principles' for a workable system, which include tough talk on 'illegal' immigration and stepped up border
enforcement."[24]

The Democratic get-tough strategy was, according to Senator Schumer
and his colleagues, the only way to pass immigration reform. The strategy
made concessions not only on policy but also on language. Democratic leaders often employed the language of their adversaries to argue for immigration reform. For example, Senator Kennedy, a long-standing champion of immigration reform, early on framed reform as a matter of national security.
He advocated for reform in the aftermath of the September 11 attacks by arguing that the primary aim of immigration reform was to "ensure that our
borders are secure and our laws are enforced."[25] This line of argument was
replicated throughout the 2000s by Senator Kennedy and other Democratic
leaders. In addition to repeating national security discourse, Senator Kennedy
expressed determination to cede to Republican demands on enforcement and
guest workers in order to get their support for reform. Reporting on his efforts
to get a comprehensive immigration reform bill passed in 2007, the *New York
Times* recounted that Senator Kennedy "said he was shifting gears in hopes of
winning Republican support and speeding the passage of immigration legislation."[26] The Democratic Senate was therefore a supportive arena for immigrant rights advocates, but it was also one that accepted the get-tough language and policies of adversaries. Democrats were willing to make significant
concessions on internal enforcement and border security before negotiations
with Republicans even started. This was the consensus strategy of Democratic
Senate leadership, and it would go on to shape the Obama administration's
approach to the issue.

Levels of Democratic support in the House of Representatives were equivalent to those in the Senate. The leading House Democrats on immigration
were Luís Gutierrez (.81), Raúl Grijalva (.79), and Nancy Pelosi (.71). Representatives Gutierrez and Grijalva were the strongest and most consistent advocates. In spite of Democratic commitment, Republican adversaries in the
House exhibited far greater abilities to set policy and block progressive reforms. There were more Republicans dedicated to the anti-immigrant cause
than there were Democrats supportive of the proimmigrant cause, and the Republicans used immigration as an ideological litmus test. Furthermore, they
were more successful in using House rules to block reform efforts. By con-

trast, there were only a handful of House Democrats committed to progressive immigration reform, and the issue did not have the same resonance and mobilizing power that it did for Republicans. It was viewed by most House Democrats as a niche issue and the dominion of the Congressional Hispanic Caucus and of Representative Luís Gutierrez. Immigration did not become an ideological litmus test for Democrats the way it did for their Republican adversaries. Immigration was an important issue for House Democrats, but it was not one that defined the very identity of the party.

For rights advocates, the Senate held out strategic advantages, because powerful Democrats supported reform and Republicans were divided. But to garner Republican support in the Senate, Democrats were quick to incorporate tough policies into their bills. Democratic willingness to cede ground before negotiations began resulted in immigration reform bills in 2007 and 2013 with highly restrictive measures.[27] With the Senate's 2013 immigration reform bill, for instance, Democratic leaders accepted $50 billion for additional enforcement. They also accepted a policy trigger that would start the process of regularizing the status of immigrants only after the border had been secured. Senate Democrats, therefore, supported reform, but they readily supported Republicans' restrictive language and measures as negotiating tactics. The legalization of some could be achieved, according to the Democratic leadership, only if the government reinforced the illegality and exclusion of many others.

While the Senate presented immigrant rights advocates with some opportunities, so did the White House. The White House was the most favorable arena (.3) in the federal government during the period that included eight years of Republican rule. Both Republican and Democratic administrations expressed support for immigration reform. But the Obama White House was much more vocal about immigration and supportive of reform. Between 2009 and 2014, the Obama administration made 208 claims about the issue. The Bush White House made 125 claims during its two terms. In addition to being more vocal on the matter, the Obama administration also expressed more support (.42) for immigrants than did the Bush administration (.03). Although George W. Bush stood out as a strong supporter of immigration reform, he nevertheless had to balance this support with the general hostility displayed by most members of his party (especially in the House). He could not depart too far from the rhetoric of fellow Republicans if he wanted to retain their support. The Obama administration faced a supportive party on immigration matters and was therefore freer to express its backing for immigration reform. Talking about immigration favorably was also a means to bolster the Latina/o vote.

Both the Bush and Obama administrations supported immigration reform, but the Obama administration was much freer to express itself publicly and develop relationships with advocacy organizations. In spite of President Obama's strong verbal support for immigrant rights and reform, he nevertheless followed the Senate leadership's get-tough strategy. An Open Society analysis of President Obama's first term stated, "The first four years of the Obama Administration was marked by a ramp up in immigration enforcement, *operating under the assumption that increased enforcement against unauthorized immigration would create conditions amenable for legislative reforms*" (emphasis added).[28] Instead of taking advantage of the Democratic majority in Congress during his first two years in office, President Obama ramped up internal enforcement to burnish his get-tough credentials with Republicans. The strategy legitimated anti-immigrant prejudices and dramatically expanded enforcement practices while providing rights advocates with little in return.

The federal government was therefore a major force in structuring the field of national citizenship. Efforts to reassert federal government power began in the mid-1990s and continued into the 2000s. While local and state governments were keen on exerting their power on the field, the federal government fought hard both legally and symbolically to retain its monopoly over immigration and citizenship.

Nationalizing the Immigration Debate

Federal officials on both sides of the debate fashioned discourses to talk about immigration, rights, and citizenship. They all recognized the sacredness of the nation and the importance of the central state to ensure its viability in global times. But they also drew from contrasting framings of citizenship to reimagine their nation and the place of immigrants within it.

For immigration foes, the nation was imagined as one with an exceptional people having a glorious past, sacred laws, and noble traditions. It was a place that provided the people comfort and a sense of belonging.[29] Sustaining national belonging and exceptionalism required closure and sharp boundaries. As one member of the House of Representatives argued, "If a burglar breaks into your home, do you serve him dinner? That is pretty much what they do with illegals."[30] The nation, according to this perspective, was a home and the immigrant a dangerous intruder. Undocumented immigrants pierced the real and symbolic boundaries that were cornerstones of the national community. The illegality of immigrants called the lawfulness of the country into question. Representative Brian Bilbray of Washington conveyed this position.

> What part of illegal in illegal immigration do people not understand? While we may be a nation of immigrants, we are also a nation of laws and it is *absolutely absurd for anyone who has broken our laws to demand rights such as citizenship.* Rewarding illegal behavior will send a terrible message to the millions of people waiting in line for their chance to realize the American dream (emphasis added).[31]

A nation of laws, according to this view, trumps a nation of immigrants. Security became a prominent issue in the years following the September 11 terrorist attacks. Federal officials also stressed that immigrants presented an economic threat to the country. They were taking American jobs and driving down wages. The plight of the American worker was not the collapse of unions, a stagnant minimum wage, and corporate exploitation. It was the fault of a porous border and undocumented immigrants. Immigrants consequently presented an existential threat to the country. It was, in the view of these officials, a battle for the life and soul of America. The very nature of civilization and the American way of life were at stake. "We are destroying the concept of citizenship itself," cried Representative Tom Tancredo. "America, and indeed Western civilization, are in a crisis."[32] Considering the nature of the threat, the country had to banish immigrants from the national body through whatever means necessary.

Federal officials who supported immigration reform countered by drawing on liberal nationalist frames of citizenship. America was not a xenophobic country. Unlike European countries with long-standing homogenous cultures, it was a new country made up of people from all over the world. America was exceptional, but its exceptionalism stemmed from its being a nation of immigrants.[33] Whereas European nations were forged by blood, common culture, and territory, America was bound by its foreign past and the values it placed on pluralism. It was made up of immigrants who quickly found their places through the homogenizing forces of integration. "The reason America is different from other countries," argued Senator Charles Schumer, "is that we take new immigrants and turn them into Americans in one generation."[34] Having reimagined the nation as open, supportive politicians reconstructed the immigrant as good and virtuous. If anti-immigrant adversaries said immigrants were foreign invaders, advocates responded by saying they held American values. If foes said immigrants were destroying the economy, government-reform advocates argued that immigrants contributed to the economic vitality of the country. "In every century and generation," argued Democratic senator Robert Menendez, "immigrants have contributed to the progress, prosperity and vitality of this nation."[35] Reform supporters therefore employed a two-pronged approach to framing national citizenship: reimagining the nation as liberal and open, and representing immigrants as virtuous contributors to the national community. President Obama was one of the most skilled politicians to use this rhetorical tactic, especially when discussing the case of undocumented youth (that is, the Dreamers). "Just as we remain a nation of laws, we have to remain a nation of immigrants," President Obama said. "And that's why, as another step forward, we're lifting the shadow of deportation from deserving young people who were brought to this country as children. It's why we still need a DREAM Act—to keep talented young people who want to contribute to our society and serve our country."[36]

Proimmigrant officials framed restrictive policies and xenophobic positions as anathema to the American way of life. Immigrants were a problem because restrictive government measures made them so. These measures impeded good people from achieving their full potential while keeping millions in the shadows. The economic and cultural contributions of immigrants were subsequently lost to the country. Irrational restrictions compelled immigrants to stake positions on the socioeconomic margins beyond the policing capacities of the state. The more restrictive the government measures, the more immigrants moved underground. One of the Senate's leading reform advocates, Edward Kennedy, repeatedly used this line of reasoning to support the reform cause. He argued, "As business leaders and experts understand, true immigration reform must be realistic and comprehensive, strengthening our security while bringing an underground economy above ground."[37] Overreaching government restrictions therefore generated the immigrant threat because they blocked integration and consigned immigrants to the shadows. Reform would permit immigrants to integrate and assume their proper places in the national order of things.

Government advocates revised nationhood to make the nation, an essentially exclusionary concept, open to immigrants. But Senate Democrats were also willing to approve tough concessions if that would secure the support of Republican adversaries. America was indeed a nation of immigrants, but because it was still an exclusionary nation, some immigrants were more deserving than others. Some immigrants possessed the attributes that merited legalization (that is, they were culturally assimilated, making economic contributions, sharing American values, and so on), while others didn't. Immigrants with a criminal record and recent arrivals were often held up as problematic. These populations were sacrificed by government reformers even before negotiations with hard-liners began. "We want," according to Senator Kennedy, "to keep those who can harm us, the criminal element, out."[38]

Framing immigrants as deserving made some appear more acceptable to the American public. But this came at the price of magnifying the gulf between "deserving" and "undeserving" (that is, unassimilated, criminal, and precarious) immigrants. The deserving/undeserving binary became especially sharp during debates concerning undocumented youth (that is, the Dreamers). This group was held up by congressional and White House supporters as exceptionally deserving. As one elected official argued, "We're not talking about someone who just stepped off a bus and is asking for favorable treatment. We're talking about young students who exhibit the best of what we expect from all of our children: academic success and the desire to succeed even more."[39] The official supported the deservingness of these immigrants by stressing commonality with the national community ("our children") and highlighting the attributes that made them exceptional ("the best"). This exceptionalism was strengthened by drawing a negative comparison with immigrants who "just stepped off a bus" and were "asking for favorable treatment." The use of a negative comparison accentuated the exceptionalism of the good immigrant. Thus, the context shaping immigration debates resulted in a discursive strategy that stressed the deservingness of immigrants.

The debate over immigration was, and remains, a debate over the nation. *America is great.* This deep, doxic truth[40] structured how all government claimants talked about immigration. It was the master signifier that made debate and discussion between adversaries possible. There was no disagreement about whether America was great or about the sanctity of borders. The debate point was whether immigration was imperiling the nation's greatness or making it greater.

Saving National Citizenship through Comprehensive Immigration Reform

Those on both sides of the debate agreed that Congress and the White House needed to fix what most believed to be a broken system. Considering the hostile position of most Republicans, it comes as no surprise that their preferred solution was border closure and interior enforcement. Antagonistic Republicans argued that because immigrants were a threat to the country, it was imperative that the government close its borders and deport unauthorized immigrants. The emphasis on the physical border resonated with the commonly held image of a porous physical barrier and its failure to protect the country against the immigrant flood. One House Republican, Lamar Smith of Texas, rejected the argument that immigration reform would secure borders. "How can they claim that enforcement is done [with reform] when there are more than 400 open miles of border with Mexico?"[41] For House Republicans, it was impossible to conceive of a secure country without a fully enforced and militarized border.

The majority of Republicans favored restrictive measures, but an influential minority in the Senate argued that comprehensive immigration reform could fix the system. Republican and Democratic advocates maintained that comprehensive immigration reform would grant legal status to deserving immigrants and banish the undeserving ones. These undeserving immigrants were viewed as unassimilated recent arrivals, precarious and informal workers, and criminals of various sorts (from drunk drivers to murderers). Securing borders *and* legalizing deserving immigrants, reform advocates argued, was the only reasonable way forward. The alternative proposed by immigration foes was impossible in a liberal democracy. The state could not build an impermeable wall and deport its way out of the problem. Lashing out at reform opponents in 2007, Senator Edward Kennedy argued, "We know what they [opponents of immigration reform] don't like. What are they for? What are they going to do with the 12 million who are undocumented here? Send them back to countries around the world? Develop a type of Gestapo here to seek out these people that are in the shadows? What's their alternative?"[42]

Reform advocates argued that comprehensive immigration reform not only was the most reasonable and constitutional option available but also would make America whole again because of its wide-ranging reach. According to Secretary of Homeland Security Janet Napolitano (and her predecessors in the Bush White House), immigration reform was a three-legged stool that includes tougher enforcement laws against illegal immigrants and employers who hire them and a streamlined system for legal immigration, as well as a tough and fair pathway to earned legal status. Let me emphasize this: we will never have fully effective law enforcement or national security as long as so many millions remain in the shadows, the recovering economy will be strengthened as these immigrants become full-paying taxpayers.[43]

The only way to make the nation secure again, according to Napolitano, was through a comprehensive measure that would address all parts of the system at once. Reform would ensure national security because it would bring immigrants out of the shadows and make them accountable to the state. Immigrants would be transformed into full taxpaying members, which would allow them to contribute to the nation's economic recovery. If the immigrants "remain[ed] in the shadows," it would be impossible to effectively enforce laws and ensure national well-being. The only way to head off the threat of immigrants was through a comprehensive architecture that would separate deserving from undeserving immigrants, bring the good, deserving immigrants into the light of the surveillance state, and expand internal and external bordering powers to banish undeserving immigrants.

Piecemeal reforms aimed to modify specific problems with immigration policy, whereas comprehensive immigration reform was envisioned as a complete overhaul of the system. Prior to 2005 and 2006, most members of Congress had not conceived of comprehensive reform. Immigration advocates in Congress had mostly focused on smaller measures such as providing legal status to agricultural workers (through AgJOBS, for example) and enrolling undocumented youths in higher education (such as through the DREAM Act). Following the 2004 elections, President Bush initiated an effort to introduce large-scale reform. The original bill (Secure America and Orderly Immigration Act, also known as the McCain-Kennedy bill) aimed to expand the temporary workers program and enhance border security. The 2006 Comprehensive Immigration Reform Act added to this the legalization of millions of undocumented immigrants. Advocates of immigrant rights and immigration reform in Congress viewed this as the gold standard and prioritized this over piecemeal reform. Some Republican leaders in the House, like majority leader Eric Cantor, proposed piecemeal measures in response to the push in 2013 and 2014 by the White House and Senate for comprehensive immigration reform. The *New York Times* reported that "Mr. Cantor emphasized that he has always opposed 'comprehensive amnesty' but also supported an option for children brought to the United States by their guardians."[44] Even the support of this relatively uncontroversial measure was not tolerated by hard-line Republicans, costing the majority leader his seat.

One solution to the immigration problem was to build a wall and support restrictions that would make living in the country without documents impossible. The other solution was comprehensive immigration reform. Advocates of the comprehensive approach agreed that enforcement and borders would be a part of the total reform package but not the only part. The federal government simply lacked the capacities and authority (constrained as it was by the Constitution) to remove every single undocumented immigrant from the country. The government needed to legalize immigrants deemed deserving—people who were rooted in the country, possessed common cultural and moral attributes, and contributed to America's economic vitality. Policies should be designed to facilitate their integration into the national community. By legalizing and integrating deserving immigrants, the repressive capacities of the state could be mobilized to target undeserving immigrants. Thus, both sides argued for the federal government to take an active role but through different routes. Whereas one embraced repression above all, the other pushed for a more totalizing approach comprised of disciplined integration, targeted repression, and expansive surveillance of immigrant workers.

The "Good" and "Bad" Immigrant

The 1990s and 2000s marked a resurgence of the federal government in the field of national citizenship. While subnational governments attempted to appropriate the means of citizenship, the federal government responded with an enormous expansion of legal and symbolic power. The aggressive intervention of the federal government created a powerful state infrastructure that was more restrictive than ever and had the capacity to reach down and steer state and local practices. The federal government had become the prime mover in the field of national citizenship. Its power in the field was institutional as much as it was discursive. Government officials were prolific producers of statements on the problems of immigration, the meaning of citizenship, and possible government interventions to save the nation. These discourses helped lay out the spectrum of possible political actions for the social movement. On one end of the spectrum, government officials argued that immigrants represented an existential threat to the nation. The only logical response was total banishment of that population. Donald Trump staked his political career on this position, and he was able to do so because it resonated heavily with a well-developed hard-line Republican base. At the other end of the spectrum, Democrats and a handful of moderate Republicans argued that the immigration system was indeed broken, which created undue stress on the nation. They argued that banishment, as a solution, was unrealistic. It made matters worse because it kept too many people in the shadows and outside the reach of the policing state. The only way to save the nation was through comprehensive immigration reform. This would legalize "good" immigrants living in the country, facilitate the flow of needed labor, and banish "bad" immigrants. Thus, ethnonationalism and liberal nationalism marked the boundaries of acceptable and legitimate speech in the halls of political power. Rarely did proimmigrant lawmakers frame their arguments in the language of territorial personhood, and never did they use postnational language. Liberal elected officials played a decisive role in shaping the immigrant rights movement because they modeled how advocates and activists framed immigration, citizenship, and policy proposals. Proreform officials, in other words, helped set the parameters of what advocates could legitimately say within this political field.

CHAPTER 6

Entering the Field of National Citizenship

THE GROWTH OF the federal government's legal and symbolic power spurred immigrant rights advocates to enter the field of national citizenship in a more concerted way. In the early 2000s, several national organizations accumulated the economic capital to play a centralizing role in what had been a highly decentralized social movement. This allowed organizations across the country to connect to one another, develop a common identity and set of mobilizing frames, and launch a series of complex battles in the national political field. The Center for Community Change (CCC) assumed a prominent role in assembling regional immigrant organizations such as CHIRLA and CASA Maryland into a powerful national block. The CCC also worked with other national organizations including the National Immigration Forum, America's Voice, and the National Council of La Raza (NCLR). It played a pivotal role among these important groups because it provided the infrastructure and support to allow local and regional organizations to enter the national political arena. This shift in scale precipitated a change in the strategy of immigrant rights organizations. By turning their attention to the federal government, immigrant rights advocates were engaging directly in an effort to change national citizenship.

The shift in scale was possible because of the creation of an expansive social-movement infrastructure. Well-endowed and politically connected national organizations worked with regional immigrant rights organizations to form a string of new coalitions with national-level reach, such as Reform Immigration for America, the Fair Immigration Reform Movement, and the

Alliance for Citizenship. The primary goal of these coalitions was to campaign for comprehensive immigration reform. DC-based organizations sat at the helm of the coalitions and reached out to regional organizations in immigrant-rich metropolitan areas. Regional organizations cosponsored meetings, trainings, and other events. The coalitions fashioned new instruments, such as communication networks, trainings, and workshops, to transmit understanding about rights, immigration reform, and citizenship from the centers of power in Washington, DC, to immigrant communities around the country. This was a complex web that enabled those at the center of power to shape the political visions, language, and aspirations of activists across the country.

This chapter draws from several different sources to assess the formation of a national social-movement infrastructure (see the appendix for further detail). It uses documents from national coalitions and draws from Open Society documents and interviews with key sources. My research assistant and I also searched the Foundation Center website for grants made to the coalitions. These different pieces of data help map the infrastructure that played a crucial role in transforming this struggle into a sustainable national social movement.

Building a National Movement

Immigrant-advocacy and immigrant-serving organizations in the early 2000s responded to the everyday political needs of their constituents. Some early organizations, such as CHIRLA and ICIRR, were based in large gateway cities. Although these organizations and certain smaller ones connected to some national campaigns, their lack of resources bound them primarily to the local political arena. By contrast, national advocacy organizations such as the National Immigration Forum and the NCLR were heavily invested in federal policy. They focused on using their expertise and good relationships with national elected officials to lobby for narrow policies. The NCLR had local branches, but they were service-oriented organizations with limited connections to grassroots activists. Both local and national rights organizations therefore honed their political expertise and used their resources and networks in very distinctive scales and political arenas.

Most regional organizations were geographically far apart from each other during the 1990s and focused largely on local political issues. But ICIRR,

CHIRLA, CASA Maryland, and some others developed connections through various personal brokers, including itinerant immigrants, organizers, and executive directors of national organizations. For example, the CHIRLA-affiliated musical group, *Jornaleros del Norte*,[1] played at corners and day laborer hiring sites across the country. Through these performances, organizers in different cities became acquainted with CHIRLA and its organizing work. Also, immigrants who moved between cities informed organizers in one city about the work being undertaken in other cities. Ideas, materials, and organizing methods began to circulate through these weak-tie networks. Organizers came to understand that they were not alone. The early networks between regional organizations were too loose and fragile to permit high levels of national political coordination. These organizations were experts in fighting against restrictions and for the rights of immigrants in local communities. They had cultivated strong and productive relations with other local organizations in their cities. Organizers had also developed deep knowledge of the rules of the local political game. They understood which politicians to target, how to exert leverage, and who to call on for additional support. Although some regional organizations contributed to national campaigns such as Temporary Protected Status, these campaigns were short-term, one-off mobilizations for piecemeal reform. There were also state-level coalitions fighting for accommodating laws (for example, driver's licenses for undocumented immigrants) and against restrictive policies (such as Proposition 187 in California).

In 1997, the CCC launched a new campaign: the National Campaign for Jobs and Income Support (NCJIS). It aimed to push back on the Personal Responsibility and Work Opportunity Reconciliation Act (PRWORA), which imposed significant restrictions on government aid to low-income people, including immigrants. The CCC assembled a large, diverse national coalition consisting of welfare, labor, religious, and neighborhood organizations as well as regional immigrant rights organizations. Prior to this coalition, the regional organizations were, according to the CCC's director Deepak Bhargava, "definitely at the periphery of CCC's orbit of grassroots organizations around the country. They had not been a central relationship for us."[2] The CCC was aware of the regional immigrant organizations because of their innovative campaigns and highly touted worker centers. Mary Ochs, a former field organizer with CCC, played an important role in developing relations with regional organizations and recruiting them to the CCC's welfare reform coalition. She recounted an early conversation with the then-director of Chicago-based ICIRR.

> I remember Marcella who was the head of ICIRR at the time. She said to me, "Do you think actually if we did welfare reform again, we could actually get at the table and actually be heard?" And I said, "We gotta try. And I think if we move now, we actually have a shot at it. And the Center [CCC] has some relationships. We can just try to leverage those and basically say you guys have to be here. And you've gotta just take the space. Don't ask permission. You just take the space."

Alone, regional organizations lacked the resources and political relations to get a seat at the table. NCJIS would help pry open the doors to the halls of national power and provide scrappy, resource-poor organizations access. The regional organizations, consequently, responded positively to CCC's invitation. "They were extremely enthusiastic," remembered the CCC's director, "and became part of the steering committee of the national campaign."[3]

While regional immigrant organizations were brought into the fight against PRWORA, the issue of immigration became important to nonimmigrant groups. Welfare and antipoverty nonprofits had constituencies that were increasingly made up of undocumented immigrants. One longtime organizer with CHIRLA and CCC remembered that "many of the groups that were not immigrant rights organizations that had multi-ethnic, multi-racial low-income memberships, their neighborhoods and communities were changing because of migration."[4] These organizations incorporated more immigrants and became entangled with immigrants' specific needs. Immigration was no longer a peripheral issue; it was an issue that directly affected the operations of a wide variety of progressive organizations. Regional organizations such as ICIRR and CHIRLA provided welfare organizations with some support and insight on immigration. The CHIRLA/CCC organizer recounted:

> It was very raw. . . . They [welfare organizations] had their heart in the right place and they were organizers in their own right. They knew that they just needed to learn a little bit. . . . They were trying to figure out what to do with immigrant people that were coming to the churches, that were coming to the workplace, that were coming to the neighborhoods. They said, "This is an opportunity to organize." We said, "We have a lot to teach on how to organize these people."[5]

Immigrants were moving away from the geographic areas they had traditionally settled in and were taking the issue of immigration with them. Consequently, immigration ceased being an issue only for immigrant rights organizations and became important to a broad array of organizations engaged in
the fight for equality and social justice.

Immigrant organizations and their close allies formed the Legalization
Subcommittee within the broader NCJIS coalition, and this subcommittee
later became the Immigrant Organizing Committee. It provided unique opportunities and resources for regional organizations to engage in national-
level politics. Through the Immigrant Organizing Committee, executive
directors continued to express a strong interest in addressing local and state-
level issues, but many began to shift to the possibility of changing federal legislation. Members of the Immigrant Organizing Committee identified common long-term goals. One participant in these discussions recalled, "We said,
'What do we have in common?' You need to have something to build around.
The issue of a lack of documents became the common issue."[6] The Immigrant
Organizing Committee set as its long-term goal the legalization of undocumented immigrants. The executive director of the CCC remembered:

> We were propositioning them to be part of the economic justice networks.
> They propositioned CCC to say, "Hey, no one wants to talk about legalization
> of the undocumented in Washington, D.C. We need a national organization
> to take up this cause and back us up, bring us together, to support us." It was
> a big issue for the organizations, not one that CCC had worked on previously.
> Really, it was kind of them coming to us and saying we need what CCC can
> bring. We eventually said yes.[7]

Although regional organizations were brought into the national social justice
fold to fight against welfare reform, the immigrant rights organizers pushed
this network and the CCC to invest more resources in the fight to legalize the
status of undocumented immigrants. The shift to immigrant rights and reform precipitated some debate within the CCC, with some arguing that those
issues took the organization away from its historical focus on welfare and social justice. Ms. Ochs from the CCC recalled that "among our field staff and
staff in general, there was a sense that the Center was getting too deeply into
immigration and immigrants were viewed as competitive with our other areas."[8] In spite of these concerns, the CCC went on to invest heavily in immigration reform.

Consolidating a National Network:
The Fair Immigration Reform Movement (FIRM)

NCJIS succeeded in creating the basic structure for today's immigrant rights movement. After the campaign's demise, the Immigrant Organizing Committee became its own independent entity and was renamed the Fair Immigration Reform Movement (FIRM) in 2003.

The Coalition Structure

FIRM members consisted mostly of regional immigrant rights organizations, but it operated under the fiscal sponsorship of the CCC, which launched FIRM, staffed it, financed it, and assumed leadership functions.[9] Clarissa Martinez De Castro of the NCLR explained that "FIRM was an internal coalition from the Center for Community Change. In other words, I think in some cases FIRM is seen as if it was a standalone entity, but it's actually a column, if you would, that was created by the Center for Community Change. It's not its own organization, it's part of that family."[10]

FIRM began with a handful of organizations but expanded over time. Based on various coalition documents that include information on affiliation, approximately 306 different organizations were connected to FIRM in one way or another between 2004 and 2015. The strength of affiliations varied. On one side of the spectrum, the majority (244) had only one direct connection to the coalition. The single connection itself was weak, consisting of a signature on the coalition's "Organizations Endorsing FIRM Principles" in 2008 or on one of its other petitions. Several other organizations had moderately stronger ties to the coalition, having signed two to three of FIRM's petitions. Weakly connected organizations nevertheless received regular materials, email blasts, and information about different campaigns, but their participation in events, campaigns, and leadership roles remained limited at best. On the other side of the spectrum, several organizations had strong ties to the coalition. These were organizations that signed most petitions, sat on the leadership council, and participated in many FIRM-sponsored campaigns and events. These organizations included CHIRLA, ICIRR, CAUSA Oregon, New York Immigration Coalition, Massachusetts Immigrant and Refugee Advocacy Coalition, Idaho Community Action Network, Voces de la Frontera, National Korean American Service and Education Consortium, Tennessee Immigrant and Refugee Rights Coalition, CASA Maryland, Sunflower Community Action,

Colorado Immigrant Rights Coalition, One America, Florida Immigration Coalition, and Nebraska Appleseed. The regional organizations had regular contact with one another throughout the coalition's existence. The director of CASA Maryland noted,

> With FIRM, we have had weekly conference calls for the last 15 years. That is how we connect with the Center for Community Change, which created and still plays a major role to bring us together. Right now, I am the co-chair of FIRM and every Thursday at 11:00, we have conference calls to develop strategies to organize how we are going to stop the deportation of our families, how we are going to develop comprehensive immigration reform strategies, how we are going to engage other organizations at the national level.[11]

The core organizations formed increasingly strong ties, which reinforced commitment and obligations to national-level campaigns.

FIRM served as a vehicle for regional organizations to tap into national networks and reach beyond the confines of their localities. The CCC provided not only connections and an infrastructure but also financial support to attend meetings with national organizations and elected officials in Washington, DC. "We [the CCC] were able," remembered Ms. Ochs, "to come up with the money to help people with plane tickets . . . so that someone like Angelica Salas [the executive director of CHIRLA] could go every month if necessary to DC to be in certain things."[12] The opportunity to tap these national networks allowed regional organizations such as CHIRLA and ICIRR to acquire valuable information and then diffuse it to their local allies and affiliates. The CCC also benefited from FIRM. The regional organizations had great legitimacy in large immigrant communities. They were thickly embedded in the grassroots and possessed high mobilization capacities in major immigrant regions (for example, Los Angeles, New York, Chicago, Miami, and Baltimore–Washington, DC). The well-connected members of FIRM provided the CCC entry into the thick underbrush of immigrant civil society. Without these organizations, the CCC lacked the legitimacy and social capital to develop its own outreach machine in these communities. The CCC also lacked the immigrant faces and stories needed to legitimately represent immigrants in Congress, the White House, and the national media. Regional organizations could supply these people and stories. Ms. Ochs, the former CCC organizer remembered, "The national groups have a lot of wisdom, but they are often hard-pressed. And they used to use the local groups, and I don't mean use in a negative way, although sometimes it was. Use local groups to get the stories that they would then go and tell."[13] Thus, whereas FIRM provided regional organizations with a number of benefits, the CCC benefited by gaining direct access to immigrant working-class communities across the country and by enhancing its own legitimacy in the federal arena.

FIRM attracted substantial support from foundations, especially in the earlier years. It received at least $10.5 million from the time of its creation up to 2014. The Ford Foundation was the most prominent funder, followed by Open Society. The peak of 2007–2009 coincided with the effort to mount campaigns to pass comprehensive immigration reform.

FIRM in Political Action

During the early years, there were few political opportunities at the federal level. The Bush administration had initiated talks with Mexico during its first six months in office, but September 11 shifted the policy focus away from immigration reform. The years following the attacks resulted in a massive increase in border security measures.[14] Facing limited opportunities for national reform, the CCC and the coalition partners directed their efforts to buttressing local and state-level campaigns (for example, securing driver's licenses and in-state tuition for undocumented students). Clarissa Martinez De Castro from the NCLR remembers, "There wasn't a comprehensive immigration reform bill before 2005. A lot of the effort was focused on either moving pieces at the state level and/or trying to fix what had been done in the '90s."[15]

The new coalition also helped establish new organizations in new destination regions and reinforce the mobilization capacities of long-standing regional organizations. For instance, FIRM and the CCC helped create the Tennessee Immigrant and Refugee Rights Coalition and the Florida Immigration Coalition to spread the struggle for immigrant rights to areas outside traditional gateway cities. In particular, Ms. Ochs of the CCC played a pivotal role assisting the new organizations. She encouraged the Ford Foundation to visit fledgling organizations and provide support.

> She was at Ford at the time and extremely supportive of those groups, but also when I said to her, "I'm going to Tennessee to help this young guy who's trying to build something down there, and I want you to come, they're having this big meeting." She was like, "Okay, I'll be there." She was wonderful. We were able to get some money to the South.[16]

During these early days, advocates were concerned primarily with strengthening the capacity of existing organizations in traditional gateway cities and assisting the creation of immigrant organizations in new destinations.

In 2005, when the window of political opportunity opened wider, FIRM, the CCC, and others were in a good position to respond. In the months following his second inauguration, President Bush signaled that large-scale immigration reform would be a top priority. He met again with President Vicente Fox of Mexico and pledged that Congress would come up with a "rational, common sense immigration policy."[17] His political advisors believed that passing immigration reform would bolster the Republican Party's fortunes with Latinas/os. Although the 2005 initiative failed to garner enough GOP support, the highly punitive House bill, the Border Protection, Anti-Terrorism and Illegal Immigration Control Act (also known as the Sensenbrenner Bill), passed in the House of Representatives with resounding support. FIRM participated in organizing mass protests against the Sensenbrenner Bill. Thus, the federal government was showing signs of greater activism on immigration, and the immigrant rights organizations were now prepared to respond.

In 2006 Republican senator Arlen Specter introduced the Comprehensive Immigration Reform Act of 2006. The bill consisted of three components: a revamped guest-workers program, legalization of eligible immigrants, and enhanced resources for enforcement. President Bush framed immigration reform as a matter of national security. Regularizing undocumented immigrants would, he went on to argue, encourage them to "assimilate" into the national community: "One aspect of making sure we have an immigration system that works, that's orderly and fair, is to actively reach out and help people assimilate into our country. That means learn the values and history and language of America."[18]

The CCC, FIRM, NCLR, NILC, National Immigration Forum (NIF), and approximately thirty other organizations formed a coalition to push for this vision of comprehensive immigration reform. This group was called the Coalition for Comprehensive Immigration Reform. The CCC and its allies assumed a leading role in these efforts, pursuing a top-down political insiders' strategy to negotiate reform measures. The leading organizations specialized in different areas and developed a loose division of labor. The NCLR began to focus on the legislative process, NILC specialized in the analysis of bills, NIF worked on communication, and CCC and FIRM focused on building capacities in the field and mobilizing grassroots support across the country. In spite of efforts to push reform and persuade House Republicans to support it, the reform advocates ultimately failed to overcome entrenched Republican resistance.

There was another attempt to pass comprehensive immigration reform in 2007. Supportive senators such as Ted Kennedy and Arlen Specter crafted a new bill that spoke to the concerns of House Republicans. They introduced a trigger that would enact legalization only after the borders had been officially secured. The bill also rolled back the rights of immigrant guest workers, increased the resources for border and internal enforcement, and introduced important restrictions on family reunification. The Coalition for Comprehensive Immigration Reform supported the 2007 Senate bill. "The machinery out of the DC national organizations were all pretty much in support," according to Marielena Hincapié, the director of the National Immigration Law Center (NILC). "I think there was a feeling that it was better than not having anything."[19] In spite of the general consensus, a handful of coalition members raised problems with the bill. Ms. Hincapié explained her organization's position.

> In 2006 and 2007 we were very much part of the coalition discussion, but we actually made a very difficult decision to oppose the bill in 2007. . . . The long-term consequences were just too much for us to be able to publicly support. We also didn't believe in the strategy that the bill was going to get better in the House. We had no doubt that it would actually get worse and move further to the right.[20]

Some high-profile Democratic senators, such as Bernie Sanders, rejected the measure outright, whereas others, such as Barack Obama, supported the AFL-CIO's line that there were insufficient protections for immigrant workers.[21] While progressives were divided over the 2007 reform proposal, anti-immigrant groups (for example, Numbers USA and FAIR) and their congressional allies were united in their opposition. They worked with radio and television media to press congressional representatives to reject immigration reform. Thousands of calls and letters poured into the congressional offices, helping to sink reform efforts. Divisions within the immigrant rights coalition and comparatively weak outreach undermined the abilities of reform advocates to counterattack. The 2007 effort to pass comprehensive immigration reform ended in a third defeat in as many years.

Reforming Immigration for America

Reform Immigration for America (RIFA) was officially launched in June 2009. RIFA was a direct descendent of the Coalition for Comprehensive Immigration Reform and the principal vehicle to push for comprehensive immigration reform. The immigration system, according to RIFA's documents, was broken and in desperate need of reform. RIFA maintained that comprehensive immigration reform was needed to regularize the status of deserving immigrants, improve the position of (immigrant) workers, and create a workable visa system as a means to close down unlawful immigration channels.[22]

The Coalition Structure

The emerging leadership of the immigrant rights movement met in the spring of 2008 to discuss the way forward after the previous year's legislative debacle. An Open Society memorandum summarizing the meeting reported, "Bruised but undaunted, leading national and local advocates have come together in multiple retreats and planning meetings to conduct an extensive analysis and to develop a new immigration reform strategy."[23] The memorandum went on to note that "the timing is right for a significant intervention by funders to capitalize on the efforts and investments made last year and the opportunity 2009 offers."[24] Open Society and its funding partners largely agreed with leading advocacy organizations. A senior official with the Atlantic Foundation remarked,

> After that setback [the failure to pass reform in 2006 and 2007], Atlantic provided funds for the key advocacy groups we support—including the Center for Community Change, National Council of La Raza, National Immigration Forum and Asian American Justice Center—to regroup and come back with a proposal for strengthening their efforts next time. The result was Reform Immigration for America (RIFA), a strong coalition with resources provided by Atlantic . . . and other funders that have enabled the movement to field an unprecedented campaign.[25]

Following a string of defeats, foundations and leading organizations came back and doubled down on comprehensive immigration reform.

Reform advocates believed that the 2007 campaign made strategic errors. The strategy employed in 2007 failed because of its inability to mobilize the grassroots and the general public. The director of the CCC remembered that "our inability to match the nativist forces toe-to-toe in 2007 is unquestionably what cost us the bill. I think even people who had a view that the best thing is the insider way behind closed doors realized, uh oh, we have to have mobilization capacity that's like the capacity that the nativists have or we won't get this thing done."[26] He went on to note that

> RIFA was sort of like the 2.0 if you will for this effort. It was much more based on the philosophy that we needed the majority of the House, 60 Senators and one president. It was very much a field-based campaign. That included mobilizations around the country. That included building a massive list of immigrant rights supporters that still exists. It's a 1.5 million person activist list to generate calls to Congress. It had a much more equal balance between insider and outsider strategies.[27]

National players hoped to design a coalition that could effectively harness the grassroots. But they also believed that national political officials would take immigrants seriously only if they increased voter turnout. "Much of that [turnout]," according to Rich Stolz of the CCC, "wasn't taken very seriously in Congress. Congress's take and their opponent's take was that those folks don't vote, they're undocumented."[28]

Learning from their failures, the leading organizations and funders designed RIFA to be more centralized, broader, and deeper-reaching in the grassroots. It was the broadest immigrant rights coalition of its kind. Between 2009 and 2012, 818 organizations had some kind of affiliation with the coalition. These organizations ranged from very small rights-focused groups to large multi-issue advocacy organizations. Two DC-based organizations served in key leadership roles: the CCC and NIF. Rich Stolz, RIFA's managing director, was a staff member of both organizations. The spokesperson, field director, and digital director of RIFA were also staff members of CCC. The chairperson was Ali Noorani, the executive director of NIF.

The RIFA coalition was organized according to specialized pillars. Ali Noorani described the structure: "The infrastructure of RIFA we called it, 'Four Pillars.' It was a four pillar campaign structure. . . . Each pillar had a lead organization that was responsible for drawing together table conversations within that pillar of organizations of the local and/or national levels."[29] The four pillars were (1) the promotion of citizenship and voter mobilization, (2) policy development with strong research and advocacy components, (3) a communication wing to "create a powerful narrative to support reform," and

(4) a cohesive field of grassroots organizations to pressure federal legislators.[30] FIRM and the CCC assumed responsibility for mobilizing the grassroots field. The Center for American Progress and the NCLR led policy and legislative strategy. The CCC and the NCLR assumed responsibility for voter mobilization. Finally, America's Voice led on communication. The management team oversaw and coordinated the different pillars. "The driver of the campaign," reported one Open Society memo, "is the Management Team, which consists of organizations playing cross-pillar leadership roles. The Management Team is chaired by the National Immigration Forum (the Forum)."[31] Staff were assigned to each of the pillars to ensure the effective implementation of the strategy. "We staffed out each pillar's set of work," according to NIF's executive director, Ali Noorani. "Without the staff in place, nothing happens. The staff would be in charge of organizing phone calls, email chains, making sure strategies were developed and executed and organizations were accountable for the work that they said they were going to do."[32]

Trusted regional organizations played an essential role, individually and through FIRM. Gustavo Torres, the director of CASA Maryland, remembered that "CHIRLA of course was part of that, CASA, of course. The Illinois coalition played a very, very important role in this process as well. Pretty much those were the organizations that played a very important role."[33] Without the regional organizations, the national leadership would not have had access to real immigrant communities. FIRM and the CCC assumed responsibility over the field pillar. They divided the national map into state and regional districts, and different members assumed responsibility for connecting, mobilizing, and training organizations within them. According to RIFA's then director,

> With RIFA, part of the structure was we had regional organizers. There were organizers for each region of the country assigned to provide support and help to drive work in the different states. Their job was to spend a lot of time with the different organizations in the different states. Key organizations were identified in each state, sometimes groups of organizations to organize coalitions within those states, so that whatever primary organization was working directly with a campaign there was a much larger network in each state of additional organizations.[34]

For example, RIFA created an Illinois political director staffed by Artemio Arreola, a member of ICIRR. There was also an Illinois senior organizer staffed by Salvador Cervantes, an employee of the CCC. State and regional directors covered strategic geographic areas for the purposes of maintaining connectivity and control over the hundreds of organizations making up the coalition.

RIFA also had extensive reach to different organizations across the country. Of 818 affiliates, 602 retained some form of affiliation during the years of its existence. Even most of the smaller organizations that possessed relatively weak ties to RIFA remained connected through petition drives, campaigns, trainings, and so on. RIFA also had clear lines of control between core national leaders (mostly in Washington, DC), regional organizations, and smaller grassroots groups. This structure provided the coalition with the capacity to connect hundreds of affiliates and steer them to exert pressure on their legislators. Rich Stolz remembered that "there were whole series of conversations to different community based organizations. We basically put down a challenge. Could you move enough of your own representatives and senators to support a comprehensive immigration reform strategy?"[35]

From 2009 to 2014, RIFA received approximately $11.45 million in funding from three foundations: Atlantic, Tides, and Open Society. This figure does not include supplemental funds allocated to RIFA's leadership to assist with new campaigns. Most of the reported funding was allocated in 2010, when the coalition started its campaign to pass comprehensive immigration reform. RIFA was therefore a broad, well-structured, and well-financed coalition. It tied local groups into a national debate over immigration reform in a way that reflected the vision, ideology, and norms of the leadership.

RIFA in Political Action

Soon after President Obama's inauguration, regional and national advocates believed that the new administration would pass comprehensive immigration reform within the first nine months. This optimism was expressed in an Open Society "Weekly Update."

> Senator Chuck Schumer (D-NY) has recently taken over the chairmanship of the Senate Immigration Subcommittee and last week held a hearing to kick off the immigration debate in the 111th Congress. The hearing demonstrates the continued momentum for advancing comprehensive immigration reform this year, an Obama Administration commitment that was underscored again by the President in his day 100 press conference last week. Schumer strongly be-

lieves that reform legislation can pass this year and is committed to leading the effort.[36]

The administration ultimately prioritized other issues, including the Affordable Care Act and the economic stimulus package. Nevertheless, RIFA and its allies hoped that immigration reform was possible in 2010. Senators Schumer (Democrat) and Graham (Republican) were working on a bipartisan agreement, and several moderate Republicans in the Senate expressed their support for these efforts. RIFA's longtime congressional ally, Representative Luis Gutierrez, also introduced a reform bill in the House. Despite the hopeful signals emanating from Washington, the Senate bill failed to materialize, prompting RIFA to organize a large immigrant rights march in the spring of 2010.

In spite of these efforts, the coalition was unable to move reform forward because of, according to one Open Society document, "a crowded Senate calendar, the challenge of positioning immigration as part of an economic recovery strategy rather than as irrelevant or harmful to job creation, and not least the 'fear factor' about doing anything big that has swept through Democratic ranks in the wake of the MA [Massachusetts] special election."[37] This last factor referred to the unexpected victory of a Republican candidate for the seat of Senator Edward Kennedy in 2010. To wary Democrats, this signaled that immigration reform was a losing issue.

RIFA was one of the most sophisticated social-movement infrastructures of its time. It brought hundreds of different organizations and thousands of activists into a common campaign. This infrastructure was then used to diffuse norms, discourses, and strategies to activists in distant locales. Such a vast framework allowed large national organizations to mobilize hundreds of smaller organizations around the country. This marked an important change in the immigrant rights movement. "What began as a legislative campaign," remarked Frank Sharry of America's Voice, "is transforming into a social movement."[38]

Narrowing the National Leadership: Alliance for Citizenship (A4C)

Alliance for Citizenship (A4C) was the last of the large mainstream coalitions of the Obama era. Created in December 2012, it was a successor of RIFA and adopted RIFA's legislative goal of passing comprehensive immigration reform. Coalition leaders maintained that a clear "path to citizenship" should be a core goal of any comprehensive immigration measure.[39] Like its predecessors, though, A4C failed to achieve its ultimate goal.

The Coalition Structure

A4C adopted the same goals and political targets as RIFA, but it developed a different mobilization strategy. Rather than federalize the movement (and have a central command with regional districts), it concentrated more power in the hands of a smaller cluster of organizations. The number of affiliated organizations grew from forty to forty-nine between 2013 and 2016, and twenty-nine of those trusted advocacy organizations were located in Washington, DC. The only national organization not headquartered in DC to make it into the leadership ranks was the Los Angeles–based National Immigration Law Center (NILC). Of the regional organizations that made up the network—CHIRLA, CASA Maryland, and CAUSA Oregon—all had already played leading roles in FIRM and RIFA.

One important innovation was the coalition's emphasis on including what they termed nontraditional allies. These included conservative groups such as the US Chamber of Commerce, evangelical churches, and sheriffs' organizations. NIF led this effort by creating a separate network called Bibles, Badges, and Business for Immigration Reform (BBB). Ali Noorani, the organization's executive director, reached out to these actors and built common ground. BBB received strong support from funders, the media, and even President Obama. According to one Open Society report, "Its [NIF] bibles, badges and business (BBB) campaign has been particularly successful in mobilizing Christian evangelicals, law enforcement, and business leaders to support immigration reform and provide cover to conservative leaders who are proponents of reform."[40]

CCC staff and alumni dominated A4C's managing directorship in 2013. Its first campaign manager (Susan Chinn) and deputy campaign coordinator (Aimee Nichols) were from the CCC. Jorge Neri worked for A4C as deputy campaign manager, but he had previously worked as an immigrant rights campaign coordinator for the CCC (2008–2011) and served as Barack Obama's Nevada state field director for Organizing for America in 2012. He later worked in the White House's Office of Public Engagement and then held a position at A4C (February 2013–January 2014). Professional consultants also assumed major positions on the A4C staff, reflecting Edward Walker's important observations of the significance of hired consultants in contemporary social movements.[41] Felipe Benítez, the deputy campaign manager, was affiliated with Mi Familia Vota, which originated as an SEIU-sponsored Latina/o voter registration organization in the 2000s. Mr. Benítez himself was an expert in mass communications and had worked for a wide variety of large organizations. According to his website profile, Mr. Benítez "has more than 15 years of experience designing and implementing strategic communications programs to enhance and protect the reputations of organizations, governments, companies, and brands."[42] A4C's development manager, operations manager, and deputy campaign manager for policy and legislation were employed by professional consulting and lobbying firms, such as the Raben Group, and had little to no experience with local grassroots organizing. The Raben Group worked with a range of clients, from Fortune 500 companies to NIF. The A4C organizational structure, therefore, took a decided shift toward professionalization and centralization.

A4C had fewer organizations to coordinate than RIFA and more resources with which to do so. According to one 2013 document, "A4C has an annual budget of $32 million, of which they have already raised $21.5 million."[43] The Atlantic Foundation and Open Society were two of the largest funders. Foundations also channeled grant money directly to the parent organizations for the purposes of running A4C campaigns. For instance, the same 2013 document remarked that "SEIU has devoted millions of staff resources toward the current round of immigration reform efforts, which is not counted in A4C's budget."[44] Moreover, the Advocacy Fund made supplementary grants (approximately $7.3 million) to organizations for their work on the A4C campaign. Some funders expressed concern over A4C's spending and pointed out that their coffers were not limitless. One Open Society document reported that "philanthropy has been encouraging A4C to develop a more realistic budget given limited fundraising prospects as philanthropy will not be able to sustain A4C's current burn rate."[45]

Alliance for Citizenship in Political Action

The A4C campaign began with great optimism. In November 2012, President Obama won a resounding victory, partly due to high Latina/o voter turnout and support. The Latina/o vote had made itself known, and advocates now expected something in return from the administration. Moreover, leading Republicans believed that it would be difficult to win future presidential elections without Latina/o support. The day after the election, House Speaker

John Boehner announced, to the consternation of hard-liners, that Republicans needed to support some version of immigration reform if they wanted to remain competitive. Other leading Republicans such as Senator John Kyl employed reformist frames when arguing that "relegating a potentially productive portion of the population to the shadows is neither humane nor good economic or social policy."[46] Just as importantly, the White House communicated to members of the DC advocacy community that immigration reform was a top priority. An Open Society memorandum reported that "Mr. Bhargava [the executive director of the CCC] cautioned that while comprehensive immigration reform will not be as easy as it may appear at present, he understood that the White House considers it the single issue that can be successfully resolved in 2013."[47]

Advocacy organizations and foundations were heartened by seemingly bipartisan support for comprehensive immigration reform. "As of this writing," the Open Society memorandum went on to say, "the so-called Senate Gang of Eight is about to introduce their bill, and this bipartisan starting point bodes well, though I emphasize that the process going forward will be complicated and challenging."[48] Funders and advocates believed that they had the organizational capacity to push the legislation through. Another Open Society report noted that

> since December, staff has consulted with a wide spectrum of immigrant leaders, policy advocates, and congressional lobbyists to assess the performance of A4C and the larger immigration advocacy field. Staff [from Open Society] believes that A4C possesses the field capacity, beltway savvy, communications expertise, and reach to vital allies needed to ensure success.[49]

Funders and lead organizers believed that they possessed the know-how and means to achieve their goal. Thus, considering A4C's political opportunities and organizational capacities, different stakeholders in the immigrant rights movement were very optimistic in 2013. "We," one Open Society document noted, "continue to have the best opportunity to enact meaningful immigration reform in over a decade."[50]

A4C lobbied federal legislators to support the Senate bill. They mobilized most of their forces in fall 2013 and focused on pressuring the House leadership to allow the bill to come up for an open vote. Frank Sharry of America's Voice noted, "We're . . . going to push really hard for votes this fall and negotiations with the Senate." He explained the timing by saying that "we never figured we'd have an opportunity in September because of the budget stuff and with the debt ceiling."[51] A4C and its regional affiliates targeted House members they believed to be susceptible to pressure. According to an Open Society memorandum, "A4C and its partners have identified a target list of House Republicans and are pursuing intensive efforts to move these members through a combination of field action, lobby visits, grass tops advocacy, and communications efforts—all designed to secure enough House Republican support to bring the issue to a vote by the end of the year."[52] CHIRLA, for example, headed an effort to pressure the Republican House Whip, Kevin McCarthy, in his California district. The organization led caravans from Los Angeles to McCarthy's office in Bakersfield. They protested and lobbied heavily, with CHIRLA's members occupying the office of the high-ranking Republican.

Strong relations between the leaders facilitated their work. They knew how to work with one another and possessed enormous levels of trust. The director of the CCC stressed as much in saying, "These are people with deep, long bonds of relationships and trust with each other, which can facilitate a level of deep conversation and honesty that is hard to do when you don't really know what's motivating people and you don't have that basis of trust. That's the relational fabric that's been built over a very long period of time in this network."[53] The strong ties facilitated quality exchanges between the directors of leading organizations. This provided them with unity even when disagreements arose. Bhargava went on to say,

> The different leaders had different views though we rarely ended up taking votes. I think once or twice we might have ended up taking votes, but the premium was to try to get to some kind of agreement about what our strategic stance was. . . . That didn't dilute our power when we were in rooms with senators or the President or whatever; we were speaking with one voice. That was very much how it played out. It was absolutely a week to week, month to month rolling discussion and the stances change and evolve and people change and evolve as they heard other people's ideas.[54]

The strong bonds among the leading organizations produced a deep reservoir of trust and collective knowledge, which made it easier for them to make complex strategic decisions and maintain a unified front in government negotiations.

These relationships made A4C into one of the most sophisticated legislative campaigns in the history of the immigrant rights movement. An Open Society report asked, "How successful were advocates?" It went on to answer,

> In the days following the successful Senate Judiciary Committee vote, immigration reform opposition leader Senator Jeff Sessions remarked to The Hill: "I've never seen a more calculated, cold-blooded p.r. campaign managed to advance a piece of legislation than this one." Sessions went on to say that "the political consultants and pollsters and people (managing the bill) . . . anticipated everything that was going to occur. . . . They planned on careful attacks to neutralize critics."[55]

Strong relations with coalition partners, intimate knowledge of the political field, and generous support from funders allowed A4C to run a sophisticated legislative campaign.

In spite of A4C's sophistication and resources, obstinate Republicans in the House refused to support the Senate's comprehensive immigration reform bill. House Whip Kevin McCarthy expressed some sympathy for the cause, but he would not allow a bill onto the House floor for a full vote without the majority support of the Republican caucus because of the Hastert Rule. The House Majority Leader Eric Cantor also expressed cautious sympathy. A4C still held out hope that a compromise bill was possible, but in the summer of 2014, two events extinguished whatever hope remained. A sharp increase in Central American refugees and unaccompanied minors soured the national mood on immigration and provided anti-immigrant organizations fodder for their campaign to block reform. And just as important, Representative Cantor lost in a primary election due to his mild support for piecemeal immigration reform. His loss terrified other Republicans who had considered supporting immigration reform.

A4C was leaner and better resourced than any previous coalition before it. It was made up of sophisticated leaders who had worked with one another for more than ten years. The leaders knew and trusted each other. They had a common understanding of what they should prioritize, and they possessed tacit knowledge of how to organize a complex national campaign. The coalition enjoyed strong support in the White House and Senate, and 63 percent of Americans supported legislation that offered undocumented immigrants a path to citizenship.[56] In spite of these major advantages, A4C was unable to break the stranglehold of hard-liner Republicans in the House. The A4C campaign would be the last effort to pass comprehensive immigration reform in the decade.

Dissent from the Left Flank

The coalitions laid down a sophisticated, well-funded, and well-capacitated infrastructure. But generating such a centrally coordinated infrastructure resulted in a hierarchy between those who were leaders—many of whom were removed from working-class immigrant communities—and those who were led—most of whom came from such communities. Additionally, the leadership emphasized sticking to a single strategy and goal in a movement made up of radically plural ideologies, tactical preferences, strategic priorities, and temperaments. As leaders worked to enact their unified vision, factions that had at first been favorable to the leadership quickly pushed back.

Dissident Dreamers

In 2010, congressional support for comprehensive immigration reform sank. Several senators, however, indicated support for the DREAM (Development, Relief, and Education for Alien Minors) Act. The piecemeal bill was narrower and provided certain undocumented immigrants (youth with postsecondary education or military service) a path to citizenship. The RIFA leaders had long supported the DREAM Act but believed comprehensive reform needed to be prioritized. Many worried that it would be easier to pass comprehensive reform if the DREAM Act were part of it. The undocumented youth were the part of the unauthorized immigrant community that elicited the most sympathy. Pulling them out of the comprehensive reform package would make it more difficult to pass the larger measure. As recounted in my previous book,[57] a number of Dreamers grew frustrated with RIFA's insistence on prioritizing comprehensive reform in the face of diminishing opportunities. Hundreds of Dreamers broke away from the RIFA strategy in the spring of 2010 and pushed for the DREAM Act as a stand-alone bill.[58] RIFA leaders pushed back on the dissidents and demanded unity across all sectors of the movement. By the end of the summer of 2010, however, it became apparent that comprehensive immigration reform was not possible and that the DREAM Act was the next best thing. RIFA eventually pivoted and put its weight behind this measure, but it was too late. The DREAM Act failed to pass in 2010.

The dissident Dreamers demonstrated that RIFA's focus on a single reform option blinded it to other viable opportunities. They also revealed that RIFA's top-heavy structure made it difficult to change course when one window of opportunity closed (comprehensive reform) and another one opened (the DREAM Act). Dissident Dreamers were flexible and able to nimbly adjust strategies in response to a changing playing field. As a massive operation, RIFA was more susceptible to getting bogged down in costly path-dependent traps. The dissidents, therefore, exposed RIFA's weaknesses. They criticized the leadership and the hierarchical nature of the coalition and called the leadership a "nonprofit industrial complex" that silenced undocumented people.[59] Although they fell short of achieving the DREAM Act, they successfully pushed the Obama administration in 2012 to enact an executive order—Deferred Action for Childhood Arrivals (DACA)—that would provide undocumented youths relief from deportation.

Resisting Enforcement

Comprehensive immigration reform had become the ultimate goal for the mainstream immigrant rights movement. But many organizations continued to engage in pitched battles against subnational and national immigration enforcement. Organizations such as the National Immigration Law Center (NILC), Border Network for Human Rights, Detention Watch Network, National Day Laborer Organizing Network (NDLON), Mexican American Legal Defense and Educational Fund (MALDEF), Immigrant Justice Network, and United We Dream (UWD) invested important resources in fighting the sharp uptick in local, state, and federal enforcement measures. These organizations also worried about the concessions that Democrats would make to enforcement hawks in their negotiations over comprehensive immigration reform.

A number of these organizations worked with one another to advance enforcement reform through a new coalition, Campaign for a Moral, Balanced Immigration Overhaul (CAMBIO). Coalition members believed that the singular focus on comprehensive immigration reform eclipsed the need to push back on the Obama administration's aggressive enforcement policies. Some also complained that mainstream leaders such as the CCC, the NCLR, and NIF would agree to enhanced enforcement in exchange for a path to citizenship. The NILC went on to assume leadership of CAMBIO, and several organizations joined the steering committee, including NDLON, UWD, the Border Network for Human Rights, and the Detention Watch Network.

In spite of funders' support of CAMBIO, the enforcement-reform flank was also constrained by its positioning within this social movement. It was conceived as a niche within the general immigrant rights movement. "The nature of enforcement issues," according to one Open Society report, "requires specific, targeted interventions, and each of these organizations occupies an important niche that the broader-based, and often more moderate, immigrant rights organizations cannot fill because of their topline goal of securing comprehensive federal reform."[60] Conceived as a niche rather than a leading force of the immigrant rights movement, funders granted CAMBIO substantially less financial support than RIFA or A4C. Moreover, CAMBIO's members were hemmed in by their dependence on many of the same foundations that financed the DC-based organizations. Funders would not be pleased if one set of grantees (CAMBIO, for instance) criticized and undermined the abilities of another, better funded set of grantees (A4C, for instance) to achieve its goals. The enforcement-reform left flank could certainly express frustration with the mainstream movement's leadership, but it had to weigh forceful criticism against the alienation of their financial patrons. Finally, several organizations from CAMBIO, especially the NILC and UWD, were also members of A4C. The Dreamer organization UWD, for instance, was active in both coalitions. An Open Society report described the situation this way: "Grantee United We Dream, was founded to address the inequities and obstacles faced by immigrant youth and other DREAMers, but it has since expanded its work to include not only CIR [comprehensive immigration reform] but also working against deportation and justice for all immigrants."[61] The competing loyalties of these organizations restricted their abilities to come out and fully criticize the immigrant rights movement's centrist leadership. Thus, the enforcement-reform left flank was not only subordinate to the mainstream leadership but also depended on the mainstream movement for money and alliances, which limited the extent of its criticisms of the leadership.

Among the organizations that made up the enforcement-reform wing, NDLON was the most vocal and determined. Its staff and member organizations had long been fighting local and state enforcement measures that heavily impacted day laborers. In the late 2000s, NDLON worked with Tonatierra, one of its member organizations in Arizona, to push back on the aggressive crackdown on day laborers and undocumented immigrants by the Maricopa County Sheriff's Office. The suburbs of Phoenix subsequently became a front line in the battle against restrictive and discriminatory local policies. In 2009, NDLON, MALDEF, the ACLU, and Tonatierra launched a campaign to draw national attention to Sheriff Arpaio's aggressive use of the federal government's 287(g) program. Pablo Alvarado, the executive director of NDLON remembered:

> And then came Napolitano [then secretary of Homeland Security in the Obama administration] negotiating a 287(g) agreement with Arpaio. Arpaio took advantage of his new powers and began doing all the shit that he was doing. That's when we drew him into that little fight, because we knew that what he was doing was paving the way for all the sheriffs and chiefs of police in the country. We saw that in Arizona he would be the determinate factor in the fight for immigration reform from the rights perspective.[62]

The campaign against Sheriff Joe Arpaio generated an infrastructure that was then used to fight Arizona's highly restrictive anti-immigrant law, SB 1070 in 2010.

The Arizona campaign coincided with RIFA's campaign for comprehensive immigration reform. Mr. Alvarado recounted, "We had big conflicts with the national organizations because they said this fight in Arizona was deviating from the fight for comprehensive immigration reform, and that in some instances it undermined it." He went on to say, "They [the national organizations] called funders to block funding for us, for our immigration work."[63] Eventually, funders and RIFA called NDLON to Washington for a mediation. The mediation, according to Mr. Alvarado, failed to resolve differences over priorities, strategy, and messaging. "We couldn't get to terms," he remembered. "And of course, they sent their political machine to Arizona [to launch the Promise Arizona campaign] to deviate our messaging."[64]

Organizations with a strong immigrant base were concerned with the mainstream leadership's willingness to accept concessions on enforcement. NDLON and its local member organizations were particularly sensitive to the issue. Many day laborers were poor, culturally unassimilated, and weakly affiliated with established communities, and they lacked documents (for example, pay slips, utility bills, and rental receipts) to prove duration of residency in the United States. Some workers had criminal records because day laboring had been criminalized in many cities during the previous two decades. Their marginal position in American society would make day laborers and similarly precarious immigrants ineligible for legalization. One former CCC organizer commented, "I'm not criticizing them [NDLON] for having a different point of view. Many day laborers, no matter what [reform legislation] passes are potentially left out because they'll either have trouble proving things or they're newer and they might not fit, and it sucks."[65]

Lacking a clear path to legal status, day laborers and other precarious immigrants would be the first to suffer the effects of enhanced interior enforcement. Concessions on enforcement, in other words, would be paid for by day laborers and other immigrants in similarly dire situations. Mr. Alvarado expressed his organization's concern by noting that "some people are fixated with CIR [comprehensive immigration reform]. And our main concern . . . is the bargaining chip, and that's a big problem for us, because essentially the bargaining has been around enforcement. And our first priority is for day laborers. When you give in on all of this stuff [enforcement] without getting anything in return, that's very problematic for us".[66]

The Senate introduced a bill in 2013 that provided many immigrants a pathway to citizenship. But bipartisan support for the bill was secured by guaranteeing $50 billion in additional enforcement funding. NDLON expressed its deep frustration with the concessions made by Senate Democrats. "We are," Mr. Alvarado explained to a reporter, "deeply disappointed with the unnecessary concessions made by Senate Democrats that have bent to the fears of xenophobes and weakened the reform that so many have struggled for." While placing responsibility on Senate Democrats, Mr. Alvarado also called out the movement's leaders for failing to push back on Democrats. As he put it, "If undocumented day laborers can stand up to a Sheriff like Arpaio, the leaders in the beltway should be able to find at least a fraction of that same courage."[67]

NDLON initiated an enforcement-reform campaign in 2013: Not One More. The campaign strongly criticized President Obama for his administration's harsh enforcement policies. Not One More activists generated messaging concerning Obama's betrayal of immigrant communities, his reputation as the greatest deporter in history, and the possibility of counterbalancing his abysmal record with a broad executive action. Mr. Alvarado argued that the "history books will blame the president and not Congress for a hypocritical and shameful period of immigrant expulsion."[68] An NDLON organizer and the Not One More campaign manager, Marisa Franco, argued, "He [Obama] has campaigned as the champion of our community. He's overseen record deportations. It's unacceptable. He cannot call himself champion when he's deporter in chief."[69] The slogan "deporter in chief" was used by activists to place responsibility squarely on the president. The slogan first appeared in August 2011 but gained wide traction following a Not One More banner drop on May 29, 2013, in Chicago.

The campaign demanded the end of deportations and the use of the president's executive authority to grant all undocumented immigrants relief from detention and deportation. DACA, they argued, created the precedent, and now they demanded that all undocumented immigrants be made eligible for a DACA-like program. "DACA for all" was, according to Mr. Alvarado, "a necessary step to reverse the pain caused by Napolitano's DHS, and it would be a helpful advance for reform efforts."[70] NDLON and its allies were also critical of how the Dreamer movement resulted in the political construction of the good and bad, deserving and undeserving immigrants. Poor, unassimilated, and unaffiliated immigrants were not well served by this messaging. Chris Newman, NDLON's head attorney protested, "Either you are an innocent Dreamer who wants to go to Harvard, or you're a criminal. It's a false choice, and there is something the president can do about it."[71] "DACA for all," they argued, would help remedy such problematic discourses.

The leadership of the mainstream movement recognized the importance of stopping deportations but believed that there was a real opportunity to pass comprehensive immigration reform and that the legislative strategy should be prioritized. Focusing on deportations would distract the coalition from its primary goal of passing comprehensive immigration reform. But the increasing visibility and intensity of the Not One More campaign and the declining probability of comprehensive reform prompted the national organizations to pivot and demand that the president use his executive authority. In March 2014, the executive director of the NCLR, Janet Murguía, used the slogan "deporter in chief" to condemn President Obama's deportation policies. She complained that his policies were leaving "a wake of devastation for families across America."[72] Youth activists aligned with the Not One More campaign responded to Ms. Murguía's announcement by stating, "Finally! But now NCLR needs to ask for all deportations to be stopped not just settle for low hanging fruit."[73]

The NCLR was a very influential organization and a central component of the A4C coalition. Ms. Murguía's direct, critical stance marked a monumental departure from the traditional messaging that had placed blame solely on Republicans. America's Voice executive director, Frank Sharry, tweeted in response to Murguía's statement, "It's bad news for @barackobama @whitehouse when NCLR calls you the 'deporter-in-chief.'"[74] Her use of the term in such a public setting signaled to other DC-based organizations that they needed to increase their pressure on the White House. Soon thereafter, the executive director of the CCC asserted, "We assumed that a Democratic president who wanted to move immigration reform would not pursue a strategy of deporting the people who he was intent on legalizing. That was a totally wrong assumption. And there is a lot of anger about that."[75] Frank Sharry went on to directly adopt NDLON's messaging, asking, "Does he [Obama] really want to go down as the 'deporter in chief,' and the only thing that happened during his second term was beefed-up enforcement and deportations? He's the president. He's got to take action."[76]

As the year progressed, some national organizations began to fully embrace Not One More's calls for executive action to stop deportations and provide relief to the country's undocumented immigrants. The president of the AFL-CIO, Richard Trumka, who had already backed NDLON's position on halting deportations, further pressed the issue in the press and with the Obama administration. As early as February 4, 2014, Mr. Trumka told a reporter, "If I were president, I would have said the following: 'It's a broken system. Except for violent criminals, no more deportations until you help me fix a broken system.'"[77] As with Ms. Murguía's use of the slogan "deporter in chief," the AFL-CIO's formal support for this effort marked another important inflection point in the movement's veer to the left. *Politico* reporter Reid Epstein described this turn in his 2014 report on the movement: "But in this low-grade civil war over immigration messaging, those who want the president to act [sign an executive order to stop deportations] increasingly own the narrative."[78]

Once it was clear in the summer of 2014 that comprehensive immigration reform was dead, A4C provided full support for executive action. Mr. Bhargava, the CCC's executive director, recounted,

> I would say the lion's share of the resources of the network in 2013 went to the legislative fight because it seemed like we might win it. I think it was not really clear until Eric Cantor's primary in 2014 became the last nail in the coffin that the legislative path was completely closed. Between the end of 2013 and that, it was a fairly ambiguous period where our position was both the administration should not hold on doing administrative relief, they should do it the right way, and we should continue to pursue legislation.[79]

NDLON's Not One More campaign created a political space for the national organizations to step into once all hope for legislative reform had died. The messaging and momentum introduced by the left flank made it possible for the mainstream movement to pivot once comprehensive immigration reform became impossible. The movement ultimately pressured the Obama administration to pass an executive order, Deferred Action for Parents of Childhood Arrivals (DAPA), on November 17, 2014. DAPA would have extended relief to an estimated four to five million undocumented immigrants and repealed the administration's Secure Communities program. DAPA was reversed by a federal judge, whose decision was subsequently upheld by the Supreme Court.

As the immigrant rights movement became more centralized and national, many activists closer to immigrant communities pushed back. Comprehensive immigration reform was, many on the left flank believed, a noble goal. But for years, the left flank had been on the front lines of the fight against federal enforcement and local restrictions. Activists had fought against anti–day laborer ordinances for more than a decade. They spearheaded efforts to push back on Arizona's notorious anti-immigrant law and its most vocal xenophobe, Sheriff Joe Arpaio. They initiated efforts to eliminate federal programs such as 287(g) and Secure Communities. Their activism was rooted in the protection of precarious immigrant communities. The DC-based national leadership tried to impose its strategic preferences for comprehensive immigration reform on the whole movement, but the left-flank activists balked and pursued their own campaigns. The two most significant wins (DACA and DAPA) were spearheaded by these activists. In both instances, the national leadership came out in support of these efforts only after their own efforts to pass comprehensive immigration reform had failed.

Making a National Social Movement

Regional and local organizations had engaged in heavy fights for the rights of immigrants during the 1990s and early 2000s. These organizations connected to one another through weak-tie relations and the occasional campaign. This decentralized structure underwent dramatic change in the 2000s when regional organizations participated in a coalition headed by the CCC, and the landscape of immigrant rights activism changed forever. The regional organizations and the CCC developed an organizational infrastructure that allowed them to enter the national political arena. Regional organizations now had a path to connect to important political figures in the area of federal immigration policy. Moreover, they were now privy to valuable political information, which improved their abilities to formulate strategies. Participating in the coalition therefore provided the access and information necessary to become effective agents in the national field. The coalition enabled organizations to escape their local isolation and engage directly in national politics.

These regional organizations were embedded in a well-organized and disciplined infrastructure. "There's a discipline to the movement," observed ICIRR's codirector Lawrence Benito. "I think certainly the last few years are much more coordinated and deeper and broader than prior years."[80] This discipline was made possible by the focused, concerted efforts of national leaders. These leaders invested in the infrastructure, largely shaped the strategies and goals, and formulated the discursive frames used in political battles. The movement was more unified and disciplined than ever, but the discipline reflected the movement's oligarchic tendencies. Leaders had difficulty recognizing the validity of alternative strategies or mobilizing frames, even if those alternatives were generated by actual undocumented immigrant activists. This motivated some of these spurned activists to mount their own campaigns. These dissident mobilizations and networks came to form the left flank of the immigrant rights movement. While the mainstream leadership continued to command the general movement, its left flank initiated the most innovative and forceful campaigns of the decade.

CHAPTER 7

Money Makes the Movement

THE IMMIGRANT RIGHTS MOVEMENT was able to penetrate the national field because of its expansive and sophisticated infrastructure. Building such an infrastructure required enormous investments of economic capital by large foundations. "The credit for our movement," remarked the director of the Center for Community Change (CCC), "goes to immigrant leaders who had the courage to step out of the shadows. But the growth and speed of the movement was significantly aided by a small number of visionary philanthropies."[1] The funding pie grew during the 2000s, which enabled national organizations to create the infrastructure underlying the mainstream immigrant rights movement. They undertook costly research to understand the discourses and frames that would resonate with the American public. They had the resources to generate training materials and run local workshops across the country. Well-resourced organizations could afford to lobby national politicians and develop relationships with the political elite. By the early 2010s, many immigrant rights organizations were connected to one another through the vast infrastructure that had been created over the previous decade. The infrastructure could reach deep down into the grassroots and also up into the halls of national political power.

The infusion of money enabled an unprecedented level of coordination, but the wealth and professionalization of national organizations introduced a veritable class divide into the social movement. The social and cultural worlds of leading executive directors were inhabited by politicians, media workers, and elites from other advocacy organizations and foundations. Frequent interactions contributed to the convergence of policy and strategy preferences. Many of the national leaders were also far from their working-class, precarious immigrant base. Organizations grounded in immigrant communities called on the movement to prioritize enforcement reform. Geographic distance and differences in social class made it difficult for leaders to fully appreciate these urgent calls. Money certainly made political power possible, but such advances were offset by inequalities and a movement whose leadership was increasingly detached from its undocumented immigrant base.

The discussion that follows assesses the funding landscape of the immigrant rights movement. It does this through the use of a data set derived from two sources: IRS 990 forms and grants information from the Foundation Center. My research assistant and I selected forty-nine organizations for inclusion in the data set (please see the appendix for a full discussion). These organizations were selected according to two criteria: (1) prominence in the immigration reform newspaper database (organizations with four claims or more) and (2) a reputation among their fellow organizations in the movement (assessed during interviews). When selecting our sample of forty-nine, my research assistant and I excluded the ACLU, the Service Employees International Union (SEIU), and the Southern Poverty Law Center (SPLC) because of their massive revenues. Including them would have severely skewed the results. IRS 990 forms and Foundation Center data were not available for several of the remaining organizations. Most tables and graphs using IRS 990 data include forty-three organizations because several did not have 990 forms.

Centralizing Resources

Over the course of the 2000s, there was a substantial increase in the financial resources available to immigrant rights organizations. The sample does not account for all immigrant rights organizations but for only a fraction of all organizations engaged in immigrant rights advocacy. Figure 7.1 presents information derived from IRS 990 tax forms. The data points to a substantial increase in funding during the 2000s. Between 2000 and 2014, the forty-three organizations in the IRS survey raised almost $1.7 billion through various funding sources. Grants made by philanthropic foundations accounted for much of these organizations' revenue, but they did not account for all of it. Organizations generated revenue from several other sources including membership fees, government contracts, and gifts.

Based on Foundation Center data, there were approximately six hundred foundations that provided support to organizations addressing immigration

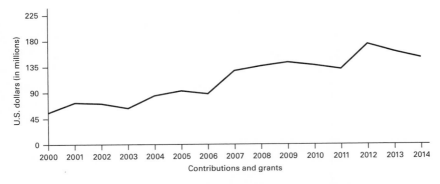

FIGURE 7.1. Contributions and grants (IRS data set). Source: Tax forms (IRS 990).

issues. These included large national foundations such as the Ford Foundation and Open Society, midsized foundations such as Atlantic and the NEO, corporations such as Walmart and PepsiCo, and smaller state and regional foundations. There was also diversity in the size of grants. In 2014, for instance, 35 percent of grants were less than $20,000; 30 percent were between $20,000 and $100,000; 30 percent were between $100,000 and $1 million; 3 percent were between $1 million and $2 million; and 1.4 percent exceeded $2 million. During this period of time, the top twenty foundations were responsible for approximately two-thirds of grants made to immigrant-serving organizations, and the top ten foundations accounted for half of the grants. The Ford Foundation, the Atlantic Philanthropies, Open Society, and the Carnegie Foundations made the greatest investments in this sector.

The influence of large individual foundations was enhanced through coordination between them. Large funders repeatedly met with one another to discuss the political field, assess opportunities, and evaluate priorities. Rather than working at cross-purposes, coordination allowed foundations to maximize their impact on the movement. As early as 2008, several foundations worked together to finance RIFA. "Funders," according to one Open Society report, "are coming together again to ensure that the investments made last year serve as the foundation to build upon for the long haul until reform is achieved."[2] During the run-up to the big push for comprehensive immigration reform in 2013, Open Society and the Ford Foundation cosponsored a funders meeting. "On December 20," one report noted, "U.S. Programs [Open Society] and Ford will co-sponsor a briefing for funders to learn more about the plans of leading immigrant rights advocates to help create a pathway to citizenship."[3] Funders also worked to showcase their grantees to other prominent foundations. "In early April, OSF, Ford, and the Carnegie Corporation coordinated a panel at the Council of Foundations annual meeting featuring A4C leadership."[4] Finally, funders worked together to advance their cause with the Obama administration. They organized several meetings between themselves, grantees, and White House officials. For instance, in the spring of 2014, Open Society collaborated with the Bill and Melinda Gates Foundation and Grantmakers Concerned with Immigrants and Refugees to "lead two funder briefings at the White House to highlight the challenges, opportunities, and the urgent need for full implementation of DACA."[5]

While elite funders coordinated at the national level, they also sought to shape funding decisions across the field. They used their size and power as leverage to influence smaller foundations to invest in the area of immigration. National foundations, for instance, provided important financial support to Grantmakers Concerned with Immigrants and Refugees. Some large foundation members also served on its board of directors. Grantmakers Concerned with Immigrants and Refugees was devised to provide smaller foundations with information and materials about immigration. In one report, Open Society remarked that "philanthropic support for immigrant rights continues to be quite limited, and the recommended renewal grant to Grantmakers Concerned with Immigrants and Refugees will help attract and coordinate resources for the immigration field to maximize the impact of limited dollars."[6] An earlier document specified the role that Grantmakers would make in the area of naturalization: "The grant to Grantmakers Concerned with Immigrants and Refugees will help OSF and its national funding partners leverage naturalization investments by securing matching support from state and local funders capable of sustaining the work."[7] In addition to assisting Grantmakers, national funders also introduced fund-matching schemes to motivate smaller foundations to donate to immigrant rights advocacy.

During this time, the funding landscape was more robust than ever. There were tens of millions of dollars more in circulation in the 2010s than there had been a decade before. There were also hundreds of different foundations making a range of grants (from small to very large sums). Most grants originated from a small group of foundations. The leading foundations also worked closely with one another to develop common funding strategies and priorities in the field. Foundations were not passive observers of the movement. They worked together to coordinate funding and influence the social movement they were financing. Liberal foundations therefore became a powerful force that shaped the trajectory of the immigrant rights movement.[8]

Privileged Relationships

Organizations with longtime connections to big funders stood a better chance of capturing resources and becoming movement leaders. Foundations such as Open Society worked directly with leading organizations like the CCC and the National Immigration Forum (NIF) to devise strategies and set priorities. Deepak Bhargava, the executive director of the CCC, was a board member of Open Society. As this foundation frequently cooperated with the Ford Foundation, Carnegie Corporation, and Atlantic Philanthropies, among others, Mr. Bhargava was in a position to interact with the most important foundations in the country. The executive directors and staff of other organizations also had close relations with the leading grant makers. Ali Noorani, director of the NIF, described the importance of these relationships: "As a managing organization for RIFA, we had budget management responsibility. As a function of that, we ended up in a place where we would be communicating quite a bit with the funders and either answering their questions or regranting and contracting dollars out that foundations would, for campaign related purposes."[9]

National funders and prominent organizations shared valuable information with one another about the field. "We would," Mr. Noorani noted, "be doing ourselves a disservice to much of the work if we weren't always looking to get the most information possible."[10] Sometimes the funders had important information for organizations, and sometimes the organizations had important information for the funders. The CCC's Mary Ochs added that advocacy organizations served as the "eyes and ears" of foundations. "It's helpful. They're making their own decisions, but they certainly were talking to each other and talking to us and others at times."[11]

The privileged relationships between funders and some grantees allowed the grantees to influence how foundations assessed political opportunities, movement capacities, and strategic paths forward. One assessment of Mr. Bhargava's role in Open Society noted that "his multifaceted role provided unique and thoughtful insights that enabled us to quickly understand complex dynamics and marshal resources, beyond what other funders could or would do, in support of immigrant rights."[12] In evaluating political opportunities in 2009, another Open Society document drew directly from the executive director of a leading organization.

> Frank Sharry of America's Voice said: "The version of immigration reform that is likely to be debated this year will focus primarily on cracking down on bad actor employers who violate immigration, labor, and tax laws, combined with the legalization of workers and families already contributing and living here in the United States. This approach will lift wages for American and immigrant workers alike, enhance tax fairness and boost revenues, and create a level playing field for honest employers."[13]

Two weeks after the publication of this document, Open Society approved $15 million of additional funding to support RIFA's campaign for comprehensive immigration reform. In the run-up to the 2013 campaign for comprehensive immigration reform, foundations drew upon the analyses of their most prominent grantees to make their funding decisions. "Staff consulted with many members of the immigration movement, congressional staffers, other funders, and the Administration and became convinced that there was a genuine window of opportunity to achieve CIR [comprehensive immigration reform]."[14] Foundations were therefore embedded in epistemic communities made up of leading advocacy organizations and policy makers, drawing from these sources as well as their own staff to devise funding priorities.

Although national organizations benefited from their privileged relationships with important funders, they also channeled resources to their national and regional allies. The CCC, for instance, made it a point early on to share revenue with the members of the FIRM network. Mary Ochs recalled that "we made a commitment that more than half of all the money that the Center might raise to work on these efforts would go back into the field."[15] In addition to sharing revenue, the CCC and other national organizations brokered relations between regional organizations and major foundations.[16] "CCC," remembered former CCC organizer Lupe Lopez, "had the contacts and the ability to funnel money into the local organizations by getting the national foundations' attention." National organizations helped convince large foundations that support for their regional allies needed to be institutionalized. In 2003, a group of national foundations created the Four Freedoms Fund. The former director of the RIFA coalition recounted that "there were conversations with Open Society, Carnegie Foundation, and others to begin to raise resources for immigration reform, and the creation of what eventually became the Four

Freedoms Fund, which was a fund or an affinity group focused on immigrants' rights, immigration reform issues."[17] The fund served as a regranting vehicle to support, according to one Open Society document, "work in resourcing and networking state and local immigrant rights organizations and coalitions."[18] National organizations worked alongside the Four Freedoms Fund to regrant money from large foundations to regional organizations. One document noted, "OSI funds through the Center for Community Change, the National Council of La Raza, and Four Freedoms Fund will support the major immigrant state-wide organizations [for example, CHIRLA, CASA Maryland, ICIRR, and NYIC]."[19] Large foundations, therefore, not only recognized the larger organizations as leaders but also provided them the authority to funnel money to their allied organizations in the field.

Regional organizations certainly benefited from these new resource streams, but many of the larger regionals, such as CHIRLA, ICIRR, and MassIRAC, also came to depend on specialized foundations like NEO Philanthropy, which itself received support from the large national foundations. They also drew in revenue from second-tier foundations, such as the Weinberg and the Marguerite Casey Foundation, as well as state and local foundations like the California Wellness Foundation. Smaller, more grassroots organizations depended on smaller, regional foundations such as the Denver Foundation, the Minneapolis Foundation, the New York Community Trust, and Los Angeles–based Liberty Hill.

More foundations were investing more money into the immigrant rights movement. These funders were coordinating their spending with one another and with smaller foundations. Relationships between funders and national organizations also served important purposes. National organizations gained access to important information about the field. They influenced the analyses of foundations and, consequently, shaped funding priorities. Just as important, they channeled money to regional organizations in the field. By serving as gatekeepers of important funding networks, the national organizations could exercise formidable economic leverage over the shape of activism within the field.

Mapping Inequalities

The infusion of foundation money was a boon for many organizations. For the first time in the movement's history, there was a concerted effort to bolster the capacity of organizations and assist in the various battles to secure

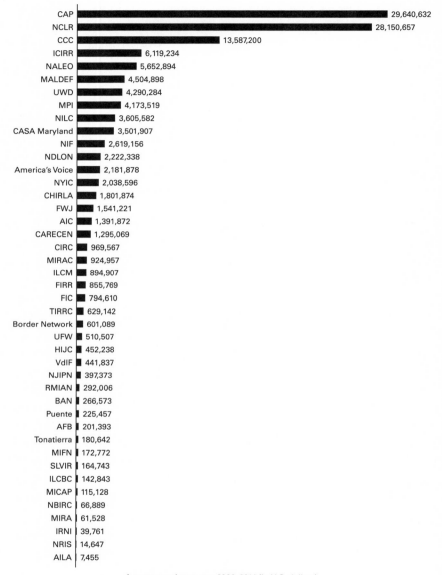

Average yearly revenue 2000–2014 (in U.S. dollars)

FIGURE 7.2. Revenue, yearly averages for 2000–2014 (IRS data set). Source: Tax forms (IRS 990).

immigration reform. Many organizations benefited from increased funding, but not all of them benefited equally. Drawing on the IRS dataset, figure 7.2 indicates that a handful of organizations (CAP, the NCLR, and the CCC) dominated the funding landscape.

The funding structure also contributed to important inequalities in the salaries of executive directors (see figure 7.3). The salary of the top executive director (of the NCLR) in 2014 was $503,715, many times more than the salary of the same position in smaller local organizations. When comparing the average salaries of the top quartile, bottom quartile, and the whole sample, we get a better understanding of salary inequalities (see figure 7.4). The average salary of all executive directors increased from $93,378 to $128,000 between 2000 and 2014. The average salary of the top quartile more than doubled, however, increasing from $127,898 to $280,693. Meanwhile, the average salary of the bottom quartile increased from $10,339 to $35,716 over the same period of time. This was a substantial increase but not enough to close the gap with the movement's top earners.

Affluent organizations also enjoyed a diverse funding base. The organizations in the survey were ranked according to IRS-based revenue categories.[20] The average number of donors to the three organizations in the highest revenue category was 152, with a range of 109 to 211. The second highest category had an average of 38 funders with a range of 18 to 71. By contrast, organizations in the lowest revenue category (with annual revenue of less than or equal to $1 million) depended on an average of 5 donors per organization, with a range of 1 to 11. These poorer organizations received most of their funding from small grants. Wealthier organizations competed with poorer organizations for funding because they applied for large and small grants alike. For example, according to Foundation Center data, 25 percent of the CCC's funding and 30 percent of the National Immigration Forum's funding came from small grants.

Certain organizational characteristics help explain these inequalities. These characteristics include organization type, number of employees, geography, and strategy. Single-issue organizations focus on one area (such as immigrant rights), whereas multi-issue organizations may invest resources in various areas (such as immigration, housing, and worker rights). The CCC and the Center for American Progress are classic multi-issue organizations. Multi-issue organizations are often better funded because they need more money to engage in multiple campaigns, and their range of specializations

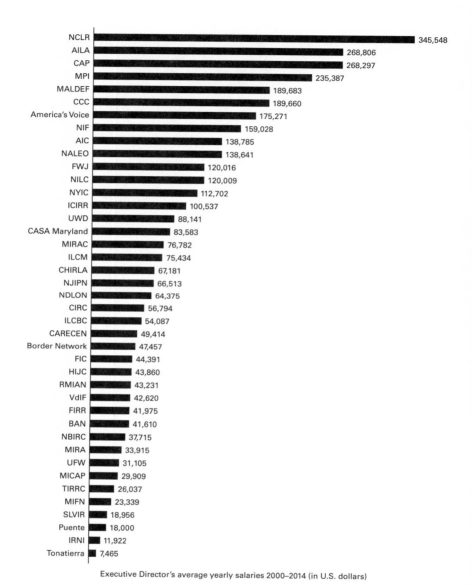

Executive Director's average yearly salaries 2000–2014 (in U.S. dollars)

FIGURE 7.3. Average yearly salary of executive directors, 2000–2014 (IRS data set). Source: Tax forms (IRS 990).

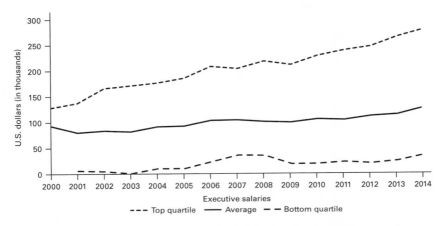

FIGURE 7.4. Salary of executive directors, average, top quartile, bottom quartile, 2000–2014 (IRS data set). Source: Tax forms (IRS 990).

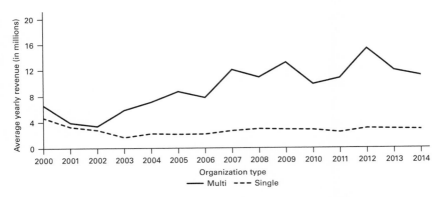

FIGURE 7.5. Organization type and average yearly revenue, 2000–2014 (IRS data set). Source: Tax forms (IRS 990).

makes them eligible for diverse grants. They can, for instance, apply for grants in areas as diverse as health advocacy, job training, and immigration. By contrast, single-issue organizations are specialized in one area, which reduces their eligibility for grants outside that area. In strict dollar terms, multi-issue organizations appeared to have a strong advantage over single-issue organizations (see figure 7.5). We find a similar gap with respect to the salaries of executive directors. The average salary of the executive directors of single-issue organizations was $91,085 in 2000, and it increased to $118,720 in 2014. Meanwhile the average salary of those in the same position at multi-issue organizations was $103,695 in 2000, growing to $206,887 in 2014.

An organization's size, as measured by the number of employees, can also help to explain for inequalities because larger organizations require more resources for more personnel. Larger organizations have greater internal divisions of labor, higher levels of professionalization, and more needs. These characteristics help them meet the requirements and expectations of foundations while also making it easier for them to respond to new funding opportunities. Table 7.1 ranks organizations into size categories (large, medium, and small) on the basis of the number of employees. Although larger organizations have a substantial per capita revenue advantage over small organizations, large organizations hold only a slight advantage over medium-sized organizations. The size of an organization also appears to have a role in shaping executive pay. Whereas the salary ratio between large and small organizations was 3.6 in 2001, it grew to 6.0 in 2014.

The geographic structure of an organization also seems to matter. Robert Putnam and others[21] argue that there was an important shift in the geography of organizations following the 1960s. In response to the increased prominence of the federal government, many national organizations shifted their headquarters to Washington, DC. They gravitated toward the center of national power and away from where their members lived. This geographic shift provided organizations with important locational advantages. In addition to being close to elected officials and their staff, advocacy organizations could also tap into funding, media, and other advocacy networks. The growth in revenue of DC-based organizations has been strong and consistent when compared with those in other geographic categories, such as national organizations

TABLE 7.1. Size of organizations and yearly revenue (IRS data set)

	Number of employees	Revenue	Per capita
Large (50–249 employees)	114	$11,258,184	$98,756
Medium (10–49 employees)	20	$1,943,387	$97,169
Small (0–9 employees)	4	$284,815	$71,204
Average	**40**	**$3,669,078**	**$91,727**

Source: Tax forms (IRS 990).

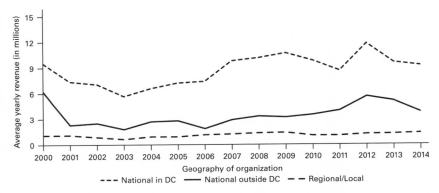

FIGURE 7.6. Geography of organization and average yearly revenue, 2000–2014 (IRS data set). Source: Tax forms (IRS 990).

headquartered outside DC and regional/local organizations (see figure 7.6). The advantages of DC-based organizations were also reflected in the salaries of executive directors. In 2000, the salaries of executive directors of national organizations headquartered *inside* DC, national organizations headquartered *outside* DC, and regional/local organizations were $110,807, $121,944, and $48,401, respectively. By 2014, the salaries of DC-based directors grew to $270,964 while rising to $133,854 and $64,570, respectively, for national organizations outside of DC and for regional/local organizations.

Finally, funders provided strong support to organizations engaged in the fight for both comprehensive immigration reform and enforcement-reform work. As noted in the previous chapter, funders conceived of enforcement-reform activism as a niche campaign within the general immigrant rights movement. Conceived as a niche, foundations provided important levels of support to organizations invested in hard-charging, direct-action campaigns like Not One More. Most funding, however, went to organizations invested in the fight for comprehensive immigration reform. "The CIR [comprehensive immigration reform] work," according to one Open Society document, "was where most of the resources and attention were focused."[22] These organizations were closer to funders and shared the common goal of passing a massive piece of legislation that would fix the broken system once and for all. Enforcement-reform organizations were, by contrast, thought to be filling a niche. Consequently, they were provided sufficient resources to engage in important campaigns but not enough to make the left-flank into a dominant force in the immigrant rights movement. That position was reserved for those invested in the fight for comprehensive immigration reform.

Larger, multi-issue, DC-based organizations focused on comprehensive immigration reform were better positioned to capture a bigger share of financial resources. They could use these resources to invest in programs and infrastructure, expand the number of employees and salaries, and plan and invest in costly campaigns. Therefore, although the funding windfall benefited most organizations in the movement, the national organizations in DC were able to use their preexisting advantages to maximize their gains.

A Stratified Social Movement

Inequalities resulted in a four-tier, class-like structure. At the top of this hierarchy stood DC-based advocacy organizations that focused mostly on the passage of comprehensive immigration reform. These organizations had a diverse, robust funding base and enjoyed strong relations with important institutions such as the Ford, Open Society, Carnegie, and Atlantic Foundations. Their ample, diverse funding base provided them with greater stability and security. Losing one of their grants was by no means catastrophic. Financial certainty allowed them to invest in longer-term strategies, build organizational capacity, hire college-educated staff, invest in policy research, and develop complex communications operations, among other things. These capacities and attributes made the organizations more competitive for large and small grants alike. Their privileges were used, in other words, to accumulate more financial resources. This, along with their close relations to funders, allowed the national organizations to capture a disproportionate amount of funding. In addition to their favorable positions, most staff did not hail from working-class, immigrant communities. With the exception of Dreamers, the socioeconomic status and legal precarity of undocumented immigrants made most ineligible for professional jobs in prominent DC-based organizations. Staff typically possessed middle-class habitus and dispositions, acquired through upbringing or university experience. High salaries for senior staff magnified the social distance between those in the leading organizations and the immigrants they represented.

Many national organizations outside of Washington, DC, such as MALDEF, NILC, NDLON, and the Border Network for Human Rights, worked on enforcement reform and found themselves in a contradictory position. The foundations praised their work but viewed their campaigns as niche rather than as leading forces of the movement. Organizations working on these issues merited funding but not at the same level as organizations advancing comprehensive immigration reform. National organizations headquartered outside Washington DC competed with DC-based organizations for recognition, resources, and the strategic direction of the movement. But their DC-based competitors had stronger relationships with the most important financial patrons of the movement, and foundations did not want to see one set of grantees undermine the abilities of another, better funded set. These organizations therefore launched their campaigns and coalitions and competed with the DC-based leadership for resources and recognition, but they ultimately occupied a subordinate position in the funding structure.

Regional organizations benefited from the funding system. The staff of these organizations often hailed from working-class immigrant communities. During the 1990s and early 2000s, they struggled to secure sufficient resources to maintain basic operations, pay staff, and finance their ambitious projects and campaigns. For instance, in the early 2000s, the city of Los Angeles cut much of its funding to CHIRLA, which led to a severe crisis in the organization.[23] By participating in a network such as FIRM, CHIRLA and similar organizations gained access to new and more reliable sources of funding, allowing them to escape the burden of perpetual financial penury and uncertainty.

At the bottom of the hierarchy stood small, local organizations like Arizona's Tonatierra. These local organizations depended on smaller grants from a narrow range of funders. This resulted in high levels of scarcity and uncertainty. Losing a single grant would send such an organization into a crisis. These organizations had difficulty meeting minimal salary obligations to their directors, let alone to employees. This made it hard to hire and retain professionally qualified staff, and many disadvantaged organizations depended on the sheer dedication of impoverished staff and volunteers to continue their work. This increased burnout rates, prompting talented staff to either find opportunities in richer organizations or drop out of the struggle altogether. The difficulty of hiring and retaining staff reinforced instability, ultimately weakening organizational capacities and undermining the ability to make long-term plans. They were locked into competition for smaller pots of money not only with organizations like themselves but also with larger, wealthier organizations with significant advantages. This funding structure placed the smaller, poorer organizations in a perpetual cycle of insecurity, with few options to move up and out of their marginal positions. They were compelled to focus simply on surviving in an increasingly competitive funding environment.

This funding structure contributed to a hierarchical, class-like organizational structure. At the top of this structure stood professional advocacy organizations, mostly located in Washington, DC, and mostly campaigning for comprehensive immigration reform. They had strong relationships with the large funders and successfully competed for large and small grants alike. At the bottom of the hierarchy were poor, local organizations embedded in working-class immigrant communities. Their lack of resources made it difficult to sustain a professional staff, build capacity, and sponsor long-term campaigns. These disadvantages made it hard to compete with higher-performing organizations for the same pots of money. The lack of resources placed them at a structural disadvantage in the never-ending struggle for money. Thus, the rich organizations enjoyed conditions that allowed them to continuously accumulate resources, while the poor organizations were placed in a vicious cycle of perpetual precarity.

The Downsides of Inequalities

Most national leaders, with the exception of United We Dream, were middle class and embedded in networks of professionals, and they worked for large organizations made up of few if any undocumented immigrants. The leadership turned to professional advocates like themselves, to foundations, and to elite policy makers to develop strategic priorities (such as comprehensive reform) rather than to the actual immigrants being affected by the Obama administration's enforcement policies. By contrast, organizations rooted in immigrant communities experienced enforcement in a visceral way, as an urgent matter that needed to be addressed forcefully. For many grassroots organizations, fighting government surveillance, detention, and deportations was their priority. As Angela Kelley, with the Center for American Progress, explained, "It's easier to understand why the grassroots groups are focused on administrative relief because they are the ones seeing the day in and day out harm of deportations. They are speaking for those families that can't speak for themselves. *We're a rung or two away from that so we don't feel that the same way*" (emphasis added).[24] The DC-based leadership was removed from immigrant communities and did not experience their difficulties and fears. Regional organizations such as CHIRLA and CASA Maryland certainly relayed information to the leadership from immigrant communities, but there were no mechanisms to hold the leadership accountable. Social and geographical distance, consequently, made it easier for the leadership to elevate comprehensive immigration reform as the movement's primary goal and to frame enforcement reform as a secondary, niche issue.

The privileged relationship between leading foundations and several grantees may have also resulted in a strategic bias. A 2016 Open Society report suggested that this relation could have limited the foundation's ability to weigh all the strategic options available to it: "We must also ask ourselves what the impact was of having a board member (Deepak Bhargava, executive director of Center for Community Change, a co-chair of the A4C Working Group) also be relied upon as an expert in the field advocating for CIR, as well as an interested party when it came to investments that were ultimately made."[25] There was concern that Open Society may have listened to Mr. Bhargava's particular point of view more than to alternative perspectives. "It leads me to wonder," the report's author noted, "whether our focus on CIR made us lose sight of other opportunities that presented themselves at the time."[26] Some foundation staff wondered whether higher levels of support to the movement's enforcement-reform wing would have been more effective: "I believe that more due diligence and a different allocation of funds between the CIR effort and other strategies to improve the lives of immigrants might have generated better outcomes, and the unintended consequences of our funding could have been better predicted."[27] With more resources, the report suggested, organizations could have pushed back on enforcement earlier in Obama's presidency and increased leverage for comprehensive immigration reform. Rather than conceiving enforcement reform as a niche within the broader movement, funders could have provided more capital and transformed that niche into the movement's vanguard. The report concluded that Open Society "should be careful in how it evaluates effectiveness and create mechanisms to allow a diverse set of voices to be heard."[28]

A Gilded Movement for a Gilded Age

Foundations invested heavily in immigrant rights advocacy. There were many different grant-making organizations, but several dominated funding. The dominant foundations also worked closely with one another and with the executive directors of leading organizations. The foundations came to believe in and trust the CCC, the National Immigration Forum, America's Voice, and the NCLR, among others. These organizations used their relationships to shape how foundations thought about strategies and priorities. They also worked with the foundations to create funding streams for their regional al

lies. Four Freedoms, for instance, was created at the behest of national organizations and used to fund regional organizations. DC-based organizations helped shape funding priorities and channeled resources to allies that
conformed to the leadership's strategic preferences and goals. Influence over
funding decisions allowed the leadership of the mainstream movement to exert a degree of control over the organizational field.

The prosperous organizations improved their capacities to invest in infrastructure, develop long-term plans, and mount big campaigns directed at the
national centers of political power. They were well placed to target and lobby
the federal government, develop national coalitions with regional and local outreach, finance expensive legal fights, and develop sophisticated communication strategies. Rich organizations that dominated the funding game
were, in other words, in a much stronger place to mount national-level campaigns that came to dominate the immigrant rights movement. Regional organizations participated in campaigns directed by rich national organizations
(mostly based in Washington, DC), but they lacked the capacities to become
leading players in their own right. Even the larger regionals such as CHIRLA
were stretched thin in terms of resources. They could participate in coalitions
directed by national organizations, but they faced impediments that limited
their abilities to become full-fledged movement leaders. Small organizations
with close ties to the immigrant communities were stretched even thinner.
They had limited money and few funders. The loss of a single funder could
send them into a death spiral. Material constraints imposed enormous limits on what they could do. Funding inequalities therefore reinforced the advantages of the national leadership in terms of resources and organizational
capacities.

The inequalities between organizations introduced class and cultural divides between richer organizations and their poorer comrades embedded in
working-class immigrant communities. The richer organizations were often
staffed by well-compensated professionals who were mostly removed from
the lives of low-income, undocumented immigrants. The disconnect between
social-movement elites and real immigrant communities was aggravated by
the lack of accountability. Most DC-based leaders did not have to go home
and actually talk to immigrant communities and address their grievances and
fears directly. Instead, the leaders set priorities by talking to people like themselves. The structure of the immigrant rights movement therefore elevated the
voices and priorities of those removed from actual immigrant communities.

CHAPTER 8

A Seat at the Table

THE MAINSTREAM IMMIGRANT RIGHTS MOVEMENT—or at least its leadership—was able to acquire much political capital during the Obama years. Democrats won the White House, House of Representatives, and Senate in 2008. As a candidate, then–Senator Obama assured immigrants and advocacy organizations that they could count on his administration to fight for immigrant rights and reform. "You can trust me," he told an assembly of Latina/o and immigrant rights leaders in June 2008, "when I say that I will be your partner in the White House. Because for eight long years, Washington has not been working for ordinary Americans and has not been working for Latinos."[1] National leaders and foundations believed that the new administration would take on immigration reform soon after its inauguration. Open Society mapped out the movement's historically propitious political opportunities.[2]

> The following developments suggest the need to be prepared with a legislative agenda as early as January, as well as the need to build the infrastructure for potential advocacy efforts in 2009:
>
> 1. Senator Obama has made public commitments at the annual conference of the National Council of La Raza (NCLR) and other events to make immigration reform a top priority in his first year in office; he has reiterated these commitments in private conference calls with immigrant rights leaders.
> 2. There is a growing acknowledgment among some Congressional leaders that it will be difficult to accomplish other elements of a domestic policy agenda, like healthcare reform, while immigration remains unresolved. Frustration about the size of the undocumented population is a useful tool

for opponents of health reform and other domestic policy reforms, creating an incentive to get immigration off the table early.

3. Congressman Rahm Emanuel privately told Janet Murguía of NCLR that there may well be an opening for immigration reform in the first nine months of 2009, and that if advocates are not ready with a bill, others on the Hill will prepare one.

4. If immigrant and Latino turnout in the election is as significant as anticipated, this could create additional momentum to address the immigration issue early.

Several months after the inauguration, a top White House official said that "comprehensive immigration legislation, including a plan to make legal status possible for an estimated 12 million illegal immigrants, would be a priority in his first year in office."[3]

The Obama administration provided extraordinary access to advocacy groups. Once he was elected, the leading organizations had many meetings with White House officials and congressional leaders. Leading organizations became the political representatives of the immigrant community in these elite circles. Strong ties with federal policy makers and politicians provided movement leaders with direct access to valuable information. This made leaders into gatekeepers of scarce information emanating from the highest halls of political power. A virtual monopoly over insider information bolstered the position of the leadership within the immigrant rights movement. Access also made national leaders appear powerful to the press, foundations, and various national politicians.

The aura of power did not, however, result in much political influence. During a period of unprecedented access, the Obama White House did not prioritize comprehensive immigration reform during its first term. President Obama took advice from Democratic leaders (Senator Schumer and Rahm Emmanuel, for instance) who had long sought to win the support of Republican colleagues and the public by getting tough on immigrants. The Obama administration went on to create one of the most effective deportation machines in history. Between 2009 and 2013, the Obama administration removed approximately four hundred thousand unauthorized immigrants a year. For most Democratic leaders, the deportation of millions was the price to pay for the legalization of millions more. This get-tough strategy did not pay off, as many Republicans remained steadfast in their rejection of any reform involving so-called amnesty. Thus, in spite of its access to the highest office in the country, the leadership of the immigrant rights movement was not able to exercise significant influence.

This chapter focuses on the accumulation of political capital, as measured by White House access. The chapter assesses this using data from many of the same organizations analyzed in the previous chapter. This database covers the first six years of the Obama administration (2009–2014). My research assistant and I retrieved information from the White House visitor web page.[4] We identified organizations by the names of important employees. These names were gathered through organization websites, the immigration-reform newspaper database, LinkedIn profiles, and extensive website searches. We cleaned the data set by removing visits that were not related to immigration issues. For instance, several organizations are multi-issue organizations (for example, the Service Employees International Union and the Center for American Progress) and had White House meetings that were not directly related to immigration issues. To be included in the database, the visitor had to be charged with the immigration portfolio in his or her organization or have met with a White House official with an immigration mandate. When somebody did not meet one of these criteria, we removed them from the database. One hundred such visits were removed from our original sample.

Accessing the White House

The Obama administration enacted a vigorous community outreach program early in its first term. It created the Office of Public Engagement to formalize its relationships with important constituent groups such as Latinas/os, African Americans, the LGBTQ community, and labor. The purpose of this office was, according to its website, to "create and coordinate opportunities for direct dialogue between the Obama Administration and the American public, while bringing new voices to the table and ensuring that everyone can participate and inform the work of the President."[5] This was by no means a symbolic White House agency. Its director, Valerie Jarrett, was a senior advisor to the president.

Outreach efforts contributed to unprecedented levels of access for organizations advocating for immigrant rights and immigration reform. Based on a survey of 49 organizations, there were approximately 854 individual visits to the White House from 2009 to 2014 and 503 meetings involving two or more immigrant rights organizations (see figure 8.1). There were fewer meetings than individual visits because many visits consisted of meetings of more

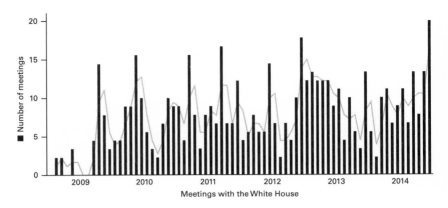

FIGURE 8.1. Number of meetings with the White House. Source: White House visitor records.

TABLE 8.1. Summary of meetings and visits to the White House.

	Number of meetings in WH	Total number of visits to the WH	Organizations present during meetings		
			1 org.	2 orgs.	>2 orgs.
2009	34	47	24	8	2
2010	80	138	55	13	12
2011	95	152	69	12	14
2012	82	135	65	7	10
2013	107	188	76	16	15
2014	105	194	73	15	17
Total	**503**	**854**	**362**	**71**	**70**

Source: White House visitor records.

than one organization. A total of 35 advocacy organizations (out of 49 in the survey) visited White House officials at least once (see table 8.1). Access to the Obama administration was unprecedented. The Bush administration supported immigration reform, but according to several prominent advocates, it granted only limited direct access to advocacy organizations. Anti-immigrant organizations also had limited access to the Obama administration. Obama's outreach efforts to the immigrant rights movement therefore disproportionately favored proimmigrant groups.

Not all organizations, however, had the same access. National organizations headquartered in Washington, DC, had the highest average number of visits between 2009 and 2014 (see figure 8.2). Six organizations (out of forty-nine in the survey) accounted for nearly half of all the visits. These included the National Council of La Raza (NCLR), the National Immigration Forum (NIF), the Center for Community Change (CCC), the Center for American Progress (CAP), United We Dream (UWD), and the Service Employees International Union (SEIU). All except SEIU were nonprofit advocacy organizations. The NCLR had the most visits with prominent White House officials, and a substantial number of its visits were with the president (36 out of 115 visits). It was the most prominent organization in terms of quantity and quality of access. Regional organizations were given more access than ever, but that access continued to pale in comparison to national leaders in both absolute and relative terms. CASA Maryland, CHIRLA, and the Illinois Coalition for Immigrant and Refugee Rights (ICIRR) each accounted for 2 percent of White House visits during the six-year period, considerably fewer than the national organizations. In spite of their growing political status, regional organizations were not the political equals of the national organizations. They had enough value to get a seat at the national table but not enough to become a major player in political discussions, as measured by frequency of visits.

Leading organizations were not only visiting more but also meeting with other advocacy organizations during their visits. As can be seen in figure 8.3,

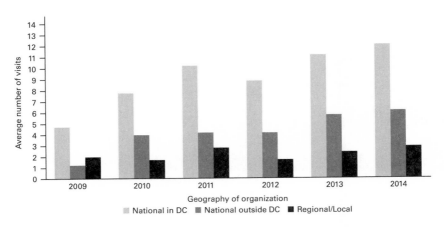

FIGURE 8.2. Size of organizations and average number of visits to the White House.
Source: White House visitor records; tax forms (IRS 990).

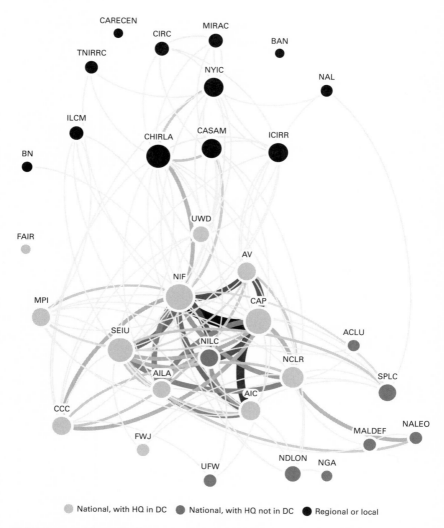

FIGURE 8.3A. Network of organizations meeting together at the White House, 2009–2011. Source: White House visitor records.

the White House became networking space for the leading advocacy organizations. The network accounts for the number of visits (indicated by the size of the circle or node) and the number of organizations copresent during meetings (indicated by thickness of lines between nodes). A large circle (showing number of visits) and several thick lines (showing the strength of ties) in-

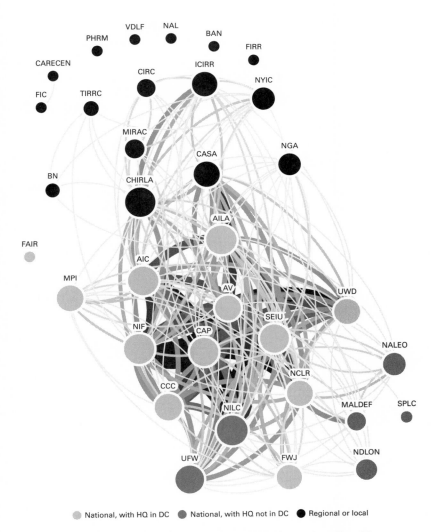

FIGURE 8.3B. Network of organizations meeting together at the White House, 2012–2014. Source: White House visitor records.

crease an organization's positioning within the network. Out of the ten most central organizations from 2009 to 2011, nine were the most central from 2012 to 2014. The group of leading organizations in these meetings was stable during these years. This leadership group was largely made up of DC-based organizations (in light gray). For national organizations outside DC (in dark gray),

NILC was the best connected and positioned. NDLON and MALDEF were positioned on the margins, with fewer individual visits and fewer connections to other important actors. NDLON's lead attorney, Chris Newman, remarked on his organization's position by saying,

> There's been no question that we've lost access. And I would say that—I don't know if we lost our innocence and we got over our incredulity about promises the Obama administration had made. We take comfort in knowing that our work is creating political space and that our presence is felt at the proverbial table, even if we have lost our golden ticket.[6]

Although regional organizations (in black) had more access than ever, many also remained on the margins.

Many White House officials working with immigrant organizations also had an intimate history with the most prominent advocacy organizations (see table 8.2). In 2014 *Cecilia Muñoz* was the director of the Domestic Policy Council and had a strong influence on shaping immigration policy. Prior to joining the White House, she was NCLR's senior vice president for the Office of Research, Advocacy, and Legislation. *Julie Rodriquez* also straddled the division between immigrant rights advocacy and the White House. She was the granddaughter of United Farm Workers founder Cesar Chavez and worked for several years as the director of programs at the Cesar E. Chavez Foundation. *Jorge Neri* was the Midwest and Southeast coordinator for the Center for Community Change (2008–2011), focusing primarily on immigrant rights advocacy. In 2012 he took up the position of Nevada state field director for Organizing for America, President Obama's reelection campaign. He then joined the White House's Office of Public Engagement. Later he became the deputy campaign manager for the field in the major immigrant rights coalition, Alliance for Citizenship, the last coalition developed by top immigrant rights organizations to campaign for the passage of comprehensive immigration reform. In 2015 he became the field representative for the Hillary Clinton campaign in Nevada. *Felicia Escobar* also had strong ties to the NCLR, starting her career with the organization as state policy analyst and representing the NCLR's state affiliates in the Texas legislature. *Lucas Guttentag* was a leading advocate of the ACLU's Immigrants' Rights Project. He led and participated in major lawsuits against federal, state, and local anti-immigrant legislation. In 2014 he became senior counselor to the director of the US Citizenship and Immigration Services (USCIS). *Janet Murguía*, the current CEO

TABLE 8.2. The revolving door between movement and White House

Name	Position in government	Organization affiliation
Cecilia Muñoz	Director of the Domestic Policy Council	National Council of La Raza's senior vice president for the Office of Research, Advocacy, and Legislation
Julie Rodriquez	Office of Public Engagement	Granddaughter of United Farm Workers founder, Cesar Chavez; Director of Programs at the Cesar E. Chavez Foundation
Jorge Neri	Nevada State field director for the Obama campaign; Office of Public Engagement; Nevada State field director for the Hillary Clinton campaign	Center for Community Change (2008–2011); deputy campaign manager for Alliance for Citizenship
Felicia Escobar	Office of Public Engagement	National Council of La Raza
Janet Murguía	Deputy assistant in the Clinton White House; campaign manager and director of constituency outreach for Al Gore's presidential campaign in 2000	Director of the National Council of La Raza
Lucas Guttentag	Senior counselor to the director of US Citizenship and Immigration Services (USCIS)	American Civil Liberties Union's Immigrants' Rights project

Source: White House visitor records.

of the NCLR, worked as a deputy assistant in the Clinton White House. This was followed by a position as deputy campaign manager and director of constituency outreach for Al Gore's presidential campaign in 2000. Thus, there was a revolving door between the worlds of party and advocacy, with many influential people moving between top advocacy organizations, Democratic campaigns, and paid government positions.

There was thus more access than ever, but organizations located in Washington, DC, had much more access than others. The organizations making up the leadership group stayed rather stable over the period. But 2014 marked a sharp decline in the number of visits for the NCLR, which, coincidentally or not, coincided with the organization's public critique of President Obama's deportation policies. Nevertheless, a stable coterie of organizations came to constitute the representative voice of the nation's undocumented immigrants inside the White House. This did not mean that they channeled the authentic desires of real undocumented immigrants, only that they expressed what they believed to be in the best interest of the community.

Access as Power

Access as a form of political capital was important because it provided advocates with a line of communication to important policy makers. Advocates hoped to use their access to better inform and influence policies. Access also provided them with rarified political information. For instance, in early 2010, advocates consulted leading elected officials and staffers about the possibility of a comprehensive immigration reform bill. The advocates then used this information not only to assess possibilities for reform but also to identify how reform would generate fault lines in the immigrant rights movement. The following excerpt from a 2010 Open Society memorandum provides an example of how such information informed the analysis of leading advocates and funders.

> Based on information from the White House, Department of Homeland Security and Congressional leadership, advocates have identified the following policy fault lines:
>
> Legalization: Concepts have surfaced that would require immigrants seeking to legalize their status to plead guilty to a criminal offense that would be expunged from their record after payment of a fine and completion of community service. There is strong opposition to this proposal on many fronts.
>
> Family Immigration: In order to clear the current backlog of applications, tradeoffs being considered include freezing family categories for several years. There continues to be discussion of imposing a point or merit-based system in lieu of the current family and/or employment-based visa categories, thus eliminating longstanding immigration priorities and values for family reunification.

Future Flow: The challenging economic environment immigration reform faces is exacerbated by tension between organized labor and business interests. Labor favors future flow of work-based immigration controlled by a commission that would base visa numbers on labor market data. Business would like economic needs to drive employment visa numbers, and is skeptical a commission would include leadership friendly to their interests. Furthermore, the controversy of guest worker visa programs remains an issue as many opponents believe all immigration should be temporary, at best.

Border and Interior Enforcement: Allies on the border (elected officials, law enforcement, faith, business and others) have grown in strength and sophistication, yet further militarization of the border is under consideration. Troublingly, interior enforcement measures may build upon existing electronic verification systems and concepts have surfaced that include national biometric identity cards.

Due Process: Scenarios may emerge where legislators trade moderate interior enforcement measures for delayed restoration of judicial review and/or discretionary waivers of removal.[7]

Having a seat at the table allowed organizations to acquire valuable information about policy and politics.

In addition to acquiring valuable political information, national organizations used their access to high-level government officials to become strategic gatekeepers within their social movement. National organizations such as the CCC, NCLR, and NIF had long-standing relationships with federal lawmakers and their staff. They worked to connect their regional allies to prominent political figures. Mary Ochs of the CCC recounted some of these early meetings: "We had meetings with staffers and I was introducing them [regional organizations] to folks. We started talking about the Dreamers and all these other issues with workers and what was going on with immigration reform. They [regional organizations] were like 'wow.'"[8] National organizations opened doors to regional organizations and shared information with FIRM members. According to the director of ICIRR, "FIRM provided the conduit to get the best intel." This intel allowed his and similar organizations "to strategize together what would be the most effective actions, most effective messaging, and specific targeting of either elected officials or other entities that we needed to move."[9] Thus, by governing the distribution of access and information within their movement, national organizations were able to assert their dominance within it.

Access could also be converted into more funding and media attention. Funders often pointed to meetings with important political officials as evidence for one of their grantees' success. For instance, Open Society approvingly discussed President Obama's praise for Ali Noorani's work cultivating alliances with conservative groups. "When Ali Noorani, the Forum's executive director participated in a meeting with President Obama and a small group of other national immigration reform advocates, the President singled out BBB efforts and said, 'You have the right strategy.'"[10] For funders, good relations with important political leaders were a marker of success, helping to justify further financial support to their prominent grantees. Access was a form of political capital that could, consequently, be converted into economic capital, and it could also raise an organization's media profile. Journalists and producers from prominent media outlets such as the *New York Times*, *Politico*, and CNN turned to the organizations that were deemed influential and had a seat at the table. Access in and of itself did not ensure a high level of media exposure, but it certainly helped.

Access was important because it provided valuable information and status. These advantages could then be used to enhance the power of leaders within the movement while ensuring continued funding and media exposure. This form of political capital was therefore a determinative resource because it could be leveraged to bolster the power of leading organizations.

The Downside of Access

The White House cultivated good relations with advocacy organizations while also working to stifle criticisms of its policies. Congressperson Luis Gutierrez, the leading proimmigrant voice in the House, remarked, "People have tried to control it [the social movement]. This administration has put inordinate pressure on people not to criticize the president on his immigration policy and not to talk about prosecutorial discretion."[11] Some advocates, mostly on the movement's left flank, argued that access to the White House was the principal instrument to control for criticism. NDLON's Chris Newman, for instance, noted that "we all have our different roles to play, but there is a perception outside of the Washington Beltway that some organizations with access have become apologists for the administration."[12] The White House was cognizant of the value placed on political access and distributed it differentially in order to contain criticisms. "I do believe that access and differential access, some of it is intentional. Much of it is intentional," remarked Tom Saenz, the director of MALDEF. "It is intended by the White House to signal power and influence."[13]

The high value placed on access increased the cost of losing it. The director of ICIRR noted that DC-based organizations were particularly worried about jeopardizing access, remarking that "the national organizations were wanting to hold on to access, the folks in DC. So, there's always the challenge of how hard to push while still maintaining access because if you push too hard you just get ignored and you no longer have access. People trade their currency on access and information."[14] Gustavo Torres, the director of CASA Maryland, remarked that the White House would signal its displeasure by excluding critical organizations from meetings.

> Interviewer: Did the White House signal that?
>
> Torres: Oh, yeah. Of course!
>
> Interviewer: They signaled that if you push on them, then you'll lose access?
>
> Torres: They don't say exactly that but we know when the next meeting, they don't invite me, or the next meeting, they move to a different strategy. We know that. They don't need to say it.[15]

Mr. Torres went on to note that if the movement pushed too hard on the president, it would not only lose access but also lose the president as an ally. "The president is deporting our families and our people, and he had the power to stop that. . . . That was the conversation back and forth about, don't touch the President because if you touch him, we lose a partner, we lose an ally."[16]

Concerns about damaging their relationship with the White House stifled public criticism of the White House (see table 8.3). National leaders, such as the NCLR and the CCC, didn't begin to criticize the Obama administration forcefully until 2014, after it became clear that comprehensive immigration reform would not pass in the House, and they pivoted to enforcement reform. Criticism of the White House, when there was any at all, was tepid. For instance, in response to the Department of Homeland Security's 2009 announcement that it would enhance enforcement measures, the NCLR was mildly reproachful, saying, "Our feelings are mixed at best. We understand the need for sensible enforcement, but that does not mean expanding programs that often lead to civil rights violations."[17] Another advocate expressed mixed feelings about the White House: "I'm trying to reconcile the stated be-

TABLE 8.3. Public criticism of executive branch and Immigration and Customs Enforcement by advocacy organizations

	2009	2010	2011	2012	2013	2014	Total
Barack Obama	0	2	2	4	2	24	34
Generic White House	1	2	0	0	0	5	8
ICE	1	4	2	2	1	0	10
Total	**2**	**8**	**4**	**6**	**3**	**29**	**52**

Source: LexisNexis.

lief of this president when he was a candidate, what he has said publicly—as recently as a naturalization ceremony last month—and what his actions are."[18] And still others provided support for the administration. CHIRLA, for example, stressed, "There is ambivalence about the president, where there really should be none."[19]

Leading organizations maintained that their relationship with the Obama administration was complex and tense. They expressed their dismay to the White House in behind-the-scenes-meetings and occasionally through protests. According to the director of the CCC, the national leadership had an adversarial relationship with the Obama administration.

> It became clear to us that the administration was not really serious about prioritizing immigration. We made a decision at the end of 2009 to organize a march, which ultimately drew 150,000 or so people to the National Mall on March 21, 2010. I think that freaked the White House out. It resulted in a meeting the President called with immigration movement leaders. I opened the meeting and there were a number of others who chimed in saying that his deportation record was becoming a moral catastrophe. He needed to both fix the enforcement problem and put his muscle behind moving legislation. Those were our kind of demands. . . . It was an incredibly tense meeting, but it was because that march was coming and they feared what the message would be of that march if they didn't meet the needs of the community or at least appear to do so. That was really, to me, the beginning of a long, challenging, up and down relationship between the president and the movement.[20]

The CCC and other leading organizations certainly faced constraints because of their proximity to the White House, but this did not necessarily stop them from registering their grievances with the administration.

Certain organizations were beholden to the Obama administration, but other organizations were not. For organizations such as NDLON, proximity to the lives of some of the most precarious immigrants motivated them to take a more critical stance, and the lack of access provided them with the freedom to do so. NDLON launched a campaign (Not One More) in 2013 that centered on denouncing President Obama—the deporter in chief—and demanding an end to mass deportations (see chapter 6).

Stuck Between a Rock and a Hard Spot

Regional organizations were trusted allies of the national leadership, but they were brought into national coalitions because of their legitimacy among local members and allies. This legitimacy allowed regional organizations to mobilize local support for national campaigns. For instance, national organizations called on regionals to mobilize immigrants to different actions and to bring some to Washington to tell their stories. The national prominence of regionals, consequently, depended partly on their abilities to retain good standing among undocumented immigrants and grassroots groups. The need to maintain local legitimacy made regional organizations accountable to the grassroots in a way the national organizations were not. "From our perspective," remarked Lawrence Benito, the director of the ICIRR, "we're a local organization and we got to do what we're accountable to our members. We couldn't necessarily care about access. We want to see results but that is part of the game."[21]

The national leadership and the grassroots, however, did not always see eye to eye on strategy, priorities, and messaging. The difficulty of being positioned between the two was exacerbated in 2013, when many local activists and smaller organizations were drawn to NDLON's Not One More campaign. Regional organizations were pitted between national leadership and grassroots allies. Mr. Benito stressed the difficulty of striking a balance between the two campaigns.

> Things can get blurry because locally there are community leaders and organizations that are aligned with Not One More. So, it wasn't like we walked in lock step with everything our national allies tell us to do. For the most part we are as much aligned as possible but there are moments where we also have to respond to what our folks locally are telling us. There were moments in which we were out in front of our national allies. Because Obama was from Chicago, we had a particular role to play.[22]

ICIRR aligned with the Not One More campaign but continued to maintain its strong ties to the national leadership. The organization launched an action directed at the future Obama presidential library in Chicago. As Mr. Benito said, "We had actions that said, if you want to build a library here then we would like to contribute to an exhibit called the Deporter in Chief exhibit."[23] The leadership was concerned about the aggressive tactics, but that did not stifle the ICIRR. Mr. Benito remarked,

> D.C. folks were a little bit squeamish about having to answer for one of the FIRM organizations that had adopted a much stronger message. At the same time, I think they realized we need to see approaches to making this work and that was the role that we embraced, a little bit later than the Not One More folks but we came to that conclusion earlier than the rest of the field.[24]

ICIRR was not invited back to the White House after its campaign.

Regional members of the large national coalitions and campaigns (for example, FIRM, RIFA, and A4C) therefore found themselves in a contradictory position. They depended on support from local immigrant communities and grassroots groups, but they also depended on their good standing in national networks for information, financial support, media coverage, and status. Criticism of the White House could result in pressure from national organizations and the likely loss of access to the White House. But not criticizing could and often did lead to the accusation that these regional groups were selling out to the "nonprofit industrial complex." Such a reputation would in turn undermine the grassroots legitimacy of regional organizations. These organizations, therefore, were in a conflicted position in this power hierarchy. Moving too much against the White House could cost valued access to the highest levels of national power. Moving too little could cost the organization its local legitimacy. All the major regional organizations had to contend with their contradictory political position and the trade-offs of moving in one direction over another.

Access and Conflict

Economic and political capital flowed into the immigrant rights movement, and the Obama administration opened the White House doors to immigrant rights groups while closing them to anti-immigrant organizations. If there ever was a golden age of access for the immigrant rights movement, it was during the Obama administration. Access grew, but it was not distributed equally to all organizations in the field. Larger, wealthier, national organizations in DC had better chances of gaining high-quality access to the White House.

The uneven distribution of access resulted in a relatively stable hierarchy dominated by a fluid yet core group of organizations. The leading core was more likely to keep its strategic focus set on the halls of national power. The continued focus on national political institutions generated important benefits, such as money and greater media exposure. Access, however, also came with trade-offs. Strong ties with the White House restricted the abilities of organizations to exert pressure on federal officeholders. A hard critique of the White House could result in ejection from the table, which would imperil access to other sources of capital. Well-connected organizations therefore had little incentive to target the Obama administration with criticism and strong incentive to direct their ire at congressional Republicans.

Organizations such as NDLON were positioned differently. They had almost no access to the White House and were accountable to some of the most precarious immigrants in the country—day laborers. Their members were the first targets of enforcement and deportation efforts. To maintain their legitimacy with their members, NDLON was compelled to take a more aggressive stance against the Obama White House and had the resources to do so. Given the position of this organization and its allies, a more critical and radical position made strategic sense. The regional organizations were stuck between the reformist flank and the left flank of the movement. They continued to be rooted in immigrant communities, but they also reaped the benefits of White House access. The regional organizations faced pressure to follow conflicting strategic lines, placing them in a state of perpetual turmoil. Thus, access not only constrained the abilities of the movement to target the White House with its grievances but also exacerbated conflicts between the various factions of the movement. As the administration was ramping up its mass deportation efforts, the movement's voice was partially muffled and increasingly divided in its stance.

CHAPTER 9

Making Immigrants American

IN EARLIER YEARS of immigrant rights activism, local activists drew from various framings—liberal national, territorial personhood, and postnational—of national citizenship to make their arguments . They deployed these framings differently according to the political situation. When pushing against police repression, they often employed a territorial personhood frame by stressing the constitutionally protected rights of immigrants. When pushing for a worker center, they often stressed immigrants' contributions to and affiliation with American communities. Rather than using a single master frame, early advocates employed a mishmash of arguments that varied across contexts, situations, and groups of people. This kind of flexible framing allowed them to generate messages that were tailored to the sensibilities of different target audiences.

Entry into the national field precipitated the selection of one master frame (liberal nationalism) over others (territorial personhood and postnationalism). Following the failure to pass immigration reform in 2007, the leadership initiated a broad campaign to change how Americans viewed immigrants. They set out to generate a disciplined message that would resonate with the hearts and minds of average Americans. Liberal nationalism provided advocates with the language, ideas, sentiments, and narratives to effectively construct a message of immigrant deservingness. America was, they argued, a nation of immigrants who possessed essential attributes that made them deserving of membership. Just as important, leading advocates felt compelled to counter the arguments of their adversaries. If adversaries maintained that immigrants were lazy freeloaders, advocates argued that they were hardworking contributors. Point-by-point counterframing reinforced the movement's embrace of liberal nationalism. Thus, efforts to craft a resonant message and counter the frames of their adversaries drove leading advocates to elevate one master frame and suppress alternatives out of fear of generating inconsistences, dissonance, or blowback.

Generating potent frames was not simply a matter of designing strong talking points. It required a sophisticated discursive infrastructure to research target audiences, construct resonant messages and stories, and ensure that the countless people involved in a movement employ messaging in a similar way. The leading organizations and their funders invested in such an infrastructure. It was a complex web that trained countless activists through workshops and special events. The infrastructure ensured that the centrally produced discourses would all be delivered to the public in the same way. Thousands of different people would use the same manuals, trainings, and language to make their claims in the public sphere.

Entering the national battle over citizenship restricted what frames were used, how they were used, and who was in charge of producing and directing their use in public debate. This chapter draws on the immigration-reform newspaper database (see the appendix for further detail), using it to identify prominent voices and their positions on different issues. In addition to this, the chapter also uses Open Society documents, documents from organizations and coalitions, and interviews with key stakeholders.

Liberalizing Citizenship

The mainstream movement invested enormous resources in communication. Frank Sharry, the director of the National Immigration Forum before going on to America's Voice, assumed a leading role in devising the communication strategy. His organizations performed surveys, polls, and focus groups to identify the political predilections of the national public. "In the middle of the 2000's, the National Immigration Forum probably had done most of the messaging research," according to Rich Stolz, then-director of RIFA. America's Voice also worked with several organizations to assess the impacts of messages on different demographics. "To evaluate the impact of the economic crisis on the immigration debate," one document reported, "polling and focus groups are underway by numerous organizations, including America's Voice, Leadership Conference on Civil Rights, and Opportunity Agenda."[1] By mapping out the norms and discursive preferences of the public, Mr. Sharry and his colleagues developed a series of messages and talking points designed to generate support from the public and national politicians.

The leadership designed a communication campaign intended to resonate with the nationalist norms of the broader public. On August 25, 2008, Open Society issued a memo on the comeback of the immigrant rights movement.[2] The memorandum reported that "the goal of the new campaign is to turn the tide of public debate and to develop policy solutions for broad immigration reform rooted in the American values of earned citizenship, the rule of law, and the promise of the American Dream."[3] The leadership believed that "the tide of public debate" could be turned by making a direct link to national values and emphasizing "earned citizenship." The memo went on to outline the five messaging themes for the upcoming RIFA campaign.

> There are five key themes that are emerging as priorities for the campaign: 1) *Who are we as a country?* Will we be defined by our ideals and the promise of the American Dream for all, or by the fear, intolerance, and the extremism of those pushing mass deportation?; 2) *Who are immigrants?* Immigrants are workers, families, taxpayers, citizens, soldiers, people of faith, Americans in all but paperwork; 3) *What policies work?* Mass deportation won't work, practical solutions including smart enforcement and earned citizenship will; 4) *What are the politics?* Anti-immigrant forces make noise but don't turn elections; immigrants vote on this issue and do influence elections; 5) *Who and what will be helped by broad immigration reform?* American workers, local communities, immigrant families, local economies, and the rule of law (emphasis in original).[4]

"Who are we as a country?" asked the authors of the memorandum. They responded by revising American values and traditions. America was reinvented as generous and open to immigrants. It was celebrated as a virtuous and cosmopolitan nation. Its core values centered on fairness, openness, and equal opportunity.[5] "The United States has always been viewed as a safe haven for those fleeing persecution," according to one RIFA document. The country's past was shaped by immigrants, and it remained open to strangers from different lands. "The United States," according to RIFA, "has a long and revered immigrant past."[6] The American nation was recast as welcoming and immigrants as "Americans in all but paperwork." There were no critiques of the nation as an essentially inegalitarian political community[7] or of citizenship's racist historical origins.[8] The leaders reimagined the nation as the cornerstone of liberal, multicultural citizenship while remaining silent on facts that would deviate from the message.

Advocates also felt compelled to counter the stigmatizing frames of anti-immigrant forces. In an analysis of past failures, advocates and funders studied how anti-immigrant forces won the battle in 2007. They determined that "proponents fought mainly a policy battle while the opposition mounted a political and cultural fight. Anti-immigrant forces garnered greater media attention, which succeeded in intimidating lawmakers on both sides of the aisle."[9] Leading advocates drew a clear lesson: the fight for immigrant rights had to be fought on cultural terms. For decades, anti-immigrant groups argued that immigrants were a threat because of their illegality and their alleged parasitical relationship to the nation.[10] These arguments drew on the stereotype of the Mexican immigrant as irredeemably other, someone who is dependent on welfare and who breaks the law. These negative attributes made immigrants ineligible for legal membership in the nation. Movement leaders countered by discursively transforming immigrants into a model minority. Immigrants, advocates argued, were deeply integrated in the country. They possessed an extraordinary work ethic and had the same family values as "normal" Americans. Their assimilation, utility, and family values made them deserving of citizenship (and therefore rights) in the United States. Rather than being a threat to all things American, immigrants were praised for being the realization of core national values.

Advocates often highlighted the cultural and moral attributes of immigrants, but they also stressed their economic contribution to the country. Liberal think tanks generated data that was consistent with the economic contribution frame. Open Society, for instance, funded a number of organizations to generate such reports, including the Economic Policy Institute, the Migration Policy Institute, and the American Immigration Law Foundation's Immigration Policy Center. A 2009 Open Society document stated, "Access to original research on the impact of immigration on the economy, and the economic benefits of legalization, is critical to the campaign's efforts to counter the growing influence of the oft-cited anti-immigration researchers."[11] Research was viewed as part of the movement's efforts to counter the stigmatizing frames of their adversaries. The document went on to provide a detailed outline of the specific contributions by immigrants to the national economy.

> With OSI support, MPI [Migration Policy Institute] will produce detailed policy recommendations on how the United States should rethink its immigra-

tion policy in the context of the current economic turmoil and future long-term trends, taking into account growing income inequality, concerns about US competitiveness, uncertain demand for migrants at all skill levels, and demographic and technological changes.[12]

Framing immigrants as economic contributors grew increasingly important over the movement's history. Coalition documents from 2007 stressed "hard-working" immigrants but discussed their economic contributions in vague terms.[13] Later documents benefited from think-tank research, providing advocates with exact numbers concerning the benefits of legalization and naturalization. One fact sheet from the Alliance for Citizenship (A4C) stated, "If the 8.5 million legal permanent residents who are eligible to naturalize did so, they would see an 8 percent to 11 percent boost in wages, leading to a $21 billion to $45 billion cumulative increase in wages, which would then ripple through the economy, creating significant gains overall."[14] Legalization and naturalization would, according to the A4C document, "generate $1.5 trillion in cumulative GDP over 10 years."[15] Immigrants had been reframed as the savior of the American Dream. "Reflected throughout this work," another Open Society report noted, "is an attempt to connect equal opportunity concerns across issues and constituencies and to demonstrate how integrating immigrants into the mainstream of society will lift all boats."[16]

Moral and economistic rationales combined to make a single powerful argument for immigrant deservingness. The Alliance for Citizenship wrote that "a reform package that includes a path to citizenship makes economic sense and is true to our ideals as a nation."[17] The cultural attributes of immigrants and their contributions to the economic vitality of the country made them deserving of membership. Citizenship needed to be earned by displaying the qualities that made a person a de facto American.[18] One document described the goals of the RIFA campaign as follows: "The goal of the new campaign is to turn the tide of public debate and to develop policy solutions for broad immigration reform rooted in the American values of earned citizenship, the rule of law, and the promise of the American Dream."[19]

Overly restrictive policies were said to stand in conflict with the country's core principles. FIRM said, "Failure to protect these fundamental rights goes against the core values of a democracy, and, therefore, the United States. For the benefit of everyone, and not just immigrants, these basic rights must be restored and protected."[20] Anti-immigrant policies and discourses conflicted with who we are as a people. A memo from Opportunity Agenda stated,

"Harsh policies that force people into the shadows are not consistent with our values. Some anti-immigrant forces want to ban undocumented immigrant families from renting apartments or sending their kids to school. These kinds of policies are unworkable and are not consistent with our values."[21] The continued exclusion of 11 million undocumented immigrants was wrong because it barred people who deserved a fair shake, and it restricted the country's capacity to reap their full economic value. During the 2013 battle for immigration reform, the executive director of the Florida Immigrant Coalition, a close ally of A4C, argued that the denial of citizenship to qualifying immigrants was "un-American" because it created a second-class citizen with diminished rights and a precarious status. "We either have a path to citizenship or a path to hell," she claimed. "To codify a person who lives in this country but will never have an opportunity for citizenship creates a second class. It seems completely un-American,"[22] she further argued. National values were used as the metric to evaluate the morality of the country's immigration policies.

The leadership recognized that a nation—no matter how open and cosmopolitan—needed borders. Borders for their reimagined and socially just nation merely needed to be fairer and more transparent. According to one FIRM document, a border strategy should emphasize "training, accountability and competency that rejects militarizing the border with Mexico."[23] The question was not if we should have borders but how to make borders more consistent with the nation's values. An A4C document argued that there is a need to "ensure enforcement measures to protect American and immigrant workers, advance due process and fair treatment, and that are consistent with American values."[24] The statement recognized the protective functions of border enforcement but stressed that enforcement needed to be brought into line with the values of the nation. Far from imagining citizenship beyond the bordered nation, leading advocates proposed reforms that were well within the confines of a liberal yet exclusionary nation-state.

Thus nationalism, albeit a liberal, pluralistic version, was the grammar through which claims were made. The Opportunity Agenda—a project closely aligned with the national leadership—issued a so-called messaging memorandum in 2011 titled "Real Solutions, American Values: A Winning Narrative on Immigration." It stated,

> Over the past three years, pro-immigration advocates and communications experts have developed and pushed out a pro-immigrant narrative designed to move hearts, minds, and policy. With the president revisiting comprehen-

sive immigration reform, it is crucial that we continue this drumbeat so that our echo chamber of values and solutions that work for all of us reverberates in the national conversation.[25]

A discursive strategy centered on American values would, leading advocates believed, help turn the tide of public debate by moving hearts and minds. Policy could then be developed to open the gates to undocumented immigrants and integrate them into the nation. Although the leadership of the movement constructed a compelling argument for why immigrants deserved national membership, it reinforced the idea that citizenship should be given only to those who had earned admission to the nation-state. Those lacking cultural, economic, and moral attributes would, by default, be deemed less deserving of citizenship and, by extension, basic rights.

Fixing the Broken System with Comprehensive Immigration Reform

How would undocumented immigrants actually become members of the national community? As noted in the previous chapters, comprehensive immigration reform was introduced by government officials as a way to fix the broken system. Early talk of comprehensive reform surfaced from bilateral talks between Mexico and the United States in 2001, but the talks were derailed after the terrorist attacks of September 11. The White House and its congressional allies revived immigration reform discussions in 2005, resulting in the Secure America and Orderly Immigration Act (also known as the McCain-Kennedy Bill). This bipartisan measure, strongly supported by the Bush White House, addressed several problems simultaneously. By rationalizing access to needed immigrant workers, the government would be in a much stronger position to monitor and control foreigners residing in the country. Legalizing deserving immigrants would take pressure off the border, which would enhance the government's capacities to combat undeserving immigrants. Immigration reform for government officials was first and foremost a method to exert greater state control over national borders.

Before the period 2005–2006, proimmigrant organizations (that is, nonprofits, unions, and religious groups) argued for reforms, but these consisted mostly of piecemeal measures such as improving the guest workers program, Temporary Protected Status, and the DREAM Act and granting refugee status to various national groups. During the first half of the 2000s, the concept of comprehensive immigration reform had not solidified in the political imaginaries or discourses of most civil society organizations. Following 2006, however, there was a sharp increase in claims for comprehensive reform and a decrease in claims for piecemeal reforms. This overlapped with government efforts to push for immigration reform and the growing consolidation of a national movement leadership. There was thus a strong preference for comprehensive immigration reform even if it meant forgoing more obtainable piecemeal reforms.

The supporters of comprehensive immigration reform believed it to be the most rational solution available to the country. The immigration system was, according to one FIRM document, "broken" because of the "mismatch between outdated policies and the economic realities of our country."[26] The divergence between past policies and current realities violated American values and denied the country the full economic benefits of hardworking immigrants. Bad policies had resulted in a plethora of short-term fixes across the system, which had generated a "patchwork of mismanaged and broken policies and programs"[27] that inflicted huge burdens on immigrant communities and high costs on the country. The problem was the poor design of policies and institutions used to regulate citizenship rather than the exclusionary nature of national citizenship itself. According to the Opportunity Agenda memorandum, "We need workable solutions that uphold our nation's values, and move us forward together. We need to fix our system so that individuals who contribute and participate can live in the United States legally. That means creating a system where undocumented immigrants can register, get legal, learn English and contribute fully."[28] Only a big, exhaustive law would be capable of "matching institutions with American values. The nation-state did not need to be abandoned or its borders torn down. Reform was not revolution. The system just needed reform to make "our immigration policy . . . consistent with reality."[29]

Advocates stressed that comprehensive reform was pragmatic, realistic, and supported by the public. In a 2013 document, A4C claimed, "Polls have shown that the majority of the American people want Congress to provide a *sensible* solution to our nation's broken immigration system, including a path to citizenship" (emphasis added).[30] Terms such as *sensible, rational, reasonable, realistic,* and *workable* assumed great prominence in coalition documents. National leaders had a reform preference that set the agenda of the immigrant rights movement. Left-wing alternatives (for example, stopping all deportations) to comprehensive reform were mostly ignored, and piecemeal measures were disqualified as Band-Aids and short-term fixes. Anti-immigrant policy measures were likewise denounced as "irrational," "impossible," and "un-American." Given the alternatives on the left and right, comprehensive reform was framed as the sensible, pragmatic, and fully American way forward.

By 2010, comprehensive immigration reform was virtually hegemonic among immigrant rights advocates, but several organizations questioned its primacy. As noted in previous chapters, enforcement-reform organizations and radical Dreamers questioned the movement's dogged embrace of comprehensive immigration reform. Another organization, the Mexican American Legal Defense and Education Fund (MALDEF), was one of the most important organizations to put forth an alternative piecemeal strategy. Tom Saenz became its director in 2009, a period when RIFA was consolidating itself as the undisputed leader of the immigrant rights movement. Mr. Saenz remarked, "I wasn't sure what made sense for us." At the time, Mr. Saenz sat for an interview with the Associated Press. He identified the limits of comprehensive immigration reform and embraced what he called a "down payment" strategy. This strategy consisted of four different piecemeal reforms that would be pushed as separate bills. Because these reforms were smaller and had more bipartisan support, they had a higher likelihood of passage when they were introduced separately rather than put together in one large, comprehensive package. Such smaller reforms included the Development, Relief, and Education for Alien Minors Act (the DREAM Act) and the Agricultural Job Opportunities, Benefits and Security Act (AgJOBS)—bills that would provide undocumented immigrant youth and farm workers a path to legal status. A *San Francisco Gate* article reported Mr. Saenz as arguing that

> "the immigration debate has been coarsened, and President Obama is apparently trying to avoid controversy. . . . There seems to be a perception that (immigration) is somehow the third rail of politics." . . . He said immigrants' rights supporters have de-emphasized some lesser measures while concentrating on their main goal, and it might be wise to refocus on those [lesser] measures in the coming year.[31]

According to Mr. Saenz, there was no reason why immigration advocates couldn't push for small "down payments" on their way toward a larger comprehensive measure.

Many of the leading RIFA organizations feared that pursuing the different reforms rather than a single comprehensive package would pull organizations in different directions. The leadership also believed that the down-payment strategy would motivate important elements of the comprehensive immigration reform coalition (youth, farmer workers, and growers) to leave the coalition once they received legal status. Many reform advocates in Congress shared this perception. In response to efforts to pass AgJOBS in 2010, a newspaper reported, "There's also resistance in the Congressional Hispanic Caucus, many of whose leaders fear that passing an agriculture bill now would pull a key group—the grower lobby—out of the campaign for comprehensive immigration reform."[32] Ali Noorani, the executive director of NIF, argued directly against the down-payment strategy by saying, "The environment, the way we've seen it . . . makes us increasingly confident that we're going to see comprehensive immigration reform." He went on to suggest that "instead of a down payment, we should be talking about a major investment."[33]

RIFA initially reached out to Saenz in 2009 but cut contact once he advocated a down-payment strategy. "Then, they lost interest when I did the Associated Press interview. . . . I departed apparently very seriously from the established orthodoxy of the coalition. At the time, the message was comprehensive or nothing," Mr. Saenz said. Then he added, "You know I would be told by a third party that, in your event I hope you won't say down payment. Then the inquiries about what role we would play in RIFA ended. . . . It was quite clear after that that I had broken the rules as it were. Left the circle of trust, if we were ever there. We got marginalized."[34] MALDEF, one of the country's oldest and most important Latina/o civil rights organizations, was pushed to the margins of the movement's leadership circle.

Disciplining Voice

For the leadership, discipline and consistency were absolutely necessary to effectively deliver their message to the public and to national politicians. But creating a movement and running campaigns with thousands of different activists presented a big challenge to presenting a consistent voice. The leadership produced an infrastructure to disseminate claims to thousands of activists across the country. Such an infrastructure would make it possible to diffuse talking points and messages and train activists to use them in a uniform way. The repetition of similar claims and messages by many different actors would, leaders hoped, create an echo chamber in the public sphere.

The CCC and its closest allies, including the National Immigration Forum, America's Voice, and the National Council of La Raza, assumed leadership in creating the discursive infrastructure. They staffed leading positions, provided material infrastructure, invested heavily in building and strengthening organizations across the country, and oversaw hundreds of communication trainings. These leading actors used meetings to lay the foundations for RIFA and A4C. They sponsored or cosponsored a variety of events, protests, workshops, trainings, and meetings that connected national, regional, and grassroots organizations. These events were designed to connect activists to one another, strengthen bonds, and set the agenda and strategic priorities of locals in ways that aligned with the national leadership. These were essential activities for diffusing centrally produced discourse across a geographically, organizationally, ideologically, and socially diverse activist network.

The CCC modeled its trainings and workshops on a program devised by Marshall Ganz. Ganz was a veteran community organizer, an architect of the grassroots strategy for Barack Obama's 2008 presidential campaign, and a senior lecturer at Harvard University. One Open Society document recommended funding Mr. Ganz and his associates.

> Ganz began his career working with Cesar Chavez and was one of the primary architects of the Obama organizing strategy. We recommend providing resources to these organizers and other innovators to develop a series of workshops for our grantees, especially organizations well-placed to expand public participation in policy reform efforts. We could target this training in regions where we are already funding significant clusters of advocates to ensure that their work has maximum impact at the state and federal levels. [35]

Marshall Ganz worked closely with the CCC and the New Organizing Institute to develop a program to train grassroots activists across the country to support comprehensive immigration reform.[36]

They devised a top-down, centralized training model. Master Trainers[37] worked for the large professional organizations such as the CCC. They trained Lead Trainers from organizations around the country who would then organize regional trainings and workshops. They were also expected to reach out and recruit people in their immediate communities. The Lead Trainers would then train all new recruits to become Lead Trainers in their own right, and these new trainers would subsequently organize their own training sessions. The process of building a grassroots base involved training participants in how to be leaders and to extend the movement's reach from the center to small communities around the country.

An organizer's job is to reach out and find leaders in your community who can help you recruit and coordinate others. These leaders will be the backbone of your local campaign. You must be able to trust them to delegate responsibility to other dedicated, reliable people, and to follow through on commitments. You may be the leader in the middle, or part of a leadership team in the middle, guiding volunteer efforts and being held accountable for outcomes, but you will be deeply reliant on your relationships with others for success.[38]

Local organizing teams replicated the divisions of labor found in national coalitions in order to avoid "duplicating and running into each other."[39] The training model was referred to as a snowflake approach because it was mimetic, creating grassroots teams across the country with the same structures and functions. These teams were then tied to one another through the Master Trainer located in a national organization.

The movement's leadership partnered with regional organizations, most of which were FIRM members, to sponsor training events and workshops. Regional partners reached down to connect to their own grassroots allies. According to the director of the Illinois Coalition for Immigrant and Refugee Rights (ICIRR), his organization served as the local representative of the national movement. "In Illinois, we were the only FIRM organization. Still are, so our member organizations and allies in the faith community and labor community basically defer to us on what was the strategy."[40] ICIRR and other regionals served as local relays of the national movement, disseminating centrally produced discourses to activist communities around the country. Reporting on its Democracy Boot Camp held in 2008 (cosponsored by FIRM and ICIRR), ICIRR reported that it had

trained 63 people from 16 states, representing 43 different immigrant rights organizations. A total of 45 of the participants were Latino (67 percent); 6 were white; 3 were Korean; 3 were Arab/Muslim; and 1 each were African American, Chinese American and Filipino (3 unknown). The group was two-thirds female and one-third male, and over two-thirds (67 percent) were in their 20's, with another 5 percent being under 20.[41]

ICIRR assumed a lead role in organizing the event, but the CCC ran many, if not most, of the actual training sessions. Nine of the ten workshops and sessions held on the first day were organized or coorganized by CCC staff members. Regional organizations held other training events in localities across the country. CASA Maryland, for instance, worked with the CCC to reach out to local organizations in the DC area. Its director remembered that "we trained in the Washington, DC area. That was like 40 various small nonprofit organizations. Our role was to make sure that they work with us pretty much with the same message."[42]

The proliferation of organizing teams was designed to have a "cascading" effect in targeted regions. Marshall Ganz and Emily Lin described how the process unfolded in Florida.

> In this first workshop, the presentation, facilitation, and coaching were provided by experienced trainers, most of whom were former students. Three weeks later, the fifteen Florida trainees had applied their learning to organize another three-day workshop of 175 young people who, deployed as thirty-six leadership teams, organized fourteen actions across Florida in which 1350 people participated to launch the campaign. By the second training, three of the fifteen original trainees had begun serving as presenters, five as coaches, and all in key leadership roles. Colorado followed a similar pattern. Encouraged by this success, a second "train the trainers" workshop was held in Washington, DC, in November, attended by one hundred young people from five more states: North Carolina, California, Nevada, New York, and Ohio. One workshop of thirty young people at the end of August had launched a twelve-state "movement building network" that was the backbone of a sustained campaign, culminating in a demonstration of some 200,000 in Washington, DC.[43]

This model was designed to extend the reach of the national leadership deep into localities around the country. Each designated leader served as another extension point of the national network. The model provided national leaders with a method to achieve a high level of cohesion and control over the language and conduct of geographically dispersed activists. It enabled thousands of activists and advocates to speak with one centrally produced and managed voice.

Leaders believed that the most effective struggles were value-based campaigns rather than issue-based ones.[44] Whereas issue-based campaigns reinforced "silos" between groups, value-based campaigns enabled people to reach across boundaries by tapping into common morals. Ganz believed that stories were the most effective vehicle to deliver value claims to the public.

> Because values are experienced—and communicated—emotionally, they are the source of the moral energy—courage, hope, and solidarity—that it takes to risk learning new things, exploring new ways. And because values that in-

spire action are communicated as narrative, each person can learn to inspire others by learning to tell their own story, a story of the experience they share with others, and a story of an urgent challenge that demands action—a public narrative.[45]

The public narrative, Ganz went on to argue, "can help us link our own calling to that of our community to a call to action now—a story of self, a story of us, and a story of now."[46] Finally, he stated that "as a practice, it [the public narrative] can be structured, learned, and shared."[47] Stories consequently became the preferred vehicle to use in communicating the shared values of undocumented immigrants with the American public.[48]

The immigrant rights movement made extensive use of collective storytelling.[49] One training manual explained, "Stories draw on our emotions and show our values in action, helping us feel what matters, rather than just thinking about or telling others what matters. Because stories allow us to express our values not as abstract principles, but as lived experience, they have the power to move others."[50] Each individual was trained to structure his or her story in an identical way: start with a morally upstanding character, present the character with a challenge followed by a choice, and finish with an outcome that conveys a compelling moral message. Training sessions consisted of a general introduction to the importance of storytelling, instructions on how to construct emotionally compelling stories, group analyses of stories by leaders, and small-group exercises that permitted new trainees to construct their own stories (that is, their stories of self).

Training manuals stressed that discipline and unity were necessary for achieving campaign goals. One manual maintained that disorganization resulted in drift, passivity, confusion, reactivity, and inaction.[51] By contrast, organization and discipline enabled purpose, participation, understanding, initiative and change. The leadership, therefore, expressed concerns with the risks posed by discursive diversity and disorganization.[52] They developed methods to ensure unity by disciplining individuals to merge their personal stories, ideas, and utterances with the central message and narrative of the movement. The micromanagement of individual speech and conduct would, the leadership believed, help overcome disorganization and allow the movement to achieve purpose, participation, and change.

This discursive infrastructure enabled national organizations to connect and steer the strategies, conduct, and discourses of countless activists across the country. It permitted the national leadership to reach deep into the immigrant grassroots and ensure strategic and discursive conformity. Thousands of activists were provided a common language to think through complex issues on immigration, citizenship, and reform. Rich Stolz, the director of RIFA, remembered, "By the time we launched Reform Immigration for America that campaign became the infrastructure to basically distribute that messaging across all the different organizations that were participating. There was a fair amount of message discipline across the campaign."[53] Disciplined messaging allowed many different actors, whether or not they were directly associated with the leadership, to replicate the central frames of the movement. This level of discipline was, according to the director of CASA Maryland, important for moving public opinion.

> For us, it was very important that we can move as many people as we can with the same message, as many people as we can all around the nation, communicating comprehensive immigration reform, communicating citizenship for all, communicating the contributions of our families and our community in the economy, in the culture, in the social fabric of this nation. For us, the communication strategy is an essential component of anything to pass immigration reform.[54]

Thus, the strong belief in generating a unified and disciplined voice, underpinned by a common story, resulted in a vertically integrated and rationalized organizational structure that enabled the center (that is, the leaders of the national coalitions) to steer activities, words, and even emotions in countless localities across the country. With thousands of different actors communicating the same message in the same way, the leadership hoped to create an echo chamber in which their central message would reverberate loudly in the public sphere.

Representing Immigrants

The national leadership helped craft the representations of the movement and ensure that activists would employ these frames in very similar ways. The leadership also assumed an important role in actually employing these frames in the public sphere. A relatively small group of organizations dominated the representations of immigrants and of arguments for immigration reform in the national media. They developed strong relationships with producers, editors, and reporters, effectively becoming the go-to advocacy organizations on the issue of immigration. "The Communications Pillar," according to one

Open Society document, "is working through mainstream and ethnic television, radio, online and print media."[55] By 2013, the mainstream immigrant rights movement's media prowess had become well established. Another document reported on the campaign's media success.

> A4C and its member organizations have generated approximately 720 unique media hits in both English-language and Spanish-language media outlets. This number includes more than 60 TV segments in national and local markets, including key swing districts. A4C's spokespeople are quoted regularly in top outlets including: Associated Press, Reuters, Bloomberg, the *New York Times*, the *Washington Post*, the *Wall Street Journal*, *Huffington Post*, *Politico*, the *Guardian*, Univision, and Telemundo, among many others.[56]

The movement had transformed into a communications powerhouse.

Of 5,422 claims included in the immigrant-reform newspaper database, nongovernmental organizations (pro- and anti-immigrant nonprofit organizations, unions, religious organizations, and businesses) accounted for 32.7 percent of claims made between 2000 and 2014. Nonprofit organizations (pro- and anti-immigrant) were the most prominent among these. Religious organizations, especially those associated with the Catholic Church, were moderately active throughout the time span. The prominence of unions declined relative to the growing importance of nonprofit organizations. Although there were year-to-year swings, levels of influence remained relatively steady over this period of time.

When examining only nonprofits, unions, and religious organizations (and excluding businesses), proimmigrant claims were more prominent than anti-immigrant ones (see figure 9.1). Whereas pro- and anti-immigrant claims enjoyed similar levels of influence in the beginning of the decade, the gap between them grew substantially starting in the middle of the decade. By 2014, 71 percent of all claims were made by organizations favorable to immigration. There were 305 proimmigrant civil society organizations (including nonprofits, religious groups, and unions but excluding business) that made 962 claims. Ten percent of these organizations accounted for 48 percent of all claims made between 2000 and 2014 (see figure 9.2). In 2005, the top 10 percent accounted for 30 percent of all claims made that year. By 2014, the share of the top 10 percent more than doubled, accounting for 62 percent of all claims. Thus, the growing prominence of proimmigrant claim and the concentration of discursive power by leading organizations overlapped directly with the consolidation of the immigrant rights movement.

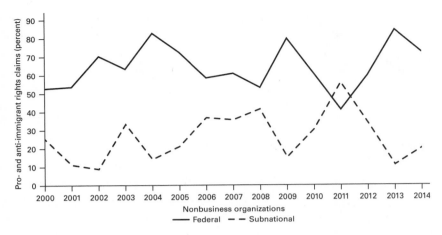

FIGURE 9.1. Pro- and anti-immigrant rights claims (percent) by nonbusiness organizations. Source: LexisNexis.

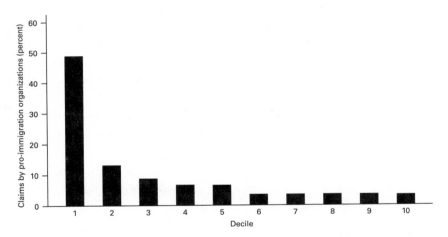

FIGURE 9.2. Percentage of claims by proimmigration organizations per decile, 2000–2014. Source: LexisNexis.

The established DC organizations were an important part of the leadership pack, but so too were national unions (the AFL-CIO and the SEIU) and established regional partners (for example, CHIRLA, ICIRR, and NYIC). The most vocal immigrant rights organization was United We Dream (UWD), established in 2009 by Dreamers with the support of the National Immigration Law Center. The organization's prominence is remarkable considering its short existence. Only 1 claim can be attributed to UWD in 2009, placing it on the margins of the organizational field that year. From that time, UWD became the most prominent organization in the proimmigrant camp, accounting for 17.6 percent of all claims made by proimmigrant organizations in 2014.

When comparing proimmigrant organizations on the basis of geographic location (national organizations headquartered in Washington, DC, national organizations outside DC, and local/regional organizations), we see that national organizations in DC started their surge to dominance in 2010 (see figure 9.3). At the beginning of the century, national organizations *outside* DC and local and regional organizations enjoyed greater prominence. The mega marches of 2006 appeared to have boosted the position of local and regional organizations, largely dominating public claims until the end of the decade. Their prominence collapsed in 2010 as national organizations inside and outside Washington surged. National organizations inside DC sat on the margins of public debate in 2005 and 2006, but this changed after 2010 when they experienced accelerated growth and surpassed local and regional organizations.

When assessing the people who have assumed a prominent role in representing immigrants, Frank Sharry of the National Immigration Forum and then America's Voice stands out as a uniquely powerful individual. Among all the individuals making public claims, Mr. Sharry was the most prominent. UWD had several spokespersons, which diluted their individual standing in national media. Mr. Sharry was a longtime employee (since 1990) and executive director of the National Immigration Forum. He helped create America's Voice in 2008, and it was there that he designed the mainstream immigrant rights movement's communication strategy. A memo documenting the creation of RIFA stated that "America's Voice will coordinate the communications efforts, including the work being done by the Four Freedoms Fund's Communications Initiative, the Opportunity Agenda, Media Matters, and others."[57] Mr. Sharry became both the architect and one of the most important mouthpieces of the mainstream immigrant rights movement.

A relatively small number of organizations within the immigrant rights camp therefore enjoyed discursive power and served as representational leaders of the movement. They took an active role in constructing a discursive space that would allow for the dominance of their frames. The period of unquestionable dominance coincided with the culmination of more rationalized and centralized coalitions in the late 2000s. This process seems to have contributed to enhancing the discursive powers of national organizations located

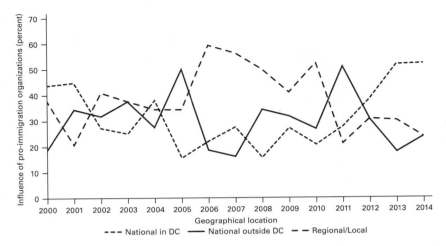

FIGURE 9.3. Influence (percent) of proimmigration organizations by geographical location. Source: LexisNexis.

in Washington. Regional organizations such as CHIRLA with close links to national leaders could and did become more prominent in the national media. The vast majority of regional and local organizations, however, experienced a decrease in media presence after 2010. The growing concentration of discursive power in the hands of national leaders allowed them to dominate representations of immigrants and their struggle for legal status. They could use this position to articulate visions of national citizenship that cohered with their ideological and strategic preferences.

De Facto Americans

Proimmigrant advocates became important players in the field on national citizenship. Groups advocating for immigrant rights and legalization began to organize immigrants across the country. The leaders of the mainstream movement drew primarily from liberal nationalism to express their claims. They argued that immigrants deserved legalization in this plural, multicultural, and liberal nation. Immigrants, they argued, stood to make an important contribution to the nation because they were good, hardworking people who ascribed to American values. Continued efforts to restrict and banish immigrants were morally wrong and wholly un-American.

Leaders believed that they needed a disciplined message that spoke to the core values of the national public. They feared that diverse strategies and messages would create dissonance. Without unity there would be countless different voices saying different things, resulting in a cacophony of utterances and actions that would resonate with few if any Americans. To avoid this dissolution into noise, the leadership created a discursive infrastructure to ensure unity across the different parts of the network. The different activists and advocates were trained to talk about themselves, immigration, and the country in very similar ways. They were encouraged to align the narrative arc of their own lives with the one manufactured for the movement.

Enormous resources were needed to produce a resonant message and the infrastructure to articulate it. Cultural capital was needed to understand the discursive rules of the game and American norms. Human capital was needed to devise strategies. Economic capital was needed to perform surveys and focus groups to test the effectiveness of different messages. Even more capital was needed to finance hundreds of trainings carried out in towns and cities across the country. Consequently, well-endowed, highly professionalized organizations assumed responsibility for representing immigrants. They produced the words to say, directed how to say them, and inserted the messages in major news outlets. This representational elite played a pivotal role because it produced the voice of the immigrant in the public sphere. Although there were certainly more radical voices that surfaced, the leadership of RIFA and then A4C assumed dominance over the production, training, and public diffusion of representations. They helped reproduce national citizenship by employing nationalist language and training thousands of activists to think and talk about rights through a national lens.

Conclusion

Where We Stand

WE ARE NOW well into the Trump administration. Politically, President Trump owes nothing to immigrant communities and everything to a xenophobic base. Undocumented immigrants, who won some victories but endured many deportations during the Obama administration, have been forced to contend with a man who launched his presidential campaign by calling Mexican immigrants criminals and rapists. One of the Trump administration's first executive orders rescinded the previous administration's policy of prioritizing violent criminals for deportation. A fact sheet released by the Department of Homeland Security in 2017 stated, "Under this executive order, ICE will not exempt classes or categories of removal aliens from potential enforcement. All of those present in violation of the immigration laws may be subject to immigration arrest, detention, and, if found removable by final order, removal from the United States." In President Trump's first year in office, the number of noncriminal aliens detained by ICE increased by 171 percent from the previous year.[1] Everybody has become a target.

The administration and its allies in the right-wing media have framed undocumented immigrants as the enemy of the people. They may be inside the country, but their illegality places them outside the legal and moral order.[2] They were being placed "beyond the line," where, as Wendy Brown notes, force can be conceivably used "freely and ruthlessly, with indifference to law."[3] Conceiving of undocumented immigrants as "beyond the line," the Trump White House believes that it can legitimately employ the state's vast armory of legal violence to terrorize well-embedded communities. ICE and Customs and

Border Patrol (CBP) agents have separated children from their parents, while others have detained immigrants performing everyday tasks such as dropping off children at school, going to court, shopping, going to the hospital, and driving. There are no areas of life that are out of bounds to the repressive arm of the state. One case concerned a man who went to buy some drinks at a 7-Eleven in Southern California. There happened to also be a group of ICE agents at the store, and they requested documentation from the unlucky customer. The man could not furnish documents and was subsequently detained and placed into deportation proceedings. Another man was arrested by ICE agents in front of his daughter's school weeks after President Trump's inauguration. His daughter filmed the arrest and posted it to YouTube. The video was viewed by thousands and sparked a campaign for his release. These and many other accounts have been passed on between undocumented immigrants through social media, Spanish-language media, and gossip chains. Facts and rumors have circulated freely and blended into one another, forming a cloud of uncertainty and fear.

"Real power," according to President Trump, "is—I don't want to use the word—fear."[4] The president employs the fear of immigrants to bolster his base while using the repressive powers of the state to instill fear in immigrant communities. Maximizing fear in different publics (that is, nationals and immigrants) has become the singular logic for governing national citizenship in the age of Trump.

What Went Wrong?

In a conversation with me during the summer of 2018, a Los Angeles–based activist marveled at the state of things. Her organization had been working on deportation defense and various sanctuary measures in local and state arenas. There were certainly some wins to be happy about, but they were hard-fought and required vast resources, energy, and time. She also felt that local protections in the form of sanctuary laws were not enough to protect immigrant communities from the full weight of state violence. During the course of our conversation, she grew somewhat nostalgic for the Obama years. The Obama administration, according to her, was bad, but at least it offered room for negotiation. There had also been the hope of passing an immigration reform law that would legalize the status of millions. "If only we had secured immigration reform," she murmured wistfully, "we would not be in the mess we are in now."[5] Although she saw herself as part of the movement's left flank, she had hoped, if not expected, for some kind of reform to pass during those years. Throwing her hands in the air, my interlocutor looked to me and asked, "What the hell went wrong?"

Part of the answer, and the answer preferred by the DC-based leadership, is bad timing. Democrats controlled both chambers of Congress during the first two years of the Obama administration, which coincided with a massive recession. The urgency of economic recovery squeezed out all other legislative items except for health care reform. In a bid to keep the movement on board, the Obama administration promised that it would move comprehensive immigration reform forward. In various speeches and meetings, White House officials such as Rahm Emmanuel expressed strong support for immigration reform within the first two years of Obama's term. But the White House strung the movement along until it was too late. An emboldened and radicalized Republican Party won both chambers of Congress in 2010, effectively shutting down the legislative path for reform. The 2013–2014 campaign to pass immigration reform was blocked by House Speaker John Boehner's refusal to allow to the floor a bill that had broad Senate support. According to this account, bad political timing and the intransigence of strategic Republicans robbed the movement of immigration reform.

The movement's left flank has another account, placing responsibility on the bad choices of the mainstream movement's leadership. In this version, the Obama administration played the movement because the movement's leadership allowed itself to be played. President Obama and his Senate allies embraced a get-tough, enforcement-first strategy as a means to win Republican support for immigration reform. The strategy was no secret. Senate leaders such as Charles Schumer described the strategy to the press, advocacy organizations, and anybody else who cared to listen. In spite of being rather transparent, the movement's leadership refused to openly criticize the Obama administration until the spring of 2014. Some critics on the left flank have long maintained that more aggressive mobilization tactics targeting the Obama administration, especially after 2010, would have at least helped to stop deportations and provide protections to communities under siege. Such tactics proved to be effective in persuading the White House to introduce the movement's only wins during this period: Deferred Action for Childhood Arrivals (DACA) and Deferred Action for Parents of Childhood Arrivals (DAPA). More concessions, the argument goes, could have been extracted from the administration if the movement as a whole had been quicker to escalate pressure on President Obama. Instead, the leadership steered the movement into a more conciliatory and subordinate relationship.

The Rules of the Game

The explanations above attribute blame to bad timing and bad choices. The mainstream leadership places responsibility on the recession and the surge of reactionary Republican leaders. The left flank blames President Obama and his so-called apologists in the immigrant rights movement. There is certainly some merit to both explanations, but the book takes a different approach. Rather than place responsibility on the contingencies (timing and choices, among others) that confronted this social movement, the book maintains that the field of national citizenship presented rules of political engagement and that following such rules resulted in an unsatisfactory outcome. Prominence in the field of national citizenship required the accumulation of economic and political capital as well as cultural capital expressed in the form of professional credentials and national habitus. It also depended on crafting frames that resonated with core national values. Following the rules helped to produce a social movement that was richer, better connected, and more popular than ever. But these important gains came with the trade-off of making leading organizations increasingly dependent on the resources and discourses of the system it had originally sought to transform. The more the movement followed the rules of the game (resource accumulation and discursive conformity) and the more it ascended in the political field, the more it became part of that field and the less it was able to demand significant change. The movement ceased being a force of transformation and became an engine of political reproduction, albeit in a more liberal direction.

Caging Organizations

The immigrant rights movement was entrenched in grassroots struggles. The organizing model that developed in the 1990s centered on recruiting working-class immigrants, building coalitions within metropolitan regions, and pressuring local and state-level politicians to enact accommodating policies. The working-class members of organizations were the primary source of their power. The more people that organizations could mobilize, the greater their status with other organizations and their abilities to pressure the government. As a consequence, recruiting and retaining members was vitally important for these early organizations. Proximity—social, cultural, and geographic—

between leaders and members was essential for building the levels of trust needed to recruit and retain members. Successful organizations were those with leaders and organizers who could relate to working-class members and employ common cultural dispositions (for example, language, taste, styles, music, and sports). The grassroots-organizing model was effective in politicizing and empowering even the most marginalized immigrants, such as day laborers.

There were, however, limits to this model. As federal policy became stricter in the late 1990s, local and regional grassroots organizations lacked the capital, capacity, and expertise to shift scale and enter the national political field. The growing investment of national organizations such as the Center for Community Change in the immigration fight was propitious because they had the economic, political, and cultural capital needed to be effective players in the national field. Regional organizations such as CHIRLA and CASA Maryland could use the infrastructure of these national organizations as a ladder to scale up their own political struggles. The national organizations provided them with a ready-made vehicle in which to bring the fight for immigrant rights to Washington. Eschewing a partnership with national organizations would, many believed, have locked immigrant organizations in the local trenches, far from the centers of political power. Partnerships with organizations such as the CCC, therefore, allowed local and regional organizations to escape the local trap and enter national political battles.

Mobilizing at the national scale was different from mobilizing in the local arena. In the national field, organizations needed to acquire more economic capital to expand organizations, hire costly college-educated professionals and consultants, build a brand-new social-movement infrastructure, develop and implement a communications strategy, and mount a series of high-profile campaigns. The need for financial resources resulted in a growing dependency on a relatively small number of foundations. Just as important, organizations needed political access to the White House and Congress in order to influence immigration policy. Political access also bolstered one's status among other advocacy organizations, major funders, and the media, effectively converting political capital into more money, exposure, and influence.

The resources of power were controlled by a handful of elite institutional actors. A handful of prominent funders mapped out the political field, developed strategic priorities, and funded organizations that advanced those priorities. They favored highly professionalized organizations with enormous reservoirs of political capital. Moreover, political elites understood the value of political access and used it as leverage over organizations. Not inviting an unruly organization back to the White House sent an unmistakable message that deviations would not be tolerated. As the sources of economic and political capital were controlled by a handful of elite actors, upwardly mobile advocates were encouraged to embrace a model that centered on large, professional, and politically consenting organizations.

The worlds of elite advocates, funders, and elected officials overlapped, creating a veritable "power elite"[6] that exercised inordinate influence over how other advocates and activists thought about citizenship. Organizations adopted similar strategies and began to adopt similar norms and worldviews. The salaries of many executive directors paralleled or even exceeded those of funders and White House and congressional staff. Many attended similar universities, lived in similarly middle-class neighborhoods, ate and drank at similar restaurants, and sent their children to similar schools. A sizable number of advocates also rotated between the worlds of government, foundations, and advocacy, effectively blurring the lines between these different spheres. Tastes, dispositions, moralities, and political perceptions converged in a world that was far removed from the trials and tribulations of most undocumented, working-class immigrants.

"The revolution ain't cheap," an activist once told me. By this, he meant that changing federal policy is costly. The methods required to obtain essential resources imposed constraints on what organizations could do and say within the field. The leadership of the mainstream movement essentially traded off more resources for more compliant tactics, greater professionalization, and greater social distance from the base.

Fighting for the Nation

The fight for the rights of immigrants within the field of national citizenship also favored a nationalist framing of citizenship. If the movement's goal was to pass favorable legislation, it would have to pressure Congress by creating broad support for immigrants and comprehensive immigration reform. Nationalist framings of citizenship were, many believed, much better at winning over supporters than were arguments calling for the disassembly of the nation-state. The movement was also working to counter the narratives of its anti-immigrant opponents. Pro- and anti-immigrant forces were bound to one another in a tug-of-war over the meaning and boundaries of citizenship. Thus, the need to create resonant discourse combined with movement-countermovement dynamics to lock in the movement's embrace of nationalism.

As anti-immigrant forces represented the nation as narrow and immigrants as polluters, proimmigrant forces countered by investing millions of dollars and countless hours in reimagining the nation and the place of immigrants within it. The mainstream immigrant rights movement was engaged in a serious fight over the meaning of the nation-state. There were indeed core national values, but these values were rooted in openness to the immigrant and the embrace of fairness, justice, and pragmatism. Ethnonational depictions of the country were, according to this argument, un-American. With the country reframed this way, immigrants were reconceived as Americans-in-waiting. They were hardworking, family-loving, God-fearing, upstanding people. They not only possessed core American values but also rejuvenated the morality, civic values, and economy of the country, making them deserving of legal status. The mainstream immigrant rights movement was therefore far from radical. It sought to bolster one particular version of national citizenship (liberal nationalism) and make it dominant in the United States. In doing so, there was agreement that exclusionary borders were a necessary condition of this political community. There could certainly be a large wall, as long as it was accompanied by a large door for those deemed deserving of national membership.

The frame of liberal nationalism came with trade-offs. The use of such a master frame helped to reify the nation-state and buttress its exclusionary boundaries. It prioritized national belonging as the basis of political community while crowding out frames that eschewed the bordered nation-state. In its celebration of America as the land of the free, the movement papered over the reality that racism and xenophobia are as much part of the nation's values and traditions as are pluralism, tolerance, and openness to immigrants. Rather than critically interrogate the dark side of national citizenship, movement leaders believed that winning over public support required remaining silent about its deeply inegalitarian underpinnings. The leaders wagered that a critical and realistic communication strategy would have fallen on deaf ears at best or have repelled target audiences at worst. Having made such a wager, the mainstream immigrant rights movement inadvertently became a propagator of a sanitized, sacralized depiction of the nation.

The discursive rules governing the field of national citizenship, therefore, present a dilemma that is difficult to resolve. One framing of national citizenship reifies an exclusionary political community but is capable of winning the hearts and minds of millions. More radical frames are quite effective at inspiring a committed base by articulating visions of an egalitarian political community, but they also alienate large parts of the public. Facing the hard dilemma, leading advocates erred on the side of nationalism.

The book places much of the blame on the rules of the political game, but leading advocates had some agency regarding the choice of strategy. The field certainly constrained strategic options, but it did not eliminate them. The executive director of MALDEF proposed the down-payment strategy in 2009, the rebellious Dreamers embraced a stand-alone DREAM Act in 2010, and NDLON sponsored the Not One More campaign to denounce the Obama administration's enforcement policies in 2013. The first two were not particularly radical and did not depart too far from the rules of the game. The third was more radical because it called for the end of all deportations, anticipating "Abolish ICE." The DC-based leadership pushed back equally on all three and counseled foundations to prioritize the strategy of pushing for comprehensive reform and targeting Republicans with criticism. They had a vested interest in pursuing their strategy and viewed the alternatives as competition and distractions. Consequently, DC-based leaders chose to use their prominent positions and access to elite funders and politicians to crowd out alternative strategies and double down on their own.

Splintering the Movement

Many activists on the movement's left flank loathed candidate Trump but were also hesitant of a Hillary Clinton presidency. They believed that her government would have largely followed the tough policies of the Obama administration. Grassroots activists denounced Trump for overtly racist statements, but they also stressed that mainstream Democrats had betrayed them in the past and were likely to do so again. Some suggested that if candidate Trump were to win, the movement would not be so easily co-opted by the White House and would stand united against a common political enemy.

The Trump administration has closed down all access to proimmigrant organizations. After a brief spate of negotiations between President Trump, Senator Charles Schumer, and Congressperson Nancy Pelosi over the fate of the Dreamers, extremist voices in the conservative media objected. Commentators at Fox, Breitbart, and other outlets called on their readers, viewers, and listeners to protest. President Trump backtracked and pulled out of negotiations. He quickly understood that moving to the center on immigration would cost him his base without picking up much support from Independents and centrist Democrats. The President's political survival has come to rest on his ability to villainize immigrants and pursue acts of cruelty. "Immigrants are coming over the border to kill you" has become, one pundit mockingly noted, his only speech.[7]

As political openings have closed, the immigrant rights movement has fractured. Deepak Bhargava, the executive director of the Center for Community Change, had transformed his organization into one of the leading immigrant rights organizations in the country, but in March 2018, he announced his retirement following the November midterm elections. Ali Noorani of the National Immigration Forum has continued his efforts to court middle-of-the-road and conservative voters by launching a tour for his recent book, *There Goes the Neighborhood: How Communities Overcome Prejudices and Meet the Challenge of American Immigration*. He has also created a new podcast on immigration, *Only in America*, and has made frequent appearances in different media outlets, including Fox News. The other DC-based organizations are providing services, developing policy proposals, lobbying Democratic and Republican congressional leaders, and registering immigrant voters. No new DC-based coalitions have arisen to fight the Trump administration. The leading organizations had developed their skills, knowledge, and professional norms largely as insiders of the political game. Cast from the halls of power, they have displayed some difficulty adapting to their outsider status.

Some organizations have become active in the fight to save DACA. United We Dream and several regional organizations, including CHIRLA and CASA Maryland, have led campaigns to pressure politicians to support a legislative solution for DACA. But given the intransigence of most Republicans, advocates have recognized that the prospects for a legislative solution are nearly nonexistent and have challenged the rescission of DACA in court. New York, California, the University of California, CASA Maryland, and the NAACP, among others, have mounted legal challenges that have, for the moment, stopped DACA's termination.

CARECEN and NDLON have also launched a campaign to protect immigrants, many of whom are Central Americans, with Temporary Protected Status (TPS). In March 2018, nine immigrants with TPS and five children

.ders filed a lawsuit against the Trump administration's termina-
TPS program. The lawsuit was filed for them by NDLON and the
undation of Southern California. Along with the lawsuit, NDLON
and CARECEN organized TPS holders into a national activist network. Many
of the newly incorporated activists come from families with deep roots in the
country. They have homes, jobs, community relations, and children born in
the United States. The federal government had given these immigrants a life
in the country, and it was now taking that life away. This expression of punitive power precipitated the political mobilization of TPS holders.

Others have responded with a series of state and local mobilizations. In
California, for instance, a broad coalition spearheaded by the Asian Law Caucus, the California Immigration Policy Center, and NDLON successfully
campaigned for the Values Act (SB 54). The Values Act, sometimes called the
sanctuary-state law, places further limitations on the levels of cooperation
with federal immigration agents while placing restrictions on enforcement
actions at public schools, hospitals, courthouses, and libraries. The California Sheriff's Association opposed the bill and forced its sponsor, State Senator
Kevin de Leon, to water down key components. Local activists and advocacy
organizations throughout the state have viewed the Values Act as securing
baseline protections for immigrants and have pushed their cities and counties
to secure additional protections. Advocacy organizations and foundations in
Los Angeles, for instance, have worked with the city and county to provide financial resources for the legal representation of immigrants in deportation
proceedings. Foundations, the city, and the county have all contributed to the
Justice Fund, which has given financial support to sixteen organizations providing legal representation to immigrants.

The disciplined messaging machine discussed in the book has largely shat-
tered. There is no longer a powerful leadership that can impose consistent
messaging across the many different parts of the movement. Some prominent
advocates continue to frame the rights of immigrants through a nationalist
lens. For instance, Ali Noorani of the National Immigration Forum drew on
such a frame in a July 24, 2018, Twitter post. He wrote that "we need to make
the case [that] immigrants are protecting America, giving back to the nation and, ultimately, becoming American."[8] Although certain organizations
continue to embrace a nationalist frame, many are embracing radical frames
such as "Abolish ICE." This particular slogan has gained enormous traction
on the movement's left flank. It has turned people's attention to the histori-

cal problems of ICE, but it also strikes fear in the hearts of many middle-of-the-road Americans. It reinforces the image of immigrant rights activists as no-border radicals, far outside the boundaries of legitimate politics. President Trump and his allies were thrilled by the growing buzz of the slogan. "Pelosi and the Democrats want to abolish the brave men and women of ICE," tweeted President Trump, "[but] what I want to do is abolish the killers in ISIS."[9] Thus, the discursive infrastructure that was so central to the movement in the early 2010s has largely come apart, resulting in the proliferation of competing frames.

Social-movement scholar Charles Tilly[10] once argued that successful movements needed to achieve worthiness, unity, numbers, and commitment (WUNC). The immigrant rights movement's WUNC has been challenged under the Trump administration. The unity of the movement has come undone as hundreds of organizations and groups pursue goals, tactics, and strategies separately. The lack of unity has made it difficult to generate consistent frames that depict the cause as worthy. One part of the movement maintains that immigrants are law-abiding Americans-in-waiting, while another part calls for the abolition of ICE. The movement has also had difficulty connecting to other parts of the anti-Trump resistance, while its own ranks have thinned due to activist fatigue. Numbers and commitment have been difficult to maintain, as wins have been few and fleeting. The Trump years have not enhanced the movement's worthiness, unity, numbers, and commitment by drawing a clear line between the movement and its political foes. Instead, Trump's rule has blown open fault lines between different factions and closed down all room for negotiation. Under these conditions, legal advocacy has become one of the last and most important tools in the fight to protect immigrants' rights.

Back to the Trenches

For a half century now, international migration and globalization have pierced the walls of the nation-state. Borders had great difficulty managing the circulation of people, goods, ideas, and cultures. The weakening boundaries of the United States disturbed the security of nationals across the country. Immigrants were held responsible for the declining economic fortunes of white Americans, any and all criminal activities, and a watering down of national identity. Aggrieved citizens mobilized, and politicians capitalized on their angst.

The state responded by enacting innumerable policies and instruments to ensure territorial control. Some controls were designed to be spectacular. For instance, ICE performed massive raids on a meatpacking plant in the Midwest and ripped children from their parents' arms. These and other spectacles were intended to terrorize large communities and deter foreigners from migrating to the United States. But random acts of terror were insufficient to root out the problem population. Finer-grained surveillance methods were instituted to better control the population. Programs such as E-Verify, 287(g), and Secure Communities allowed federal enforcement agencies to acquire information about immigrants passing through local employment and law enforcement systems. These programs also allowed locals to contribute to the detention and deportation of undocumented immigrants. Local governments initiated their own programs to tighten the government's stranglehold on this population. Such policies included enacting bans on soliciting work in public, requiring landlords to verify the immigration status of prospective tenants, and enforcing existing quality-of-life ordinances. Through these various controls, responsibility for keeping foreigners out was transmitted to the cellular level of society. Local police officers, landlords, and employers, among others, assumed a fundamental role in certifying the pedigree of the population and deciding whether people should stay or go. The Trump administration has only intensified the long trend of territorial securitization.

In spite of the mounting pressure on immigrant populations and the splintering of the social movement, the will to resist will continue. State power involves the production of discourses and techniques to differentiate and rank populations by their proximity to the national norm. It establishes limits on who can and cannot live within a territory. But by creating categories to distinguish good and bad, deserving and undeserving, and normal and abnormal populations, the state constructs the deviant subject and provides it with the grievances and moral outrage to resist its exclusion. Producing the power of the nation-state is therefore bound to produce resistant subjects. There is, according to Foucault, "no power without potential refusal or revolt."[11] At each point in which power is enacted against an "illegalized" subject—whether on the street corner, at a job interview, at a city hall, or at a detention center—the seeds of resistance and counterpower are planted. These seeds will grow into localized revolts when they can connect to and feed on the outrage of others—family members, friends, neighbors, fellow congregants, and others—injured by state violence.

The current state of the immigrant rights movement may be splintered and in partial abeyance. But the decline of a social movement does not mean an end to resistance. New points of revolt are developing and gaining momentum in different parts of the country. Such revolts can contribute to the reconfiguration of the national social movement and introduce a new model with which to mobilize for rights and equality. Localized revolts gave rise to the immigrant rights movement in the 1990s, and it will be these types of struggles that will power the movement's rebirth in the years to come.

Appendix
Methods of Investigation

Part 1 of the book examines the early immigrant rights battles through the lens of day laborer conflicts. Day laborers are people (mostly immigrant men) who sell their labor for various services including construction, gardening, home repairs, and moving. Day laborers try to find employment by standing on public street corners or in the parking lots of big-box retail stores. This public method of obtaining work has made the day laborers into a particular flash point of immigration conflicts, especially in the suburbs. For this reason, day laborers served as a window into early immigrant rights politics in the 1990s. The chapters of part 1 provide both a broad overview of day-labor conflicts across the country and an in-depth analysis of the specific dynamics that unfolded in Los Angeles, California.

To assess conflicts across the country, my research assistant (Marieke de Wilde) and I created a day-labor database. The database draws on the claims-analysis method pioneered by Ruud Koopmans and Paul Statham. The day-labor database contains claims on day-labor issues between 1989 and 2014. These claims were obtained from newspaper articles gathered through LexisNexis searches. The keywords that have been used in the searches are "day laborer" and "antisolicitation." All relevant articles on day-labor issues were included, while editorials and opinion articles were excluded. For the period under question, 1,503 newspaper articles have been included, of which 12,652 claims were extracted. Each claim is included only once, and duplicates (that is, a claim occurring in more than one newspaper article) have been removed. For the purposes of these chapters, I focused mostly on conflicts in the 1990s. The database provides information on the newspaper articles (date published, newspaper, title, author(s), brief description, and location) as well as information on the claim makers (name, affiliation, and claim). The claims have been coded for a number of aspects, including attitude toward day laborers, perceived problems (caused by the presence of day laborers), and solutions (to day-labor issues). Most of the conflicts covered were for suburban cities and towns rather than large city centers.

Although the day-labor database provides a good bird's-eye view, I also perform an in-depth case study of the local immigrant rights movement in Los Angeles and the neighboring suburbs of Pasadena. Although no two cases are identical, this case illustrates how the struggle for immigrant rights arose in response to local efforts to banish immigrants. Through a detailed empirical analysis, the chapter shows how small sparks of resistance grew into larger regional battles for immigrant rights. The case study depends on historical records of the Pasadena Day Labor Association, La Escuela de la Comunidad (Pasadena), and the Center for Humane Immigrant Rights of Los Angeles (CHIRLA). The records are derived from the archives of the Liberty Hill Foundation during the period from 1990 to 2002. Liberty Hills made these archives available through the Southern California Library in Los Angeles. The case study also uses semistructured interviews with key stakeholders to provide greater insight into the motives behind certain actions and important events.

The second part of the book analyzes the nationalization of the immigrant rights movement in the 2000s and up to the mid-2010s. This period was selected because it overlaps with the rise and consolidation of a national social-movement infrastructure. For this discussion, my research assistant and I collected a wide variety of resources.

First, we constructed an immigration-reform newspaper database to address the more general issue of immigrant rights for the 2000–2014 period. The database again employs the Koopmans and Statham method. These claims were acquired through LexisNexis, and the keywords that have been used in all searches are "immigration reform" and "immigration protest." All relevant articles on immigrant rights were included, while editorials and opinion articles were excluded. For the 2000–2014 period, 1,254 newspaper articles have been included, of which 5,422 claims were extracted. A claim is a quote or a paraphrase of a person or organization in a newspaper article. It is included in the database when the subject of the claim is immigration. The database provides information on the newspaper articles (date published, newspaper, title, author(s), brief description, and location) as well as information on the claim makers. The claims have been coded for a number of aspects, including addressee, mode (for example, protest or press release), scale (federal or local), the number of people involved in protests (if there was one), and the affiliation of the claim makers (that is, government official, advocacy organization, church, union, and so on). The database was used to address the general political and discursive trends in the national political arena, the prominence of different claims makers, and the positioning of certain organizations and people on different immigration issues, among other topics.

Second, to address the formation of a national social-movement infrastructure, we collected documents associated with the major national coalitions during the 2000s. The Fair Immigration Reform Movement (FIRM), Reform Immigration for America (RIFA), and the Alliance for Citizenship (A4C) are three national coalitions that have played a central role in nationalizing the immigrant rights movement. Using web archives of coalitions and organizations, Foundation Center data, and Google searches, we obtained documents on these coalitions and their activities. A database contains information on the leading organizations, leading persons, projects, events, and finances of FIRM, RIFA and A4C. We were able to compile twenty-two documents from the web searches. These documents helped provide information about the basic features of the social-movement infrastructure.

Third, the social movement required enormous financial resources. To assess these resources, a database containing financial information was created based on IRS 990 forms and grant information from the Foundation Center. We included a total of forty-nine immigrant rights organizations in our sample. We developed a nonrandom sampling strategy that attempted to cover many of the advocacy organizations in the country. To identify the most important organizations, we selected proimmigration advocacy organizations with four or more claims in the newspaper database. We also turned to several key informants to ask which organizations should be included in our database. The original search (for newspapers and reputations) resulted in thirty immigrant rights organizations. To broaden the sample, we generated a list of immigrant organizations based on data provided by the Foundation Center. The search was restricted to organizations that received grants because of immigration advocacy work. We also wanted to ensure that our sample included regional and local advocacy organizations. We added nineteen additional organizations derived from the Foundation Center data. The final sample consists of forty-nine immigrant organizations. It must be noted that some of these organizations are issue specific and focus only on immigration advocacy. Others are multi-issue organizations (for example, the Center for American Progress and the Center for Community Change) but have invested considerable resources in the immigrant rights movement. Considering this, we searched IRS 990 tax forms for the forty-nine sampled organizations. The tax forms provided information on the grants and contributions, salaries to executives, and the number of employees. We also searched for the forty-nine sampled organizations in the Foundation Center database and for information on grant makers, recipients of grants, and grant amounts. The data on the revenue of advocacy organizations and foundations provides important information on the sizeable financial resources flowing into the movement and which organizations benefited the most. Financial data for several organizations were incomplete or heavily skewed. We left out organizations with such problems.

Fourth, the book uses access to the White House as a measure of an organization's political capital. The White House database contains information on the visits to the White House by nonprofit organizations working on immigrant rights advocacy. The Obama administration made this available through the White House visitor web page. The Trump administration discontinued the practice. Our sample includes the same forty-nine advocacy organizations used for the revenue database. We identified organizations by the names of central employees. These names were gathered through organization websites, the newspaper database, LinkedIn profiles, and extensive website searches. Many organizations from the sample did not appear on the White House visitor page, and this was duly noted. We cleaned the database by removing visits that were not related to immigration issues. Some organizations met with White House officials that had nothing to do with immigration. For multi-issue organizations, we examined (through extensive online searches) which key employees of these organizations specialized in immigration and included only those. After compiling the original database, approximately one hundred meetings were removed because they did not meet specific requirements. Most meetings removed involved multi-issue organizations.

Fifth, to understand the basic strategy and structure of the immigrant rights movement, the book draws on twenty-six interviews with directors, organizers, and activists of various organizations. I also had many "background" conversations with activists and advocates across the country. The interviews and background conversations provide important information on the strategies of leading organizations.

Finally, we compiled a database using eighty-four Open Society Foundation and Institute project documents procured through DC Leaks (http://soros.dcleaks.com /view?div=us). The book refers to all such documents simply as Open Society. The documents span from 2008 to 2016. This period overlaps well with the period of movement nationalization. Open Society was the second most important funder of advocacy organizations. Its project descriptions give valuable information on the strategies of some of the leading immigrant rights advocates. Documents containing information on projects regarding immigrant rights have been included in the database. The Open Society database has a structure that's similar to the newspaper databases, and it contains statements addressing immigration politics and policy. My research assistant and I extracted 1,382 statements that directly addressed the issue of immigration. These statements were coded for frames, strategic preferences, partnerships with foundations and organizations, and various other discussion topics. The book employs established rules of the mainstream press concerning documents obtained through Wikileaks and similar websites. I have ensured that compromising information is not used. The interviews and the Open Society database provide context, clarification, and corroboration for trends found in the other sources of data.

Notes

Introduction

1. Sassen 2006; FitzGerald and Cook-Martín 2014.
2. Portes and Rumbaut 1996.
3. Berezin 2009.
4. Benhabib 2004, 4.
5. Gest 2016; Hochschild 2016.
6. Gest 2016, 12.
7. Hochschild 2016.
8. Gest 2016, 12.
9. Varsanyi 2011; Menjívar and Kanstroom 2013; Nicholls 2016b.
10. Lamont and Duvoux 2014, 60.
11. Chavez 2008; Massey and Pren 2012.
12. Walker and Leitner 2011; Strunk and Leitner 2013; Menjívar 2000; De Graauw, Gleeson, and Bloemraad 2013.
13. Massey and Denton 1998; Massey 2007; Carpio, Irazabal, and Pulido 2011.
14. Newman 2013.
15. Berezin 2009, 34.
16. Strunk and Leitner 2013.
17. Inda 2006; Nicholls 2016b.
18. Dean and Villadsen 2016, 63.
19. Nicholls 2016a.
20. Derby 2014; Menjívar and Abrego 2012.
21. Portes and Sensenbrenner 1993; Portes and Zhou 1993; Portes and Rumbaut 1996.
22. Portes and Sensenbrenner 1993, 1329.
23. Scott 1985, 1990.
24. Jasper 1997.
25. Pallares 2014, 17.
26. Portes and Sensenbrenner 1993.
27. Pallares and González 2011, 163.

28. Hondagneu-Sotelo 2006; Heredia 2011.
29. Nicholls 2016b.
30. Bosniak 2007, 2010; Motomura 2014.
31. Soysal 1994.
32. Seif 2010, 445.
33. Motomura 2006, 2012.
34. Snow et. al. 1986; Benford 1993; Benford and Snow 2000.
35. McCarthy 1996, 143.
36. Dean and Villadsen 2016, 63.
37. Gould 1995; Diani and Bison 2004; Nicholls 2008.
38. Walker and Leitner 2011; Strunk and Leitner 2013; Steil and Vasi 2014.
39. Foucault 1978.
40. Ong 1996; Isin 2001.
41. Miller 2000; Sikkink 2005; Tarrow 2005; Soule 2013; Wallace, Zepeda-Millán, and Jones-Correa 2014.
42. Cordero-Guzmán et al. 2008; Barreto et al. 2009; Voss and Bloemraad 2011; Voss, Bloemraad, and Lee 2011; Zepeda-Millán 2017.

Chapter 1: The Rights of Immigrants in the Nation

1. Soysal 1994; Isin 2001.
2. Brown 2014.
3. Sassen 2006; Glick Schiller and Çağlar 2009; McFarlane 2009.
4. Snow et al. 1986; Benford 1993.
5. Bourdieu and Wacquant 1992; Bourdieu 1984, 1986, 1994a, 1994b; Wacquant 2005.
6. Fligstein and McAdam 2015; Hilgers and Mangez 2015; Emirbayer and Desmond 2015.
7. Fligstein and McAdam 2011, 3.
8. Emirbayer and Desmond 2015, 82.
9. Alba 2005; Wimmer 2013.
10. Ruggie 1993; Brown 2014, 52.
11. Mouffe 1993.
12. Alexander 2006; Jaworsky 2016.
13. Alexander 2006, 60.
14. Tambini 2001, 209.
15. Abizadeh 2004, 234.
16. Arendt 1974; Benhabib 2004, 2018; Bosniak 2006; Somers 2008; H. Brown 2014.
17. Elias 1996, 155.
18. Arendt 1974.
19. Benhabib 2004; Bosniak 2006.
20. Arendt 1974, 299.
21. Ibid., 275.

22. Benhabib 2018, 20.
23. Torpey 1997, 239.
24. Ibid., 248.
25. Bourdieu 1984, 1994a; Wacquant 2005, 2015.
26. Dikeç 2004, 195.
27. Varsanyi 2008; Motomura 2014; Varsanyi 2008, 2011; FitzGerald and Cook-Martín 2014; Provine et al. 2016.
28. Varsanyi 2008.
29. Emirbayer and Desmond 2015, 124.
30. Mann 1996, 296–97.
31. Sassen 2006; Sassen 2013; Mann 2013.
32. Balakrishnan 1996; Sassen 2006; Mann 1996, 2013.
33. Foucault 2004.
34. Corrigan and Sayer 1985.
35. Torpey 1997.
36. Mann 1996, 298.
37. Elias 1996.
38. Ibid., 152.
39. Bourdieu 1984, 170.
40. Arendt 1974, 292.
41. Ibid.
42. Berezin 2009, 46.
43. Wimmer 2013, 50.
44. Benford and Snow 2000.
45. Brubaker 1992; Tambini 2001; Abizadeh 2004.
46. Fassin 2012.
47. Chavez 2008.
48. Arendt 1974; Brown 2014.
49. Foucault 2003.
50. Tamir 1993; Tambini 2001; Bosniak 2007.
51. Song 2009; Motomura 2012.
52. Tambini 2001, 203.
53. Motomura 2006; Carens 2010.
54. Motomura 2012, 376.
55. Ibid., 377.
56. Motomura 2006; Bosniak 2007, 2010; Song 2009.
57. Bosniak 2007; Varsanyi 2011; Motomura 2014.
58. Walzer 1983.
59. Bosniak 2007, 391.
60. Ibid., 396.
61. Soysal 1994, 1997; Tambini 2001; Abizadeh 2004.
62. Soysal 1997, 511.
63. Ibid.

64. McCarthy and Zald 1977.
65. Brown 2014; Kohl-Arenas 2016.
66. DiMaggio and Powell 1983.
67. Bourdieu 1984, 1986.
68. Bourdieu 1986, 1994a.
69. Benford and Snow 2000, 621.
70. Snow et al. 1986, 469; Patler and Gonzales 2015; Bloemraad and Trost 2011; Bloemraad, Silva, and Voss 2016.
71. Koopmans et al. 2005.
72. Giugni and Passy 2004, 52–53.
73. Benford and Snow 2000, 629.
74. Snow et al. 1986; Benford 1993; Benford and Snow 2000.
75. Meyer and Staggenborg 1996; Benford and Snow 2000; Feagin 2013.
76. Chavez 2008.
77. Ngai 2004.
78. Coutin 2007.
79. Honig 2006.
80. Alexander 2006, 421.
81. Benford 1993; Benford and Snow 2000; Nicholls 2013a, 2013b.
82. Polletta 2006; Fernandes 2017.
83. Rose and Miller 1992; Cruikshank 1999; Inda 2006.
84. Staggenborg 1988; Rucht 1999; Putnam 2000; Skocpol 2004a, 2004b; Jacobs and Skocpol 2005; Walker 2014.
85. Skocpol 2004b; Walker 2014.
86. Putnam 2000, 70.
87. McAdam 1986; Gould 1995; Diani and Bison 2004; Diani 2014.
88. Skocpol 2004b, 11.
89. DiMaggio and Powell 1983, 55.
90. Skocpol 2004b, 8.
91. Ibid., 11.
92. Schorske 1955, 15; see also Rucht 1999.
93. Bourdieu 1994a; Wacquant 2005; Lehman Schlozman, Brady, and Verba 2018, 144.
94. Jacobs and Skocpol 2005, 10.
95. Putnam 2000, Skocpol 2004a, 2004b.
96. McCarthy 1987.
97. Hamilton and Chinchilla 2001; Nicholls and Uitermark 2016.
98. Arendt 1974, 292.
99. Skocpol 2004a, 12.
100. Lehman Schlozman, Brady, and Verba 2018, 144.

Chapter 2: Suburbia Must Be Defended

1. Foucault 2003.
2. Phillips and Massey 1999.

3. Stevenson 1989.

4. Mitchell 1992.

5. Carvajal 1996.

6. Foucault 2003.

7. Dugger 1996.

8. Mydans 1990.

9. Babington 1992.

10. As Norbert Elias argued more than a half century ago, dominant groups often point to the physical attributes (color) and bodily dispositions (taste, accent, and hygiene) of outsiders to naturalize their own superiority. As he put it, "It appears as 'objective'—as implanted on outsiders by nature or the gods. In that way, the stigmatizing group is exculpated from any blame. It is not we . . . who put a stigma on these people, but the powers that made the world." Elias and Scotson 1994, pp. xxxiv–xxxv.

11. Guthey 1992b.

12. Emling 1992a.

13. Mydans 1992.

14. LeDuff 1997.

15. Haughney 2000.

16. LeDuff and Halbfinger 1999.

17. Reinhold 1993.

18. Haughney 2000.

19. Hochschild 2016.

20. Gross 2000.

21. Parker and McMahon 2001.

22. Guthey 1992b.

23. Cooper 1999.

24. Gest 2016.

25. McFadden 2000.

26. Chauvin and Garcés-Mascareñas 2012.

27. Reinhold 1993.

28. Stone Lombardi 1994.

29. Mydans 1990.

30. Brown 2014.

31. Ibid., 45–46.

32. Badie 2000.

33. Brown 2014.

34. Valenzuela et al. 2006.

35. Ibid., 3

36. Duggan 1992.

37. Constable 1995.

38. Ibid.

39. McDonald 1999.

40. Ibid.

41. Valenzuela et al. 2006, 3.

42. Nadia Marin-Molina, formerly of the Workplace Project, personal interview, 2016.
43. Mydans 1992.
44. Rothwell and Massey 2009.
45. Provine et al. 2016.
46. Valenzuela et al. 2006.
47. Guthey 1992a.
48. Lai 2016.
49. Guthey 1992b.
50. Nieves 1994b.
51. Hamilton 1993.
52. Petersen 1994c.
53. Ibid.
54. Anderson 1999.
55. De Sa 1999.
56. Massey 2007.
57. Nieves 1994a.
58. Carvajal 1995.
59. Sáenz, Menjívar, and García 2015, 172.
60. Brown 2014, 45.

Chapter 3: Resisting Ethnonationalism, One Town at a Time

1. Brown 2014.
2. McLaughlin 1994.
3. "Doing Jobs Citizens 'Would Never Do.'"
4. Quintanilla 1997.
5. Dugger 1996.
6. Cleland-Pero 1992.
7. Nieves 1994b.
8. LeDuff 1997.
9. McLaughlin 1994.
10. Gustavo Torres, executive director, CASA Maryland, personal interview, 2016.
11. Valenzuela et al. 2006.
12. Pallares 2014.
13. Strugatch 2004.
14. Petersen 1994b.
15. Ibid.
16. Zinko 1995.
17. Fassin 2012.
18. Stone Lombardi 1994.
19. Gustavo Torres, executive director, CASA Maryland, personal interview.
20. Schneider 1998.
21. Aguilar 1994b.

22. Moody 1988; Corona 1994.

23. Nicholls 2016.

24. Milkman 2006.

25. Mitchell 1992.

26. Levander 1994.

27. Robbins 1999.

28. Fine 2006; Milkman, Bloom, and Narro 2010.

29. Milkman 2006; Fine 2006.

30. Mary Ochs, formerly of the Center for Community Change, personal interview, 2016.

31. Nadia Marin-Molina, formerly of the Workplace Project, personal interview, 2016.

32. Ibid.

33. Ibid.

34. Heredia 2011.

35. Ibid.

36. Fassin 2012.

37. Gearty 2000.

38. Nadia Marin-Molina, formerly of the Workplace Project, personal interview, 2016.

39. Ibid.

40. Onishi 1995.

41. McQuiston 1999.

42. Ibid.

43. Dickey 1994.

44. Dugger 1996.

45. Dugger 1997.

46. Jung 1994.

47. Aguilar 1994a.

48. De Sa 1999.

49. Gearty 1997a.

50. Nieves 1998.

51. Aguilar 1994a.

52. Fay 1996.

53. Dugger 1996.

54. De Graauw 2016; De Graauw, Gleeson, and Bloemraad 2013; Carpio, Irazábal, and Pulido 2011; and Nicholls and Uitermark 2016.

55. McQuiston 1999.

56. Blake 1996.

57. Visser 1999a.

58. Witt 1997.

59. Griffith 1991.

60. Duggan 1992.

61. Tarrow and McAdam 2005.
62. Marielena Hincapié, National Immigrant Law Center, personal interview, 2016.
63. Stone Lombardi 1995.
64. Schmitz 1996.
65. Dugger 1996.
66. Emling 1992b.
67. Petersen 1994a.
68. Anderson 1999.
69. Badie 1999.
70. Guthey 1992b.
71. Gearty 1997b.
72. Woolfolk 1995.
73. Stone Lombardi 1995.
74. Woolfolk 1995.
75. Visser 1999b.
76. Bixler 1999.
77. Woolfolk 1995.
78. Ibid.
79. Petersen 1994c.
80. Petersen 1994a.
81. Petersen 1994d.
82. Wykes 1994.
83. Ibid.
84. Kiggen Miller 1999.
85. Ibid.
86. Schrade 1999.

Chapter 4: Regionalizing the Fight for Immigrant Rights in Los Angeles

1. Valenzuela 2003; Chauvin 2010.
2. Its operating budget in 1993 was $3,350, with most of that covered by membership dues. Its first substantial grant application (for $8,000) was submitted by the Liberty Hill Foundation.
3. La Escuela de la Comunidad 1993.
4. Pasadena Day Labor Association 1994.
5. Ibid.
6. José Esquivel, formerly of the Pasadena Day Labor Association, personal interview, 2015.
7. Ibid.
8. La Escuela de la Comunidad 1994.
9. Alvarado 1998.
10. William Crowfoot, formerly of the Pasadena City Council, personal interview, 2015.

11. José Esquivel, formerly of the Pasadena Day Labor Association, personal interview, 2015.

12. Ibid.

13. Ibid.

14. Vanya de la Cuba, Pasadena district representative, personal interview, 2016.

15. Ibid.

16. José Esquivel, formerly of the Pasadena Day Labor Association, personal interview, 2015.

17. "Hiring Location Opposed," 1995.

18. Pasadena Day Labor Organization 1995.

19. International Brotherhood of Electrical Workers 1995.

20. Ibid.

21. Ibid.

22. Ibid.

23. Liberty Hill Foundation 1995.

24. Jasper 1997.

25. Alvarado 1995.

26. José Esquivel, formerly of the Pasadena Day Labor Association, personal interview, 2015.

27. Pedro Cardenas, formerly of the Pasadena Day Labor Association, personal interview, 2015.

28. Theodore, Valenzuela, and Meléndez 2009.

29. Milkman 2006.

30. Meyerson 2005.

31. Milkman 2006, 2010; Nicholls 2008; Nicholls and Uitermark 2016.

32. Hamilton and Chinchilla 2001.

33. The Center for Humane Immigrant Rights (CHIRLA), the Central American Resource Center (CARECEN), El Rescate, the Korean Workers Association (KIWA), and the Southern California Institute of Popular Education (IDEPSCA), among others.

34. Milkman 2010.

35. Patler 2010.

36. Coutin 2003.

37. Coalition for Humane Immigrant Rights of Los Angeles 1989a.

38. Coalition for Humane Immigrant Rights of Los Angeles 1989b.

39. Coalition for Humane Immigrant Rights of Los Angeles 1995a.

40. Patler 2010, 77.

41. Antonio Bernabe, Coalition for Humane Immigrant Rights of Los Angeles, personal interview, 2016.

42. Ibid.

43. Mayron Payes, formerly of the Coalition for Humane Immigrant Rights of Los Angeles and currently with the Center for Community Change, personal interview, 2016.

44. Pedro Cardenas, formerly of the Pasadena Day Labor Association, personal interview, 2015.

45. Dziembowska 2010.

46. Pedro Cardenas, formerly of the Pasadena Day Labor Association, personal interview, 2015.

47. Association of Day Laborers 1997.

48. Ibid.

49. Ibid.

50. Ibid.

51. Ibid.

52. Alvarado 1996.

53. Ibid.

54. Coalition for Humane Immigrant Rights of Los Angeles 1995c.

55. Ibid.

56. Coalition for Humane Immigrant Rights of Los Angeles 1997.

57. Association of Day Laborers 1997.

58. Coalition for Humane Immigrant Rights of Los Angeles 1995b.

59. Ibid.

60. California Immigrant Welfare Collaborative 1997.

61. Coalition for Humane Immigrant Rights of Los Angeles 1997b.

62. Coalition for Humane Immigrant Rights of Los Angeles 1997d.

63. Dziembowska 2010.

64. Gustavo Torres, CASA Maryland, personal interview, 2016.

Chapter 5: The Resurgent Nation-State

1. Stumpf 2013.

2. Koopmans and Statham 1999.

3. Nevins 2002; Durand and Massey 2003; De Genova 2005.

4. Coutin 2007; Varsanyi 2008; Wadhia 2010.

5. De Genova 2004, 176.

6. Coutin 2007, 27.

7. Varsanyi 2008, 289.

8. De Genova 2014, 53.

9. Emanuel 1996.

10. Ibid.

11. Ibid.

12. Thompson 2001.

13. De Genova 2007; Massey and Pren 2012.

14. Shenon and Toner 2001.

15. Massey and Pren 2012, 10–11.

16. Meissner et al. 2013.

17. Ibid., 12.

18. National Immigration Forum 2013.

19. Meissner et al. 2013, 139.

20. Hernández 2013.

21. Meissner et al. 2013, 148.

22. Jasper 2014.

23. Thompson and Herszenhorn 2009.

24. Open Society 2009g.

25. Sachs 2001.

26. Swarns 2007.

27. Gonzales 2014.

28. Open Society 2016.

29. Duyvendak 2011.

30. Archibold 2010.

31. "Immigration Reform Caucus Responds; to Nationwide Immigration Protests" 2007.

32. Santora and Roberts. 2007.

33. Coutin 2007.

34. Bernstein 2006.

35. Herszenhorn 2010.

36. Calmes 2012.

37. Stevenson 2005.

38. Hulse and Rutenberg 2006.

39. Stowe 2007.

40. Bourdieu 1994a.

41. Preston 2009c.

42. Pear and Hulse 2007.

43. Preston 2009c.

44. Huetteman 2014.

Chapter 6: Entering the Field of National Citizenship

1. Translated as Day Laborers of the North.

2. Deepak Bhargava, Center for Community Change, personal interview, 2016.

3. Ibid.

4. Mayron Payes, formerly of the Coalition for Humane Immigrant Rights of Los Angeles and currently with the Center for Community Change, personal interview, 2016.

5. Ibid.

6. Ibid.

7. Deepak Bhargava, Center for Community Change, personal interview, 2016.

8. Mary Ochs, formerly of the Center for Community Change, personal interview, 2016.

9. Center for Community Change 2016.

10. Clarissa Martinez De Castro, National Council of La Raza, personal interview, 2016.

11. Gustavo Torres, CASA Maryland, personal interview.

12. Mary Ochs, formerly of the Center for Community Change, personal interview, 2016.

13. Ibid.

14. Massey and Pren 2012.

15. Clarissa Martinez De Castro, National Council of La Raza, personal interview, 2016.

16. Mary Ochs, formerly of the Center for Community Change, personal interview, 2016.

17. Kornblut 2005.

18. Stolberg. 2006.

19. Marielena Hincapié, National Immigration Law Center, personal interview, 2016.

20. Ibid.

21. In 2007, Obama said, "Without modifications, the proposed bill could devalue the importance of family reunification, replace the current group of undocumented immigrants with a new undocumented population consisting of guest workers who will overstay their visas, and potentially drive down wages of American workers." Santora 2007.

22. Reform Immigration for America 2016.

23. Open Society 2008.

24. Ibid.

25. LaMarche 2010.

26. Deepak Bhargava, Center for Community Change, personal interview, 2016.

27. Ibid.

28. Rich Stolz, Center for Community Change and Reform Immigration for America, personal interview, 2016.

29. Ali Noorani, National Immigration Forum, personal interview, 2016.

30. Open Society 2008.

31. Open Society 2009d.

32. Ali Noorani, National Immigration Forum, personal interview, 2016.

33. Gustavo Torres, CASA Maryland, personal interview, 2016.

34. Rich Stolz, Center for Community Change and Reform Immigration for America, personal interview, 2016.

35. Ibid.

36. Open Society, 2009f.

37. Open Society, 2010b.

38. Preston 2010.

39. Alliance for Citizenship 2016; Tobar 2013; GiveWell 2013.

40. Open Society 2013b.

41. Walker 2014.

42. Benitez Strategies 2018.

43. GiveWell 2013.

44. Ibid.

45. Open Society 2013b.

46. Baker 2012.
47. Open Society 2013b.
48. Ibid.
49. Open Society 2013c.
50. Ibid.
51. Shear and Preston 2013.
52. Open Society 2013c.
53. Deepak Bhargava, Center for Community Change, personal interview, 2016.
54. Ibid.
55. Open Society 2013c.
56. Jones et al. 2014.
57. Nicholls 2013a.
58. Ibid.
59. Unzueta Carrasco and Seif 2014.
60. Open Society 2013c.
61. Open Society 2016.
62. Pablo Alvarado, National Day Laborer Organizing Network, personal interview, 2012.
63. Ibid.
64. Ibid.
65. Mary Ochs, formerly of the Center for Community Change, personal interview, 2016.
66. Pablo Alvarado, National Day Laborer Organizing Network, personal interview, 2012.
67. Staff Reporter 2013.
68. Kim 2013.
69. Matthews 2013c.
70. Matthews 2013a.
71. Constable 2013.
72. Shear 2014.
73. Staff Reporter 2014.
74. Ibid.
75. Thompson and Cohen 2014.
76. Hirschfeld Davis and Shear 2014.
77. Nakumera 2014.
78. Epstein 2014.
79. Deepak Bhargava, Center for Community Change director, personal interview, 2016.
80. Lawrence Benito, Illinois Coalition for Immigrants and Refugee Rights, personal interview, 2016.

Chapter 7: Money Makes the Movement

1. Preston 2014.
2. Open Society 2008.

3. Open Society 2012.

4. Open Society 2013b.

5. Open Society 2015.

6. Open Society 2013a.

7. Open Society 2011.

8. Kohl-Arenas 2016.

9. Ali Noorani, National Immigration Forum, personal interview, 2016.

10. Ibid.

11. Mary Ochs, formerly of the Center for Community Change, personal interview, 2016.

12. Open Society 2016.

13. Open Society 2009e.

14. Open Society 2016.

15. Mary Ochs, formerly of the Center for Community Change, personal interview, 2016.

16. Lupe Lopez, organizer, Center for Community Change, personal interview, 2016.

17. Rich Stolz, Center for Community Change and Reform Immigration for America, personal interview, 2016.

18. Open Society 2010c.

19. Open Society 2009b.

20. Internal Revenue Service 2018.

21. Putnam 2000; Skocpol 2004a, 2004b.

22. Open Society 2016.

23. Patler 2010.

24. Epstein 2014.

25. Open Society 2016.

26. Ibid.

27. Ibid.

28. Ibid.

Chapter 8: A Seat at the Table

1. Falcone 2008.

2. Open Society 2008.

3. Preston 2009b.

4. White House 2016.

5. Ibid.

6. Epstein 2014.

7. Open Society 2010a.

8. Mary Ochs, formerly of the Center for Community Change, personal interview, 2016.

9. Lawrence Benito, Illinois Coalition for Immigrant and Refugee Rights, personal interview, 2016.

10. Open Society 2013b.

11. Epstein 2014.

12. Ibid.

13. Thomas A. Saenz, Mexican American Legal Defense and Educational Fund, personal interview, 2016.

14. Lawrence Benito, Illinois Coalition for Immigrant and Refugee Rights, personal interview, 2016.

15. Gustavo Torres, CASA Maryland, personal interview, 2016.

16. Ibid.

17. Preston 2009a.

18. Stolberg 2010.

19. Preston 2012.

20. Deepak Bhargava, Center for Community Change, personal interview, 2016.

21. Lawrence Benito, Illinois Coalition for Immigrant and Refugee Rights, personal interview, 2016.

22. Ibid.

23. Ibid.

24. Ibid.

Chapter 9: Making Immigrants American

1. Open Society 2009c.

2. Open Society 2008.

3. Ibid.

4. Ibid.

5. Ibid.

6. Ibid.

7. Bosniak 2006; Brown 2014; Arendt 1974.

8. FitzGerald and Cook-Martín, 2014.

9. Open Society 2012.

10. See Chavez 2008.

11. Open Society 2009b.

12. Ibid.

13. Fair Immigration Reform Movement 2007a.

14. Alliance for Citizenship 2013.

15. Ibid.

16. Open Society 2009a.

17. Alliance for Citizenship 2013.

18. Somers 2008.

19. Open Society 2009a.

20. Fair Immigration Reform Movement 2007b.

21. Opportunity Agenda 2011.

22. Preston 2013.

23. Fair Immigration Reform Movement 2007b.

24. Alliance for Citizenship 2013.
25. Opportunity Agenda 2011.
26. Fair Immigration Reform Movement 2007b.
27. Opportunity Agenda 2013.
28. Opportunity Agenda 2011.
29. Fair Immigration Reform Movement 2007b.
30. Alliance for Citizenship 2013.
31. Egelko 2009.
32. Kondracke 2010.
33. Egelko 2009.
34. Thomas A. Saenz, Mexican American Legal Defense and Education Fund, personal interview, 2016.
35. Open Society, 2009i.
36. Ganz and Lin 2012.
37. New Organizing Institute 2011, 4.
38. Center for Community Change 2011, 14.
39. New Organizing Institute 2011, 24.
40. Lawrence Benito, Illinois Coalition for Immigrant and Refugee Rights, personal interview, 2016.
41. Illinois Coalition for Immigrant and Refugee Rights 2008.
42. Gustavo Torres, CASA Maryland, personal interview, 2016.
43. Ganz and Lin 2012.
44. Ganz 2009, 7.
45. Ibid.
46. Ibid.
47. Ibid.
48. Nicholls 2013b; Swerts 2015; Enriquez and Saguy 2016; Fernandes 2017.
49. Nicholls 2013a; Patler and Gonzales 2015; Swerts 2015; Terriquez 2015; Enriquez and Saguy, 2016; Fernandes 2017.
50. Dream Team Los Angeles 2010, 16; emphasis in original.
51. New Organizing Institute 2011, 13.
52. Ibid., 12–13.
53. Rich Stolz, Center for Community Change and Reform Immigration for America, personal interview, 2016.
54. Gustavo Torres, CASA Maryland, personal interview, 2016.
55. Open Society 2009b.
56. Open Society 2013b.
57. Open Society 2008.

Cconclusion: Where We Stand

1. Kopan 2018.
2. Bosniak 2006, 7.
3. Brown 2014, 45.

4. Blow 2018.
5. Anonymous, personal interview, August 2018.
6. Mills 1956.
7. Lind 2019.
8. Ali Noorani, Twitter, July 24, 2018.
9. Collins 2018.
10. Tilly 2004.
11. Foucault, in Ettlinger 2011, 549.

References

Abizadeh, Arash. 2004. "Liberal Nationalist versus Postnational Social Integration: On the Nation's Ethno-Cultural Particularity and 'Concreteness.'" *Nations and Nationalism* 10(3): 231–50.

Alba, Richard. 2005. "Bright vs. Blurred Boundaries: Second-Generation Assimilation and Exclusion in France, Germany, and the United States." *Ethnic and Racial Studies* 28(1): 20–49.

Alexander, Jeffrey C. 2006. *The Civil Sphere.* Oxford, UK: Oxford University Press.

Arendt, Hannah. 1974. *On the Origins of Totalitarianism.* New York: Harcourt, Brace, Jovanovich.

Balakrishnan, Gopal. 1996. "The National Imagination." In *Mapping the Nation*, edited by Gopal Balakrishnan, 195–213. London: Verso.

Barreto, Matt A., Sylvia Manzano, Ricardo Ramirez, and Kathy Rim. 2009. "Mobilization, Participation, and Solidaridad: Latino Participation in the 2006 Immigration Protest Rallies." *Urban Affairs Review* 44(5): 736–64.

Benford, Robert D. 1993. "Disputes within the Nuclear Disarmament Movement." *Social Forces* 71(3): 677–701.

Benford, Robert D., and David A. Snow. 2000. "Framing Processes and Social Movements: An Overview and Assessment." *Annual Review of Sociology* 26: 611–39.

Benhabib, Seyla. 2004. *The Rights of Others: Aliens, Residents, and Citizens.* Cambridge, UK: Cambridge University Press.

———. 2018. *Exile, Statelessness, and Migration: Playing Chess with History from Hannah Arendt to Isaiah Berlin.* Princeton, NJ: Princeton University Press.

Berezin, Mabel. 2009. *Illiberal Politics in Neoliberal Times: Culture, Security and Populism in the New Europe.* Cambridge, UK: Cambridge University Press.

Bloemraad, Irene, Fabiana Silva, and Kim Voss. 2016. "Rights, Economics, or Family? Frame Resonance, Political Ideology, and the Immigrant Rights Movement." *Social Forces* 94(4): 1647–74.

Bloemraad, Irene, and Christine Trost. 2011. "It's a Family Affair: Intergenerational Mobilization in the Spring 2006 Protests." *American Behavioral Scientist* 52(4): 507–32.

Bosniak, Linda. 2006. *The Citizen and the Alien*. Princeton, NJ: Princeton University Press.

———. 2007. "Being Here: Ethical Territoriality and the Rights of Immigrants." *Theoretical Inquiries in Law* 8(2): 389–410.

———. 2010. "Persons and Citizens in Constitutional Thought." *International Journal of Constitutional Law* 8(1): 9–29.

Bourdieu, Pierre. 1984. *Distinction: A Social Critique of the Judgement of Taste*. Cambridge, MA: Harvard University Press.

———. 1986. "The Forms of Capital." In *Handbook of Theory and Research for the Sociology of Education*, edited by John G. Richardson, 46–58. New York: Greenwood.

———. 1994a. *Language and Symbolic Power*. Cambridge, MA: Harvard University Press.

———. 1994b. *Raisons pratiques. Sur la thèorie de l'action*. Paris: Seuil.

Brown, Wendy. 2014. *Walled States, Waning Sovereignty*. New York: Zone Books.

Brubaker, Rogers. 1992. *Citizenship and Nationhood in France and Germany*. Cambridge, MA: Harvard University Press.

Carens, Joseph H. 2010. *Immigrants and the Right to Stay*. Cambridge, MA: MIT Press.

Carpio, Genevieve, Clara Irazábal, and Laura Pulido. 2011. "Right to the Suburb? Rethinking Lefebvre and Immigrant Activism." *Journal of Urban Affairs* 33(2): 185–208.

Chauvin, Sébastien. 2010. *Les agences de la précarité. Journaliers à Chicago*. Paris: Seuil.

Chauvin, Sébastien, and Blanca Garcés-Mascareñas. 2012. "Beyond Informal Citizenship: The New Moral Economy of Migrant Illegality." *International Political Sociology* 6(3): 241–59.

Chavez, Leo. 2008. *The Latino Threat: Constructing Immigrants, Citizens, and the Nation*. Palo Alto, CA: Stanford University Press.

Cordero-Guzmán, Hector, Nina Martin, Victoria Quiroz-Becerra, and Nik Theodore. 2008. "Voting with Their Feet: Nonprofit Organizations and Immigrant Mobilization." *American Behavioral Scientist* 52(4): 598–617.

Corona, Bert. 1994. *Memories of Chicano History: The Life and Narrative of Bert Corona*. Berkeley: University of California Press.

Corrigan, Philip, and Derek Sayer. 1985. *The Great Arch: English State Formation as Cultural Revolution*. Oxford, UK: Blackwell Press.

Coutin, Susan B. 2003. *Legalizing Moves: Salvadoran Immigrants' Struggle for U.S. Residency*. Ann Arbor: University of Michigan Press.

———. 2007. *Nations of Emigrants. Shifting Boundaries of Citizenship in El Salvador and the United States*. Ithaca, NY: Cornell University Press.

Cruikshank, Barbara. 1999. *The Will to Empower: Democratic Citizens and Other Subjects*. Ithaca, NY: Cornell University Press.

Dean, Mitchell, and Kaspar Villadsen. 2016. *State Phobia and Civil Society: The Political Legacy of Michel Foucault*. Redwood City, CA: Stanford University Press.

De Genova, Nicholas. 2004. "The Legal Production of Mexican/Migrant 'Illegality.'" *Latino Studies* 2: 160–85.

———. 2005. *Working the Boundaries: Race, Space, and "Illegality" in Mexican Chicago*. Chapel Hill, NC: Duke University Press.

———. 2007. "The Production of Culprits: From Deportability to Detainability in the Aftermath of 'Homeland Security.'" *Citizenship Studies* 11(5): 421–48.

———. 2014. "Immigrant 'Reform' and the Production of Migrant 'Illegality.'" In *Constructing Immigrant 'Illegality': Critiques, Experiences, and Responses*, edited by Cecilia Menjívar and Daniel Kanstroom, 37–63. Cambridge, UK: Cambridge University Press.

De Graauw, Els. 2016. *Making Immigrant Rights Real: Nonprofits and the Politics of Integration in San Francisco*. Ithaca, NY: Cornell University Press.

De Graauw, Els, Shannon Gleeson, and Irene Bloemraad. 2013. "Funding Immigrant Organizations: Suburban Free Riding and Local Civic Presence." *American Journal of Sociology* 119(1): 75–130.

Derby, Joanna. 2014. *Everyday Illegal: When Policies Undermine Immigrant Families*. Berkeley: University of California Press.

Diani, Mario. 2014. *The Cement of Civil Society: Studying Networks in Localities*. Cambridge, UK: Cambridge University Press.

Diani, Mario, and Ivano Bison. 2004. "Organizations, Coalitions and Movements." *Theory and Society* 33: 281–309.

Dikeç, Mustafa. 2004. "Voices into Noises: Ideological Determination of Unarticulated Justice Movements." *Space and Polity* 8(2): 191–208.

DiMaggio, Paul J., and Walter W. Powell. 1983. "The Iron Cage Revisited: Institutional Isomorphism and Collective Rationality in Organizational Fields." *American Sociological Review* 48(2): 147–60.

Durand, Jorge, and Douglas S. Massey. 2003. "The Costs of Contradiction: US Border Policy 1986–2000." *Latino Studies* 1(2): 233–52.

Duyvendak, Jan W. 2011. *The Politics of Home. Nostalgia and Belonging in Western Europe and the United States*. Basingstoke, UK: Palgrave.

Dziembowska, Maria. 2010. "NDLON and the History of Day Labor Organizing in Los Angeles." In Milkman, Bloom, and Narro, *Working for Justice*, 141–53.

Elias, Norbert. 1996. *The Germans. Power Struggles and the Development of Habitus in the 19th and 20th Centuries*. Cambridge, MA: Polity Press.

Elias, Norbert, and John L. Scotson. 1994. *The Established and the Outsiders*. London: Sage Publications.

Emirbayer, Mustafa, and Matthew Desmond. 2015. *The Racial Order*. Chicago: University of Chicago Press.

Enriquez, Laura E., and Abigail C. Saguy. 2016. "Coming Out of the Shadows: Harnessing a Cultural Schema to Advance the Undocumented Youth Movement." *American Journal of Cultural Sociology* 4(1): 107–30.

Ettlinger, Nancy. 2011. "Governmentality as Epistemology." *Annals of the Association of American Geographers* 101(3): 537–60.

Fassin, Didier. 2012. *Humanitarian Reason: A Moral History of the Present*. Berkeley: University of California Press.

Feagin, Joe R. 2013. *The White Racial Frame: Centuries of Racial Framing and Counter-Framing*. New York: Routledge.

Fernandes, Sujatha. 2017. *Curated Stories: The Uses and Misuses of Storytelling*. Oxford, UK: Oxford University Press.

Fine, Janice R. 2006. *Worker Centers: Organizing Communities at the Edge of the Dream*. Ithaca, NY: Cornell University Press.

FitzGerald, David, and David Cook-Martín. 2014. *Culling the Masses: The Democratic Origins of Racist Immigration Policy in the Americas*. Cambridge, MA: Boston University Press.

Fligstein, Neil, and Doug McAdam. 2011. "Towards a General Theory of Strategic Action Fields." *Sociological Theory* 29(1): 1–26.

———. 2015. *A Theory of Fields*. Oxford, UK: Oxford University Press.

Foucault, Michel. 1978. *History of Sexuality*. New York: Pantheon.

———. 2003. *Society Must Be Defended: Lectures at the Collège de France*. New York: Picador.

———. 2004. *Abnormal: Lectures at the Collège de France*. New York: MacMillan Publishers.

———. 2007. "Spaces of Security: The Example of the Town. Lecture of 11th January 1978." *Political Geography*, 26: 48–56.

Ganz, Marshall L. 2009. "Organizing Obama: Campaign, Organizing, Movement." Paper presented at the American Sociological Association Annual Meeting, San Francisco, August.

Ganz, Marshall L., and Emily Lin. 2012. "Learning to Lead. A Pedagogy of Practice." In *The Handbook for Teaching Leadership*, edited by Nitin Nohria, Rakesh Khurana, and Scott Snook, 353–66. Los Angeles: Sage Publications.

Gest, Justin. 2016. *The New Minority: White Working Class Politics in an Age of Immigration and Inequality*. Oxford, UK: Oxford University Press.

Giugni, Marco, and Florence Passy. 2004. "Migrant Mobilization between Political Institutions and Citizenship Regimes: A Comparison of France and Switzerland." *European Journal of Political Research* 43: 51–82.

Glick Schiller, Nina, and Ayse Çağlar. 2009. "Towards a Comparative Theory of Locality in Migration Studies: Migrant Incorporation and City Scale." *Journal of Ethnic and Migration Studies* 35(2): 177–202.

Gonzales, Alfonso. 2014. *Reform without Justice: Latino Migrant Politics and the Homeland Security State*. New York: Oxford University Press.

Gould, Roger V. 1995. *Insurgent Identities: Class, Community, and Protest in Paris from 1848 to the Commune*. Chicago: University of Chicago Press.

Hamilton, Nora, and Norma Stolz Chinchilla. 2001. *Seeking Community in a Global City: Guatemalans and Salvadorans in Los Angeles*. Philadelphia: Temple University Press.

Heredia, Luisa. 2011. "From Prayer to Protest: The Immigrant Rights Movement and the Catholic Church." In *Rallying for Immigrant Rights: The Fight for Inclusion in 21st Century America*, edited by Kim Voss and Irene Bloemraad, 101–22. Berkeley: University of California Press.

Hernández, David. 2013. "Detained in Obscurity: The U.S. Immigrant Detention Regime." *NACLA Report on the Americas* 46(3): 48–63.

Hilgers, Matthieu, and Eric Mangez. 2015. *Bourdieu's Theory of Social Fields*. New York: Routledge.

Hochschild, Arlie R. 2016. *Strangers in Their Own Land: Anger and Mourning on the American Right*. New York: New Press.

Hondagneu-Sotelo, Pierrette. 2006. *Religion and Social Justice for Immigrants*. New Brunswick, NJ: Rutgers University Press.

Honig, Bonnie. 2006. *Democracy and the Foreigner*. Princeton, NJ: Princeton University Press.

Inda, Jonathan X. 2006. *Targeting Immigrants: Government, Technology, and Ethics*. Malden, MA: Wiley-Blackwell.

Isin, Engin F. 2001. *Being Politics: Genealogies of Citizenship*. New York: Routledge.

Jacobs, Lawrence R., and Theda Skocpol. 2005. "American Democracy in an Era of Rising Inequality." In *Inequality and American Democracy: What We Know and What We Need to Learn*, edited by Lawrence R. Jacobs and Theda Skocpol, 1–18. New York: Russell Sage Foundation.

Jasper, James M. 1997. *The Art of Moral Protest*. Chicago: University of Chicago Press.

———. 2014. "Playing the Game" In *Players and Arenas: The Interactive Dynamics of Protest*, edited by James M. Jasper and Jan W. Duyvendak, 9–32. Amsterdam: Amsterdam University Press.

Jaworsky, Bernadette N. 2016. *The Boundaries of Belonging: Online Work of Immigration-Related Social Movement Organizations*. London: Palgrave

Jones, Robert, Daniel Cox, Juhem Navarro-Rivera, E. J. Dionne, and William Galston. 2014. "What Americans Want from Immigration Reform in 2014." *Governance Studies at Brookings*.

Kohl-Arenas, Erica. 2016. *The Self-Help Myth: How Philanthropy Fails to Alleviate Poverty*. Berkeley: University of California Press.

Koopmans, Ruud, and Paul Statham. 1999. "Political Claims Analysis: Integrating Protest Event and Political Discourse Approaches." *Mobilization* 4(1): 203–21.

Koopmans, Ruud, Paul Statham, Marco Giugni, and Florence Passy. 2005. *Contested Citizenship. Immigration and Cultural Diversity in Europe*. Minneapolis: University of Minnesota Press.

Lai, Annie. 2016. "Confronting Proxy Criminalization." *Legal Studies Research Paper Series*, no. 2016-33, University of California, Irvine.

Lamont, Michèle, and Nicolas Duvoux. 2014. "How Neo-Liberalism Has Transformed France's Symbolic Boundaries." *French Politics, Culture and Society* 32(2): 57–75.

Lehman Schlozman, Kay, Henry E. Brady, and Sidney Verba. 2018. *Unequal and Unrepresented: Political Inequality and the People's Voice in the New Gilded Age*. Princeton, NJ: Princeton University Press.

Mann, Michael. 1996. "Nation-States in Europe and Other Continents: Diversifying, Developing, Not Dying." In *Mapping the Nation*, edited by Gopal Balakrishnan, 295–314. London: Verso.

———. 2013. *The Sources of Social Power: Globalizations, 1945–2011*. Vol. 4. Cambridge, UK: Cambridge University Press.

Martinez, Lisa. 2008. "The Individual and Contextual Determinants of Protest among Latinos." *Mobilization: An International Quarterly* 13(2): 180–204.

Massey, Douglas S. 2007. *Categorically Unequal: The American Stratification System*. New York: Russell Sage Foundation.

Massey, Douglas S., and Nancy A. Denton. 1998. *American Apartheid: Segregation and the Making of the Underclass*. Cambridge, MA: Harvard University Press.

Massey, Douglas S., and Karen A. Pren. 2012. "Unintended Consequences of US Immigration Policy: Explaining the Post-1965 Surge from Latin America." *Population and Development Review* 38(1): 1–29.

McAdam, Doug. 1986. "Recruitment to High-Risk Activism: The Case of Freedom Summer." *American Journal of Sociology* 92(1): 64–90.

McCarthy, John D. 1987. "Pro-Life and Pro-Choice Mobilization: Infrastructure Deficits and New Technologies." In *Social Movements in an Organizational Society: Collected Essays*, edited by Mayer N. Zald and John D. McCarthy, 49–66. New Brunswick, NJ: Transaction Books.

———. 1996. "Mobilizing Structures: Constraints and Opportunities in Adopting, Adapting, and Inventing." In *Comparative Perspectives on Social Movements*, edited by Doug McAdam, John D. McCarthy, and Mayer N. Zald. Cambridge, UK: Cambridge University Press.

McCarthy, John D., and Mayer N. Zald. 1977. "Resource Mobilization and Social Movements: A Partial Theory." *The American Journal of Sociology* 82(6): 1212–41.

McFarlane, Colin. 2009. "Translocal Assemblages: Space, Power and Social Movements." *Geoforum* 40(4): 561–67.

Meissner, Doris M., Donald M. Kerwin, Muzaffar Chishti, and Claire Bergeron. 2013. *Immigration Enforcement in the United States. The Rise of Formidable Machinery*. Washington, DC: Migration Policy Institute.

Menjívar, Cecilia. 2000. *Fragmented Ties: Salvadoran Immigrant Networks in America*. Berkeley: University of California Press.

Menjívar, Cecilia, and Leisy Abrego. 2012. "Legal Violence: Immigration Law and the Lives of Central American Immigrants." *American Journal of Sociology*, 117(5): 1380–1421.

Menjívar, Cecilia, and Daniel Kanstroom. 2013. *Immigrant Experiences, Critiques, and Resistance*. Cambridge, UK: Cambridge University Press.

Meyer, David and Suzanne Staggenborg. 1996. "Movements, Countermovements, and the Structure of Political Opportunity." *American Journal of Sociology* 101(6): 1628–60.

Milkman, Ruth. 2006. *L.A. Story: Immigrant Workers and the Future of the U.S. Labor Movement*. New York: Russell Sage Foundation.

———. 2010. Introduction to Milkman, Bloom, and Narro, *Working for Justice*, 1–22.

Milkman, Ruth, Joshua Bloom, and Victor Narro. 2010. *Working for Justice: The L.A. Model of Organizing and Advocacy*. Ithaca, NY: Cornell University Press.

Miller, Byron A. 2000.*Geography and Social Movements: Comparing Antinuclear Activism in the Boston Area*. Minnesota: University of Minnesota Press.

Mills, C. Wright. 1956. *The Power Elite*. New York: Oxford University Press.

Minkoff, Debra C. 1999. "Bending with the Wind: Strategic Change and Adaptation by Women's and Racial Minority Organizations." *American Journal of Sociology* 104(6): 1666–1703.

Moody, Kim. 1988. *An Injury to All: The Decline of American Unionism*. New York: Verso.

Motomura, Hiroshi. 2006. *Americans in Waiting: The Lost Story of Immigration and Citizenship in the United States*. New York. Oxford University Press.

———. 2012. "Who Belongs?: Immigration Outside the Law and the Idea of Americans in Waiting." *UC Irvine Law Review* 2: 359–79.

———. 2014. *Immigration Outside the Law*. New York. Oxford University Press.

Mouffe, Chantal. 1993. *The Return of the Political*. London: Verso.

Nevins, Joseph. 2002. *Operation Gatekeeper. The Rise of the "Illegal Alien" and the Making of the U.S.-Mexico Boundary*. New York: Routledge.

Newman, Benjamin J. 2013. "Acculturating Contexts and Anglo Opposition to Immigration in the U.S." *American Journal of Political Science* 57(2): 374–90.

Ngai, Mae M. 2004. *Impossible Subjects: Illegal Aliens and the Making of Modern America* Princeton, NJ: Princeton University Press.

Nicholls, Walter J. 2008. "The Urban Question Revisited: The Importance of Cities for Social Movements." *International Journal of Urban and Regional Research* 32(4): 1468–2427.

———. 2013a. *The Dreamers: How the Undocumented Youth Movement Transformed the Immigrant Rights Debate in the United States*. Palo Alto, CA: Stanford University Press.

———. 2013b. "Making Undocumented Immigrants into Legitimate Political Subjects: A Comparison of France and the United States." *Theory, Culture and Society* 30(3): 82–107.

———. 2016a. "Politicizing Undocumented Immigrants One Corner at a Time: Day Laborers and the Urban Roots of the National Immigrant Rights Movement." *International Journal of Urban and Regional Research* 40(2): 299–320.

———. 2016b. "Producing-Resisting National Borders in the United States, France and the Netherlands." *Political Geography* (55)1: 43–52.

Nicholls, Walter J., and Justus Uitermark. 2016. *Immigrant Rights Activism in the United States, France and the Netherlands, 1970–2015*. Oxford, UK: Wiley-Blackwell.

Ong, Aihwa. 1996. "Cultural Citizenship as Subject Making: Immigrants Negotiate Racial and Cultural Boundaries in the United States." *Current Anthropology* 37(5): 737–51.

Pallares, Amalia. 2014. *Family Activism: Immigrant Struggles and the Politics of Non-Citizenship*. New Brunswick, NJ: Rutgers University Press.

Pallares, Amalia, and Nilda Flores González. 2011. "Regarding Family: New Actors in the Chicago Protests." In *Rallying for Immigrant Rights*, edited by Kim Voss and Irene Bloemraad, 161–79. Berkeley: University of California Press.

Patler, Caitlin C. 2010. "Alliance-Building and Organizing for Immigrant Rights: The Case of the Coalition for Humane Immigrant Rights of Los Angeles." In Milkman, Bloom, and Narro, *Working for Justice*, 71–88.

Patler, Caitlin C., and Roberto G. Gonzales. 2015. "Framing Citizenship: Media Coverage of Anti-Deportation Cases Led by Undocumented Immigrant Youth Organisations." *Journal of Ethnic and Migration Studies* 41(9): 1453–74.

Phillips, Julie A., and Douglas S. Massey. 1999. "The New Labor Market: Immigrants and Wages after IRCA." *Demography* 36(2): 233–46.

Polletta, Francesca. 2006. *It Was Like a Fever: Storytelling in Protest and Politics*. Chicago: University of Chicago Press.

Portes, Alejandro, and Rubén G. Rumbaut. 1996. *Immigrant America: A Portrait*. Berkeley: University of California Press.

Portes, Alejandro, and Julia Sensenbrenner. 1993. "Embeddedness and Immigration: Notes on the Social Determination of Economic Action." *American Journal of Sociology* 98: 1320–50.

Portes, Alejandro, and Min Zhou. 1993. "The New Second Generation: Segmented Assimilation and Its Variants among Post-1965 Immigrant Youth." *The Annals of the American Academy of Political and Social Sciences* 530: 74–96.

Provine, Doris M., Monica W. Varsanyi, Paul G. Lewis, and Scott H. Decker. 2016. *Policing Immigrants: Local Law Enforcement on the Front Lines*. Chicago: University of Chicago Press.

Putnam, Robert D. 2000. *Bowling Alone: The Collapse and Revival of American Community*. New York: Simon and Schuster.

Rose, Nikolas, and Peter Miller. 1992. "Political Power beyond the State: Problematics of Government." *British Journal of Sociology* 43(2): 172–205.

Rothwell, Jonathan, and Douglas S. Massey. 2009. "The Effect of Density Zoning on Racial Segregation in U.S. Urban Areas." *Urban Affairs Review* 44(6): 779–806.

Rucht, Dieter. 1999. "Linking Organisation and Mobilization: Michels's Iron Law of Oligarchy Reconsidered." *Mobilization* 4(2): 151–69.

Ruggie, John G. 1993. "Territoriality and Beyond: Problematizing Modernity in International Relations." *International Organization* 47(1): 39–174.

Sáenz, Rogelio, Cecilia Menjívar, and San Juanita Edilia García. 2015. "Arizona's SB 1070: Setting Conditions for Violations of Human Rights Here and Beyond." In *Governing Immigration Through Crime: A Reader*, edited by Julie A. Dowling and Jonathan X. Inda, 165–80. Stanford, CA: Stanford University Press.

Sassen, Saskia. 2006. *Territory, Authority, Rights: From Medieval to Global Assemblages*. Princeton, NJ: Princeton University Press.

———. 2013. "When Territory Deborders Territoriality." *Territory, Politics, Governance* 1(1): 21–45.

Schorske, Carl E. 1955. *German Social Democracy, 1905–1917. The Development of the Great Schism.* Cambridge, MA: Harvard University Press.

Scott, James C. 1985. *Weapons of the Weak: Everyday Forms of Peasant Resistance.* New Haven, CT: Yale University Press.

———. 1990. *Domination and the Arts of Resistance: Hidden Transcripts.* New Haven, CT: Yale University Press.

Seif, Hinda. 2010. "The Civic Life of Latina/o Immigrant Youth: Challenging Boundaries and Creating Safe Spaces." In *Handbook of Research in Civic Engagement,* edited by Lonnie R. Sherrod, Judith Torney-Purta, and Constance A. Flanagan, 445–70. Hoboken, NJ: Wiley and Sons.

Sikkink, Kathryn. 2005. "Patterns of Dynamic Multilevel Governance and the Insider-Outsider Coalition." In *Transnational Protest & Global Activism,* edited by Donatella Della Porta and Sidney Tarrow, 151–74. Lanham, MD: Rowman and Littlefield.

Skocpol, Theda. 2004a. *Diminished Democracy: From Membership to Management in American Civic Life.* Norman: University of Oklahoma Press.

———. 2004b. "Voice and Inequality: The Transformation of American Civic Democracy." *Perspectives on Politics* 2(1): 3–20.

Snow, David A., Robert D. Benford, E. Burke Rochford, and Steven K. Worden. 1986. "Frame Alignment Processes, Micromobilization, and Movement Participation." *American Sociological Review* 51, 464–81.

Somers, Margaret R. 2008. *Genealogies of Citizenship: Markets, Statelessness, and the Right to Have Rights.* Cambridge, UK: Cambridge University Press.

Somers, Margaret R., and Fred Block. 2005. "From Poverty to Perversity: Ideas, Markets, and Institutions over 200 Years of Welfare Debate." *American Sociological Review* 70(2): 260–87.

Song, Sarah. 2009. "What Does It Mean to Be an American?" *Daedalus* 138(2): 31–40.

Soule, Sarah A. 2013. "Diffusion and Scale Shift." In *The Wiley-Blackwell Encyclopedia of Social and Political Movements,* edited by David A. Snow, Donatella Della Porta, Bert Klandermans, and Doug McAdam. Oxford, UK: Wiley Publishing.

Soysal, Yasemin N. 1994. *Limits of Citizenship: Migrants and Postnational Membership in Europe.* Chicago: University of Chicago Press.

———. 1997. "Changing Parameters of Citizenship and Claims-Making: Organized Islam in European Public Spheres." *Theory and Society* 26(4): 509–27.

Staggenborg, Suzanne. 1988. "The Consequences of Professionalization and Formalization in the Pro-Choice Movement." *American Sociological Review* 53(4): 585–605.

Steil, Justin P., and Ion B. Vasi. 2014. "The New Immigration Contestation: Social Movements and Local Immigration Policy Making in the United States, 2000–2011." *American Journal of Sociology* 119(4): 1104–55.

Strunk, Christopher, and Helga Leitner. 2013. "Resisting Federal–Local Immigration

Enforcement Partnerships: Redefining 'Secure Communities' and Public Safety." *Territory, Politics, Governance* 1(1): 62–85.

Stumpf, Juliet. 2013. "The Crimmigration Crisis: Immigrants, Crime and Sovereign Power." In *Governing Immigration through Crime: A Reader*, edited by Julie A. Dowling and Jonathan X. Inda, 59–76. Stanford, CA: Stanford University Press.

Swerts, Thomas. 2015. "Gaining a Voice: Storytelling and Undocumented Youth Activism in Chicago." *Mobilization: An International Quarterly* 20(3): 345–60.

Tambini, Damian. 2001. "Post-National Citizenship." *Ethnic and Racial Studies* 24(2): 195–217.

Tamir, Yael. 1993. *Liberal Nationalism*. Princeton, NJ: Princeton University Press.

Tarrow, Sidney. 2005. *The New Transnational Activism*. New York: Cambridge University Press.

Tarrow, Sidney, and Doug McAdam. 2005. "Scale Shift in Transnational Contention." In *Transnational Protest and Global Activism*, edited by Donatella della Porta and Sidney Tarrow, 121–48. Boulder, CO: Rowman and Littlefield.

Terriquez, Veronica. 2015. "Training Young Activists: Grassroots Organizing and Youths' Civic and Political Trajectories." *Sociological Perspectives* 58(2): 223–42.

Theodore, Nik, Abel Valenzuela, and Edwin Meléndez. 2009. "Worker Centers: Defending Labor Standards for Migrant Workers in the Informal Economy." *International Journal of Manpower* 30(5): 422–36.

Tilly, Charles. 2004. *Social Movements, 1768–2004*. Boulder, CO: Paradigm Publishers.

Torpey, John. 1997. "Coming and Going: On the State Monopolization of the Legitimate 'Means of Movement.'" *Sociological Theory* 16(3): 239–59.

Unzueta Carrasco, Tania A., and Hinda Seif. 2014. "Disrupting the Dream: Undocumented Youth Reframe Citizenship and Deportability through Anti-Deportation Activism." *Latino Studies* 12(2): 279–99.

Valenzuela, Abel. 2003. "Day Labor Work." *Annual Review of Sociology* 29(1): 307–33.

Valenzuela, Abel, Nik Theodore, Edwin Meléndez, and Ana L. Gonzalez. 2006. *On the Corner: Day Labor in the United States*. Chicago: Latino Union of Chicago.

Varsanyi, Monica W. 2008. "Rescaling the 'Alien,' Rescaling Personhood: Neoliberalism, Immigration, and the State." *Annals of the Association of American Geographers* 98(4): 877–89.

———. 2011. "Neoliberalism and Nativism: Local Anti-Immigrant Policy Activism and an Emerging Politics of Scale." *International Journal of Urban and Regional Research* 35(2): 295–311.

Vermeulen, Floris. 2013. "Mutualism, Resource Competition and Opposing Movements among Turkish Organizations in Amsterdam and Berlin, 1965–2000." *The British Journal of Sociology* 64(3): 453–77.

Voss, Kim, and Irene Bloemraad. 2011. *Rallying for Immigrant Rights: The Fight for Inclusion in 21st Century America*. Berkeley: University of California Press.

Voss, Kim, Irene Bloemraad, and Taeku Lee. 2011. "The Protests of 2006: What Were They, How Do We Understand Them, Where Do We Go?" In *Rallying for Immi-*

grant Rights: The Fight for Inclusion in 21st Century America, edited by Kim Voss and Irene Bloemraad, 3–43. Berkeley: University of California Press.

Wacquant, Loïc. 2005. "Symbolic Power in the Rule of the 'State Nobility.'" In *Pierre Bourdieu and Democratic Politics*, edited by Loïc Wacquant, 133–50. London: Polity.

———. 2015. "Bourdieu, Foucault, and the Penal State in the Neoliberal Era." In *Foucault and Neoliberalism*, edited by Daniel Zamora and Michael C. Behrent, 114–33. Cambridge, UK: Polity Press.

Wadhia, Shoba S. 2010. "The Role of Prosecutorial Discretion in Immigration Law." *Connecticut Public Interest Law Journal* 9(2): 243–99.

Walker, Edward T. 2014. *Grassroots for Hire: Public Affairs Consultants in American Democracy.* Cambridge, UK: Cambridge University Press.

Walker, Kyle E., and Helga Leitner. 2011. "The Variegated Landscape of Local Immigration Policies in the United States." *Urban Geography* 32(2): 156–78.

Wallace, Sophia J., Chris Zepeda-Millán, and Michael Jones-Correa. 2014. "Spatial and Temporal Proximity: Examining the Effects of Protests on Political Attitudes." *American Journal of Political Science* 58(2): 449–65.

Walzer, Michael. 1983. *Spheres of Justice: A Defense of Pluralism and Equality.* New York: Basic Books.

Wimmer, Andreas. 2013. *Ethnic Boundary Making: Institutions, Power, Networks.* Oxford, UK: Oxford University Press.

Zepeda Millán, Chris. 2017. *Latino Mass Mobilization: Immigration, Racialization, and Activism.* Cambridge, UK: Cambridge University Press.

News Articles

Aguilar, Louis. 1994a. "An Eye on the Elections; Silver Spring Voters Show Their Pride." *Washington Post*, August 11.

———. 1994b. "Outreach Runs into Neighborhood Outrage; Montgomery's Efforts to Help Day Laborers Cause Resentment." *Washington Post*, January 23.

Alvarado, Pablo. 1996. "Conversation with Day Labor Activist Pablo Alvarado." *Los Angeles Times*, September 7.

Anderson, Will. 1999. "INS Arrests Day Laborers in Marietta; Raid: Crackdown Comes Ahead of Tough City Law on Such Gatherings of Workers." *Atlanta Journal-Constitution*, June 23.

Archibold, Randal C. 2010. "Side by Side, but Divided over Immigration." *New York Times*, May 11.

Babington, Charles. 1992. "Md. Judge to Rule on Mobile Office." *Washington Post*, November 10.

Badie, Rick. 1999. "Rumors, Fear of INS Raids Rife among Day Laborers; Recent Deportations of Illegal Immigrants Arrested in Marietta Have Even Those with Documentation Worried, Hispanic Advocates Say." *Atlanta Journal-Constitution*, July 4.

———. 2000. "Gwinnett Seeks Rules for Laborers." *Atlanta Journal-Constitution*, June 2.

Baker, Peter. 2012. "Mexico's President-Elect Discusses Immigration Policy with Obama." *New York Times*, November 27.

Bernstein, Nina. 2006. "Eclectic Crowd Joins a Call for the Rights of Immigrants." *New York Times*, April 11.

———. 2010. "Democrats Outline Plans for Immigration." *New York Times*, April 29.

Bixler, Mark. 1999. "Day Laborers in Roswell Get Place to Call Their Own; Blamed for Bad Traffic and Litter, Threatened with Arrest, Latinos Find a Savvy Negotiator to Improve Things." *Atlanta Journal-Constitution*, December 19.

Blake, John. 1996. "New Women of the New South: Keen on the Community; Latino Leader a Strong Voice in Campaign to Promote Jobs for New Immigrants and Defeat Old Stereotypes." *Atlanta Journal-Constitution*, August 7.

Blow, Charles. 2018. "The Commander of Fear." *New York Times*, August 9.

Calmes, Jackie. 2012. "Obama Marks Fourth with New U.S. Citizens." *New York Times*, July 4.

Carvajal, Doreen. 1995. "Out of Sight, Out of Mind, but Not Out of Work; Town Finds Space for Welcome Mat, Postage-Stamp Size, for Immigrant Laborers." *The New York Times*, July 8.

———. 1996. "Fresh Faces Are Making an Impact on the L.I. Landscape." *New York Times*, May 5.

Cleland-Pero, Cathy. 1992. "Day Laborers Dodge Law to Seek Jobs Marietta Police Must Balance Rights of Merchants, Workers." *Atlanta Journal-Constitution*, November 5.

Collins, Eliza. 2018. "Republican Playbook for 2018: Tie Democrats to Nancy Pelosi, Medicare for All and Abolishing ICE." *USA Today*, September 4.

Constable, Pamela. 1995. "Laborers Get Clout from Force of Law; Program Helps Gain Pay from Employers." *Washington Post*, November 25.

———. 2013. "Immigrants' Experiences, in Their Own Words." *Washington Post*, July 23.

Cooper, Michael. 1999. "Laborers Wanted, but Not Living Next Door." *New York Times*, November 28.

De Sa, Karen. 1999. "Cities Crack Down Complaints Spur Los Altos to Enact Latest Ban on Hiring Along Streets." *San Jose Mercury News*, August 8.

Dickey, Jim. 1994. "Law Center Assists Immigrants Fights for the Rights of Low Income Workers." *San Jose Mercury News*, October 17.

Duggan, Paul. 1992. "Day Laborers Losing Gathering Place; Central Americans Protest Ouster from Silver Spring Parking Lot." *Washington Post*, April 19.

Dugger, Celia W. 1996. "Immigrants and Suburbia Square Off; Hispanic Residents of Mt. Kisco Say They're Being Harassed." *New York Times*, December 1.

———. 1997. "Settling Hispanic Suit, Mt. Kisco Agrees Not to Enforce Overcrowding Law." *New York Times*, August 13.

Egelko, Bob. 2009. "Group's Leader Urges New Strategy on Immigrant Rights." *San Francisco Chronicle*, November 27.

Emling, Shelley. 1992a. "Hispanic Leaders, Chamblee Officials Seeking Dialogue." *The Atlanta Journal-Constitution*, September 1.

———. 1992b. "Tensions Remain High in Chamblee A Gathering Place for Laborers Sought." *Atlanta Journal-Constitution*, September 2.

Epstein, Reid J. 2014. "W.H. Faces Rising Grass-Roots Heat." *Politico*, February 20.

Falcone, Michael. 2008. "McCain and Obama Court Hispanic Voters." *New York Times*, June 28.

Fay, Tim. 1996. "Chamblee's Day Labor Pool Spills onto Buford Highway." *Atlanta Journal-Constitution*, May 16.

Garcia, Edwin. 1997. "Labor Day New Law Aims to Bring Hiring Process Inside on Wednesday, S. J. Police Told Day Laborers Their Streetside Solicitations Will Soon Be Illegal." *San Jose Mercury News*, March 6.

Gathright, Alan. 1995. "Hispanic Group Says Funding Cut Is Anti-Immigrant La Raza Centro Legal Defends Day Laborers In San Mateo." *San Jose Mercury News*, July 20.

Gearty, Robert. 1997a. "Center Helps Immigs Shape Up Their Future." *Daily News* (NY), April 6.

———. 1997b. "Rally Hits City Where It Lives Activists Demand Homeless Shelter." *Daily News* (NY), November 26.

———. 2000. "Day Laborer Site Is Blessed Hiring Spot Set Up amid Many Prayers." *Daily News* (NY), April 14.

Griffith, Stephanie. 1991. "Suburbs 'Sit Up and Take Notice' of Hispanics' Grievances." *Washington Post*, May 28.

Gross, Jane. 2000. "For Latino Laborers, Dual Lives; Welcomed at Work, but Shunned at Home in Suburbs." *New York Times*, January 5.

Guthey, Greig. 1992a. "Comments Irk Latin Americans 8 Consuls Seek Improved Relations after 'Ugly' Statements in Chamblee." *Atlanta Journal-Constitution*, August 22.

———. 1992b. "Melting Pot Aboil. Chamblee Neighborhood Complains about Presence of Hispanic Laborers." *Atlanta Journal-Constitution*, August 20.

Hamilton, William. 1993. "Harvest of Blame; Californians Turn on Illegal Immigrants." *Washington Post*, June 4.

Haughney, Christine. 2000. "Assault on Mexicans Shakes Long Island Town; Suspects Linked to White Supremacists." *Washington Post*, November 28.

Herszenhorn, David M. 2010. "Menendez Urges Boycott of All-Star Game in Arizona." *New York Times*, May 10.

"Hiring Location Opposed." 1995. *Pasadena Star News*, May 31.

Hirschfeld Davis, Julie, and Michael D. Shear. 2014. "57,000 Reasons Immigration Overhaul May Be Stalled for Now." *New York Times*, July 16.

Huetteman, Emmarie. 2014. "'There Is a Divide' in Republican Party, Cantor Says." *New York Times*, June 15.

Hulse, Carl, and Jim Rutenberg. 2006. "2 Immigration Provisions Easily Pass Senate." *New York Times*, May 18.

"Immigration Reform Caucus Responds; to Nationwide Immigration Protests." 2007. *States News Service*, May 1.

Jung, Carolyn. 1994. "Mountain View Rejects a 'Racist' Law." *San Jose Mercury News*, November 20.

Kiggen Miller, Elizabeth. 1999. "Day-Labor Solution Rejected." *New York Times*, September 12.

Kim, Seung M. 2013. "Immigration Groups Push Action." *Politico*, September 19.

Kondracke, Morton M. 2010. "Hope Exists for Immigration 'Down Payment.'" *Roll Call*, July 29.

Kopan, Tal. 2018. "How Trump Changed the Rules to Arrest More Non-Criminal Immigrants." *CNN*, March 2.

Kornblut, Anne E. 2005. "Bush Cites Political Hurdles in Plan for 'Guest Workers.'" *New York Times*, March 24.

LaMarche, Gara. 2010. "A Growing Drumbeat from Activists Energizes Drive for Urgent Immigration Reform." *The Atlantic Philantrophies*, March 18.

LeDuff, Charlie. 1997. "Neighborhood Report: Flushing; Loitering, or Job Hunting?" *New York Times*, February 23.

LeDuff, Charlie, and David M. Halbfinger. 1999. "Slums Behind Shutters: A Special Report.; Wages and Squalor for Immigrant Workers." *New York Times*, May 21.

Levander, Michelle. 1994. "Latino Labor Movement's Quandary Unions Debate If They Should Exclude or Try to Organize Undocumented Workers in Border States." *San Jose Mercury News*, August 5.

Lind, David. 2019. "'Immigrants Are Coming over the Border to Kill You' Is the Only Speech Trump Knows How to Give." *Vox*, January 9.

Matthews, Laura. 2013a. "Immigration Reform 2013: Napolitano Spread Arizona's 'Shameful Infection Of Nativism,' Say Day Laborers." *International Business Times News*, August 29.

———. 2013b. "Immigration Reform 2013: Undocumented Handcuff Themselves to White House Fence, Promise More Civil Unrest." *International Business Times*, September 18.

———. 2013c. "Undocumented Immigrants Promise Civil Unrest to Push for Reform." *International Business Times News*, September 18.

McDonald, R. Robin. 1999. "Day Laborer Fatally Shot during DeKalb Robbery." *Atlanta Journal-Constitution*, April 8.

McFadden, Robert D. 2000. "At Rally, Suffolk Residents Protest Illegal Immigration." *New York Times*, October 15.

McLaughlin, Ken. 1994. "Prop. 187: Immigrants Face 'Ugly Time.'" *San Jose Mercury News*, October 18.

McQuiston, John T. 1999. "Immigrants Help Defeat L.I. Bill Banning Street Job Markets." *New York Times*, June 30.

Meyerson, Harold. 2005. "The Architect. Miguel Contreras, 1952–2005." *LA Weekly*, May 12.

Mitchell, Alison. 1992. "Wary Recruits: Immigrants Vie for Day Jobs." *New York Times*, May 26.

Mydans, Seth. 1989. "Los Angeles Project Aids Illegal Aliens, in Challenge to U.S." *New York Times*, October 26.

———. 1990. "Encinitas Journal; Accident of Geography Prompts Local Protest." *New York Times*, November 13.

———. 1992. "Alpine Journal; Cultural Frictions of a Border Town." *New York Times*, December 7.

Nakumera, David. 2014. "Obama Is Squeezed in Border Debate." *Washington Post*, February 4.

Nieves, Evelyn. 1994a. "Our Towns; A Contract Out on Workers' Rights." *New York Times*, October 18.

———. 1994b. "Our Towns; Laborers, Unwanted but Willing." *New York Times*, August 2.

———. 1998. "Our Towns; Day Laborer Stakes Out His Own Patch." *New York Times*, May 10.

Onishi, Norimitsu. 1995. "Neighborhood Report: College Point/Flushing; For Day Laborers, a New Hurdle." *New York Times*, February 5.

Parker, Laura, and Patrick McMahon. 2001. "Immigrant Groups Fear Backlash." *USA Today*, April 9.

Pear, Robert, and Carl Hulse. 2007. "Immigrant Bill Dies in Senate; Defeat for Bush." *New York Times*, June 29.

Petersen, Melody. 1994a. "Hispanics Confront Cops, INS over Raids in Mountain View." *San Jose Mercury News*, February 18.

———. 1994b. "INS Arrests Spur New Rights Group Sweep along El Camino in Mountain View Has Latinos Who Are U.S. Citizens Afraid to Walk along the Street." *San Jose Mercury News*, February 20.

———. 1994c. "Mtn. View Split on Illegal Laborers Some Support the INS Raids on El Camino." *San Jose Mercury News*, February 5.

———. 1994d. "Shun INS Raids, Cops Are Asked Hispanics Protest Mtn. View Cooperation." *San Jose Mercury News*, March 3.

Pols, Mary F. 2000. "Day Laborer Center Up for Study; A Proposed Haven for Undocumented Workers in Concord Sparks Debate between Union Leaders and Business Owners." *Contra Costa Times*, March 27.

Preston, Julia. 2009a. "Firm Stance on Illegal Immigrants Remains Policy." *New York Times*, August 3.

———. 2009b. "Obama to Push Immigration Bill as One Priority." *New York Times*, April 8.

———. 2009c. "White House Plan on Immigration Includes Legal Status." *New York Times*, November 11.

———. 2010. "A Potential Obama Ally Becomes an Outspoken Foe on Immigration." *New York Times*, May 28.

———. 2012. "While Seeking Support, Obama Faces a Frustrated Hispanic Elector-ate." *New York Times*, June 10.

———. 2013. "Illegal Immigrants Are Divided over Importance of Citizenship." *New York Times*, November 20.

———. 2014. "The Big Money Behind the Push for an Immigration Overhaul." *New York Times*, November 14.

Quintanilla, Blanca M. 1997. "For Latino Day Laborers, Finding Work Is Hard Job." *Daily News* (NY), June 11.

Reinhold, Robert. 1993. "A Welcome for Immigrants Turns to Resentment." *The New York Times*, August 25.

Robbins, Tom. 1999. "Union, Pols Push Immigrant Amnesty." *Daily News* (NY), De-cember 1.

Sachs, Susan. 2001. "Changes Called Likely in Policy on Immigration." *New York Times*, September 24.

Santora, Marc. 2007. "'08 Candidates Weighing Consequences as They Take Sides on Immigration Plan." *New York Times*, May 19.

Santora, Marc, and Sam Roberts. 2007. "Giuliani Shifts His Tone on Immigration." *New York Times*, April 22.

Schmitz, Tom. 1996a. "Santa Clara Takes Aim at Panhandlers City Is First in Valley to Enact Ban against Sign-Holding Beggars." *San Jose Mercury News*, March 28.

———. 1996b. "Santa Clara Targets Street Panhandlers Proposal: Law Would Keep 'Signers' Off Roadways." *San Jose Mercury News*, March 20.

Schneider, Craig. 1998. "Complexes Run Area's Lifestyle Gamut; Roswell Complex Helps Immigrants Cope." *Atlanta Journal-Constitution*, September 17.

Schrade, Brad. 1999. "Hispanics Oppose Roswell Crowd-Control Effort after Arrests; Mexican Envoy Says Law Regulating Day Laborers Is 'Dangerous for the Latino Community.'" *Atlanta Journal-Constitution*, April 7.

———. 2000. "Smyrna Mayor Backs Arrest of Bricklayers; Bacon Says Workers' Claim They Were Targeted for Being Latino 'an Excuse' for Violating Law." *At-lanta Journal-Constitution*, June 17.

Semple, Kirk. 2011. "Cuomo Ends State's Role in Checking Immigrants." *New York Times*, June 1.

Shear, Michael D. 2014. "Obama, Citing a Concern for Families, Orders a Review of Deportations." *New York Times*, March 13.

Shear, Michael D., and Julia Preston. 2013. "Immigration Reform Falls to the Back of the Line." *New York Times*, September 8.

Shenon, Philip, and Robin Toner. 2001. "A Nation Challenged: Policy and Legislation; U.S. Widens Policy on Detaining Suspects; Troubled Airlines Get Federal Aid Pledge." *New York Times*, September 19.

Sontag, Deborah. 1993. "Study Sees Illegal Aliens in New Light." *New York Times*, September 2.

Staff Reporter. 1993. "Doing Jobs Citizens 'Would Never Do.'" *New York Times*, Au-gust 25.

———. 2013. "Senate Passes Imperfect Immigration Bill by a 68–32 Margin: Debate Moves to House of Representatives." *Latino Rebels*, June 27.

———. 2014. "Immigration Activists Applaud NCLR Leader's 'Deporter-in-Chief' Obama Comments." *Latino Rebels*, March 4.

Stevenson, Richard W. 1989. "Jobs Being Filled by Illegal Aliens despite Sanctions." *New York Times*, October 9.

———. 2005. "Bush, Touring the Border, Puts Emphasis on Enforcement." *New York Times*, November 30.

Stolberg, Sheryl G. 2006. "Bush Suggests Immigrants Learn English." *New York Times*, June 8.

———. 2010. "Immigration Overhaul Advocates Question Troops." *New York Times*, May 26.

Stone Lombardi, Kate. 1994. "Parallel Worlds Collide in Mt. Kisco." *New York Times*, December 25.

———. 1995. "Debate Goes on over Protecting Residents and Workers." *New York Times*, June 11.

Stowe, Stacey. 2007. "Bill Giving Illegal Residents Connecticut Tuition Rates Is Vetoed by the Governor." *New York Times*, June 27.

Strugatch, Warren. 2004. "L.I. @ WORK; The Changing Face of the Island's Labor Force." *New York Times*, November 14.

Swarns, Rachel L. 2007. "Kennedy, Eager for Republican Support, Shifts Tactics on an Immigration Measure." *New York Times*, March 13.

Thompson, Ginger. 2001. "Fox Urges Congress to Grant Rights to Mexican Immigrants in U.S." *New York Times*, September 7.

Thompson, Ginger, and Sarah Cohen. 2014. "More Deportations Follow Minor Crimes, Records Show." *New York Times*, April 6.

Thompson, Ginger, and David M. Herszenhorn. 2009. "Obama Set for First Step on Immigration Reform." *New York Times*, June 24.

Tran, Tini. 1996. "Street Corner Laborers to Get a Home." *San Jose Mercury News*, January 1.

Visser, Steve. 1999a. "Church Welcomes Hispanics with a Parade in Marietta." *Atlanta Journal-Constitution*, May 16.

———. 1999b. "Laborers Gather as Police Make No Effort to Enforce Ban." *Atlanta Journal-Constitution*, July 2.

Witt, Barry. 1997. "Day Laborers Booted Off Some Streets City Council Says Work Seekers Block Traffic, Intimidate Shoppers." *San Jose Mercury News*, January 22.

Woolfolk, John. 1995. "Job Solicitation Curb a Flop Ineffective: Backers of San Mateo's Ban on Hiring Laborers, Mostly Hispanics, from a Car Agree It Hasn't Made a Difference." *San Jose Mercury News*, April 17.

Wykes, S. L. 1994. "Mtn. View to Weigh Cops' Role in INS Raids." *San Jose Mercury News*, March 31.

Zinko, Carolyne. 1995. "Day Laborers Start Fight against New San Mateo Law." *San Jose Mercury News*, May 10.

Documents

Alliance for Citizenship. 2013. "Easter Recess Toolkit."
———. 2016. "About." Retrieved March 16, 2016, from www.allianceforcitizenship. org/about.
Alvarado, Pablo. 1995. "Letter to Margarita Ramirez, Program Officer of Liberty Hill Foundation." May 20.
———. 1998. "Letter to Margarita Ramirez, Program Officer of Liberty Hill Foundation." April 1.
Association of Day Laborers. 1997. "Newsletter."
Benitez Strategies. 2018. http://www.benitezstrategies.com/about/.
California Immigrant Welfare Collaborative. 1997. "Grant Application."
Center for Community Change. 2011. "Ohio Movement Building Training. Participant Guide."
———. 2016. "Immigration Timeline." Retrieved March 10, 2016, from https://www .communitychange.org/real-power/immigration-timeline/.
Coalition for Humane Immigrant Rights of Los Angeles. 1989a. "CHIRLA Proposal to the Liberty Hill Foundation." March 1.
———. 1989b. "Know Your Rights Pamphlet."
———. 1995a. "Newsletter." January.
———. 1995b. "Diversity and Democracy Fund Application." August 28.
———. 1995c. "Fund For a New Los Angeles Application." November 28.
———. 1997a. "Day Laborer Newsletter."
———. 1997b. "Flyer."
———. 1997c. "Grant Application."
———. 1997d. "Press Release."
———. 2001. "Grant Report." December.
Dream Team Los Angeles. 2010. "Youth Empowerment Summit."
Emanuel, Rahm. 1996. "Memorandum to President Clinton: Domestic Policy." November 12. https://upload.democraticunderground.com/10025271739.
Fair Immigration Reform Movement. 2007a. "Reclaiming Our Communities Toolkit." January 3.
———. 2007b. "Teach In: The Fight for CIR."
———. 2009. "ACTION: Youth Organizing Trainings in CO and FL." August 6. https://fairimmigration.wordpress.com/2009/08/06/action-youth-organizing -trainings-in-co-and-fl/.
GiveWell. 2013. "A Conversation with Sue Chinn and Marielena Hincapié on July 11, 2013." July 11.
Illinois Coalition for Immigrant and Refugee Rights. 2008. "Teaching 'Chicago Style Politics': The New Americans Democracy 'Boot Camp.'" November 2.
Internal Revenue Service. 2018. "SOI Tax Stats—Charities & Other Tax-Exempt Organizations Statistics." https://www.irs.gov/statistics/soi-tax-stats-charities-and -other-tax-exempt-organizations-statistics.

International Brotherhood of Electrical Workers. 1995. "Letter from Southern California IBEW-NECA Labor Management Cooperation Committee to the American Friends Service Committee." April 13.

La Escuela de la Comunidad. 1993. "Grant Application for Liberty Hill Foundation." August 31.

———. 1994. "Follow Up Questionnaire and Report for Liberty Hill Foundation." July 8.

LaMarche, Gara. 2010. "A Growing Drumbeat from Activists Energizes Drive for Urgent Immigration Reform." *The Atlantic Philanthropies*, March 18.

Liberty Hill Foundation 1995. "Grant Report on the Pasadena Day Labor Association." November.

National Immigration Forum. 2013. "The Math of Immigration Detention: Runaway Costs for Immigration Detention Do Not Add Up to Sensible Policies." August 22.

New Organizing Institute. 2011. "Power Shift Organizing Training—Northeast." March 18–20.

Open Society. 2008. "Special Funding Request for Immigration Comeback Strategy." August 25.

———. 2009a. "End of the Year Strategic Plan." August 8.

———. 2009b. "Grant Recommendations for the 2009 Immigration Reform Campaign." April 29.

———. 2009c. "Memo Grant Recommendations for the 2009 Immigration Reform Campaign." April 4.

———. 2009d. "Memo Grant Recommendations for the 2009 Immigration Reform Campaign." April 9.

———. 2009e. "Seize the Day Initiative Weekly Update." April 15.

———. 2009f. "Seize the Day Initiative Weekly Update." May 6.

———. 2009g. "Seize the Day Initiative Weekly Update." July 7.

———. 2009h. "Seize the Day Initiative Weekly Update." September 10.

———. 2009i. "Special Funding to Seize This Transformative Moment." February 12.

———. 2010a. "Comprehensive Immigration Reform Update." February 2.

———. 2010b. "Comprehensive Immigration Reform Update." February 13.

———. 2010c. "Equality and Opportunity Fund Docket II." July 19.

———. 2011. "Memorandum: Recommended Naturalization Grantmaking for 2011." November 11.

———. 2012. "Board Book." December 18–19.

———. 2013a. "Board Book." December 17–18.

———. 2013b. "Open Society U.S. Programs Board Meeting." May 8–9.

———. 2013c. "Open Society U.S. Programs Board Meeting." September 3–4.

———. 2015. "Board Book." February 20–22.

———. 2016. "Open Society U.S. Programs Board Meeting." May 4–6.

Opportunity Agenda. 2011. "Real Solutions, American Values: A Winning Narrative on Immigration; Messaging Memo." May 10.

———. 2013. "Quick Tips for Talking Immigration Issues." July.

Pasadena Day Labor Association. 1994. "Grant Application for Liberty Hill Foundation." August 29.

———. 1995. "Liberty Hill Follow Up Questionnaire." March 6.

Reform Immigration For America. 2016. "About the Campaign." Retrieved March 16, 2016, from http://reformimmigrationforamerica.org/oabout//.

Tobar, Pili. 2013. "Alliance for Citizenship Launches New Campaign to Win Citizenship for 11 Million Immigrants." *America's Voice*, February 19.

White House. 2016. "White House Visitors." https://open.whitehouse.gov/dataset/White-House-Visitor-Records-Requests/p86s-ychb#column-menu2016.

Interviews

Pablo Alvarado, National Day Laborer Organizing Network
Lawrence Benito, Illinois Coalition for Immigrant and Refugee Rights
Antonio Bernabe, Coalition for Humane Immigrant Rights of Los Angeles
Deepak Bhargava, Center for Community Change
Pedro Cardenas, formerly of the Pasadena Day Labor Association
Steven Choi, New York Immigration Coalition
William Crowfoot, Pasadena city councilmember
Vanya de la Cuba, Pasadena district representative
Adrienne DerVartanian, Farmworker Justice
José Esquivel, formerly of the Pasadena Day Labor Association
Fernando Gonzales, Pasadena Day Labor Association
Marielena Hincapié, National Immigration Law Center
Lupe Lopez, Center for Community Change
Nadia Marin-Molina, formerly of the Workplace Project
Angel Martinez, formerly of the Pasadena Job Center
Clarissa Martinez De Castro, National Council of La Raza
Eva Millona, Massachusetts Immigrant and Refugee Advocacy Coalition
Christine Neumann-Ortiz, Voces de la Frontera
Ali Noorani, National Immigration Forum
Mary Ochs, formerly of the Center for Community Change
Mayron Payes, formerly of the Coalition for Humane Immigrant Rights of Los Angeles and currently with the Center for Community Change
Thomas A. Saenz, Mexican American Legal Defense and Educational Fund
Angela Sanbrano, Central American Resource Center
Rich Stolz, Center for Community Change and Reform Immigration for America
Gustavo Torres, CASA Maryland
Arturo Vargas, National Association of Latino Elected and Appointed Officials

Index

Page numbers followed by f or t indicate material in figures or tables.

joining economic justice networks, 133; Jorge Neri, 144, 184; leadership role of, 140; Mary Ochs, 163; as multi-issue organization, 167, 231; and NCJIS, 106, 131–33; need for mobilizing grassroots, public, 139–41; Rich Stoltz, 140; and RIFA, 139; Salvador Cervantes, 142; statements on Obama administration, 189–90; Susan Chinn, 144; and voter turnout, 140

Center for American Progress (CAP), 141, 167, 174, 179, 181, 231

centralization of power, 111–12, 116, 145, 196

Cervantes, Salvador, 142

Cesar E. Chavez Foundation, 184

chain migration, 23

Chamblee, Georgia, 45–46, 51, 60, 68, 76–77

Charlottesville attacks, 2

Chavez, Cesar, 184, 205

Chicago, Illinois, 59, 66, 71, 85, 97, 154. *See also* ICIRR; Obama, Barack

children: citizen children of immigrants, 24; DACA (Deferred Action for Childhood Arrivals), 2, 150, 154, 156, 162, 217, 223; family reunification issues, 138, 186, 244n21; family separations, 2, 216, 226; nutritional assistance for, 99; with Temporary Protected Status, 223–24. *See also* DREAM Act/DREAMers

Chinn, Susan, 144

CHIRLA (Center for Humane Immigrant Rights of Los Angeles): aiding welfare organizations, 132; and CCC, 129; and DACA, 223; Day Laborer Organizing Project, 103–4; Day Laborer World Cup, 102; day-worker projects, 73, 97, 99–100; difficulties for, 174, 176; and FIRM, 134–35, 141, 144, 173; foundation funding for, 165; founding and focus of, 71–73, 98; Immigrant Campaign for Civil Rights, 104; know-your-rights campaign, 99; lawsuits, 79; leadership position of, 211, 213, 219; managing work centers, 99–100; national action by, 105–7, 130–31; neighborhood improvement projects by, 104; and Obama White House, 181, 190; opposing antisolicitation ordinance, 99; in Pasadena, 100–102; pressuring Rep. McCarthy, 147; regional and national

work of, 78, 85–86; union issues with, 97–98; using popular-education methodology, 102–3; working with existing network, 98. *See also* Los Angeles, CA; MIWON

Christmas posadas, 89

churches, 64–66, 77, 83–84, 210

Church of the Resurrection (Farmingville), 65

CIR (comprehensive immigration reform) work, 151, 153, 164, 171, 175

Citizens for Action, 47, 50

Citizens for the Preservation of Local Life, 50

city officials and day laborer issues, 43, 53–54, 70, 75–76, 80–82, 100

city size and immigrant issues, 69

civil rights issues, 24, 80–81, 104, 189

class divide in immigration movement, 27–28, 58, 159–60, 172–76, 218–20

Clinton, Bill, 112–14, 185

Clinton, Hillary, 1, 118, 184, 222

CNN, 188

Coalition for Comprehensive Immigration Reform, 137–39

collective action, 11, 18, 50

collective storytelling, 96, 208

Colorado Immigrant Rights Coalition, 135

common identity as foundational concept, 17–20, 89, 129

common language, narratives for activists, 73, 209

commonsense politics, 21, 30, 71

"Communications Pillar, The," 209

Communication Workers of America (California), 62

Community Charities (Roswell, Georgia), 61

Comprehensive Immigration Reform Act (2006), 126, 137–38

comprehensive immigration reform (CIR) work, 151, 153, 164, 171–72, 175, 189, 201–4

Congressional Hispanic Caucus, 120, 204

conservatives, 4, 13, 69, 144, 188, 222–23

constitutionally protected rights, 127; of all people, 70, 79–80, 101–2, 106; Fifth Amendment rights, 24; First Amendment rights, 76, 79–80, 101–2; Fourteenth Amendment rights, 24;